Life, Literature, and Thought Library

ENGLISH BIOGRAPHY IN THE SEVENTEENTH CENTURY

CONTEMPORARY PEN DRAWING OF JOHN AUBREY NOW
IN THE ASHMOLEAN MUSEUM, OXFORD
By kind permission of the Bodleian Library

English Biography in the Seventeenth Century

SELECTED SHORT LIVES

EDITED BY
VIVIAN DE SOLA PINTO

Biography Index Reprint Series

BOOKS FOR LIBRARIES PRESS
FREEPORT, NEW YORK

First published 1951 as part of the Life, Literature and
Thought Library by George G. Harrap & Co. Ltd.

Reprinted 1969 by arrangement

STANDARD BOOK NUMBER:

8369-8007-7

LIBRARY OF CONGRESS CATALOG CARD NUMBER:

72-101833

PRINTED IN THE UNITED STATES OF AMERICA

FOREWORD

THIS series aims at presenting in an attractive form English texts which have not only intrinsic merit as literature but which are also valuable as manifestations of the spirit of the age in which they were written. The plan was inspired by the desire to break away from the usual annotated edition of English classics and to provide a series of books illustrating some of the chief developments in English civilization since the Middle Ages. Each volume will have a substantial introduction, which will relate the author to the main currents of contemporary life and thought, and which will be an important part of the book. Notes, where given, will be brief, stimulating, and designed to encourage the spirit of research in the student. It is believed that these books will be of especial value to students in universities and in the upper forms of schools, and that they will also appeal very much to the general reader.

Grateful acknowledgment is made of the valuable help given to the series in its early stages by Mr S. E. Buckley.

VIVIAN DE SOLA PINTO
General Editor,
Life, Literature and
Thought Library

PREFACE

THE Introduction to this book is designed to give some account of the antecedents of English biography and of the remarkable development of this kind of writing which took place in England in the seventeenth century. The Lives that follow have been selected to illustrate that development; they have also been chosen as records of eight of the most interesting figures of a great age. It is hoped, therefore, that the book will serve the twofold purpose of introducing readers to a highly significant but somewhat neglected chapter of English literary history, and of placing within their reach vivid contemporary accounts of eight great Englishmen, which have not hitherto been easily accessible to the ordinary reader.

The texts are presented in seventeenth-century spelling and punctuation, which do not differ sufficiently from modern usage to cause any difficulty to an intelligent modern reader. For the *Life of George Herbert* the text of the second (revised) edition of 1675 has been used, and for *Some Passages of the Life and Death of John Earl of Rochester* that of the first edition of 1680. Walton's short introduction to his *Life of Herbert* and Burnet's preface and moralizing "Conclusion" to his *Rochester* have been omitted. Hill's *Life of Isaac Barrow* is given in the text prefixed to the edition of Barrow's *Works* published in 1683, where it first appeared. Certain passages were added to this biography in the third edition of 1716, the last published in Hill's lifetime. I have inserted these passages in the text of this edition, but have enclosed them in square brackets. It is impossible to tell whether they formed part of Hill's original draft of his biography and were omitted from the first edition because they were considered too intimate or undignified, or whether Hill added them to the text of the biography when he was preparing the third edition because he had obtained fuller information.

Aubrey's *Brief Lives* present formidable problems to the modern editor. They survive in four folio volumes in the Bodleian Library (MS. Aubrey 6, 7, 8, 9), containing a jumble of MS. notes full of abbreviations, lacunæ, repetitions, deletions, and alternative words and phrases. Any modern printed version, if it is to be readable, must be in some measure a selection from, and a rearrangement of, these notes. The text presented here is based on photostats of the Bodleian MSS., and is a selection and reconstruction designed to present to the modern reader a continuous text preserving as far as possible the idiosyncrasies of Aubrey's spelling and punctuation, but expanding his contractions, and rearranging his notes as it might have been supposed he would have rearranged them if he had prepared them for publication. Where a word or date has been added which is not in Aubrey's text it is enclosed in pointed brackets. In this work of reconstruction I have been greatly helped by Andrew Clark's valuable edition (Oxford University Press, 1898) and by the text of the "Life of Milton" printed by Miss Helen Darbishire in her *Early Lives of Milton* (Constable, 1932).

My special thanks are due to Professor John Butt and to Mr G. R. Hibbard for reading the book in typescript, correcting my mistakes, and making many useful suggestions, which I have been glad to adopt. Professor Butt has generously placed at my disposal his unrivalled knowledge of the background of Walton's "Lives," and I am particularly grateful to him for revising the notes to *The Life of George Herbert* and adding some valuable and interesting information. I am also grateful to Bodley's Librarian for providing me with excellent photostats of the Aubrey MSS., and I acknowledge my debt to those two great monuments of English scholarship *The Oxford English Dictionary* and *The Dictionary of National Biography*.

V. DE S. P.

CONTENTS

INTRODUCTION

ANTECEDENTS

BIOGRAPHY is defined by the *Oxford English Dictionary* as "the history of the lives of individual men, as a branch of literature." As history biography should be the product of critical intelligence, detached curiosity, and the careful sifting and analysis of records. As literature it should have organic unity, and should satisfy standards of æsthetic judgment by its style and structure. As the study of individuals it should be informal and intimate, though opinions will differ as to the degree of frankness which is permissible, or desirable, in a biography. This "most delicate and humane of all the branches of the art of writing," as Lytton Strachey calls it, is necessarily a very late development in literature. It presupposes a society with a detached curiosity about human life, and a conception of every human being as an individual worthy of respect, as well as a tolerance and a freedom of speech that are only possible in secure and highly civilized communities. Dr Johnson, in his admirable essay on biography (No. 60 of *The Rambler*, 1750), the first notable study of the subject in English, writes that

> the business of the biographer is often to pass lightly over those performances and incidents, which produce vulgar greatness, to lead the thoughts into domestick privacies, and display the minute details of daily life, where exterior appendages are cast aside, and men only excel each other in prudence and virtue.

James Boswell, the greatest of English biographers, wrote, in his *Life of Johnson* (1791):

> I cannot conceive a more perfect mode of writing any man's

life, than not only relating all the most important events of it in
their order, but interweaving what he privately wrote, and said,
and thought; by which mankind are enabled as it were to see him
live, and to "live o'er each scene" with him, as he actually
advanced through the several stages of his life.

"I will venture to say," Boswell affirmed of the subject of
his own great book, "that he will be seen in this work more
completely than any man who has ever yet lived. And he
will be seen as he really was; for I profess to write not his
panegyric . . . but his life." To show a human being as a
unique individual, "as he really was," seems to us to be the
natural aim to the biographer, but this aim represents a conception of the art which is only two or three centuries old in
Europe, though there are some remarkable foreshadowings of
it in the writings of certain Greek and Roman authors at the
end of the third and beginning of the second century B.C.

The earliest literary records of human beings are mythical:
the stories of the 'god-like' heroes of the Greek epics, the
patriarchs and kings of Israel in the Old Testament, and the
warriors and chieftains of Germanic and Celtic saga. Another
kind of primitive life-record is to be found in the traditions of
the teaching and acts of sages and saints, such as the prophetic
books of the Hebrew Scriptures, the sayings of the Buddha,
and the Analects of Confucius. The accounts of the life and
teaching of Socrates, given by Plato and Xenophon in Athens
in the fourth century B.C., may be regarded as a development
of this kind of record of a great teacher. Incomparable portraits of Socrates and his associates are to be found in the
Dialogues of Plato, but their main interest is philosophical
rather than biographical; the *Memorabilia* of Xenophon, however, though certainly not a biography in the modern sense of
the word, is a series of sketches of the philosopher which are,
at times, almost Boswellian in their intimacy and vividness.
Another literary form practised by classical Greek authors,
which may be regarded as a kind of embryonic biography,

was the encomium, or funeral oration. The chief surviving examples of this kind of writing are the *Agesilaus* of Xenophon and the *Evagoras* of Isocrates. In works of this kind the achievements of the subject of the encomium are recounted briefly with exaggeration (αὔξησις) in order to heighten the praise of his virtues, the aim of the author being not accuracy but panegyric. The ghost of the Greek encomium continued to haunt European literature down to the nineteenth century, and its latest degenerate descendants were those two-volume Victorian biographies which suggested to Lytton Strachey "the cortège of the undertaker" in their "slow funereal barbarism."

The first European author who is remembered primarily as a biographer was Plutarch of Chæronea (*c.* 50 A.D.—120), a Greek philosopher, antiquarian, and man of letters, who lived under the Roman Empire in the days of Titus, Domitian, Nerva, and Trajan. His most famous and influential work is his *Parallel Lives*, a series of forty-six biographies of ancient Greek and Roman statesmen and soldiers, arranged in pairs, with a comparison between each pair. This collection is one of the most fascinating works of antiquity, and certainly one of the main fountain-heads of the European biographical tradition. Plutarch seems to have been the first author to have a clear conception of biography as a separate type of literary composition. He distinguishes it sharply from mythology on the one hand and history on the other. In his *Life of Theseus* he compares himself to the geographers who

> crowd on the outer edges of their maps the parts of the earth which elude their knowledge, with explanatory notes that what lies beyond is sandy desert without water and full of wild beasts,

and adds:

> now that I have traversed these periods of time which are accessible to probable reasoning, and afford a basis for a history dealing with facts, I might well say of the earlier periods what lies beyond

is full of marvels and unreality, the land of poets and fabulists, of doubt and obscurity.[1]

In the *Life of Alexander*, he makes it clear that his function is not that of the historian:

> It is not Histories I am writing but Lives; and in the most illustrious deeds, there is not always a manifestation of virtue or vice, nay a slight thing like a phrase or a jest often makes a greater revelation of character than a battle where thousands fell or the greater armaments or sieges of cities.[2]

Plutarch's *Lives* are certainly the nearest approach in ancient classical literature to the modern conception of biography. In them, as Dryden says:

> You are led into the private lodgings of the Heroe; you see him in his undress, and are made familiar with his most private actions and conversations. You may beheld a *Scipio* and a *Lælius* gathering cockle-shells on the shore, *Augustus* at play at bounding stones with Boyes; and *Agesilaus* riding on a hobby-horse among his children.

Nevertheless Plutarch's *Lives*, in spite of all their vividness and charm, fall short of the Johnsonian and Boswellian ideals. His view of life is not that of the detached spectator interested in the unique individual "as he really was"; he is primarily a moralist and a student of politics. Even if he shows his heroes in undress they are always ethical types, and his main objects are to exalt the Doric and Early Roman virtues and provide lessons for future statesmen. As Archbishop Trench writes, "Vivid moral portraiture, this is what he aimed at, and this is what he achieved. It is not too much to affirm that his leading purpose in writing those lives was not historical but ethical."[3]

A less interesting collection of late Greek biographies is

---

[1] *Plutarch's Parallel Lives*, translated by B. Perrin (11 vols.; Loeb Classical Library, 1914–26), vol. i, p. 3.   [2] *Op. cit.*, vol. vii, p. 225.
[3] *Plutarch, his Life, his Lives, and his Morals* (Macmillan, 1873), p. 43.

The Lives of the Philosophers, by Diogenes Laertius (*c.* A.D. 200—250), a dry compilation which is, however, enlivened by some good anecdotes. The amusing but probably fictitious life of the sage and magician Apollonius of Tyana by the rhetorician Philostratus (*c.* A.D. 181—200) is really a kind of historical novel, based on the tradition of the life-record of a great teacher preserved by his disciples.

The art of biography was also practised by Latin writers under the Empire, and the stately and penetrating life of the soldier-statesman Agricola by his son-in-law, the historian Tacitus, a contemporary of Plutarch, is the most notable extant example of this kind of writing in classical Latin literature. This work is certainly influenced by the tradition of the Greek encomium, and the beautiful and moving epilogue in which Agricola is directly addressed suggests the manner of the funeral oration. The bulk of the work, however, is devoted to a straightforward record of the career of Agricola, together with a long digression containing a description of Britain and the previous Roman conquests in the island, leading up to Agricola's own achievements as administrator, general, and explorer.[1] Agricola is treated throughout as a public figure, and the book is really a kind of mixture of the 'ethical-type' biography with the historical monograph of the encomium. Like Plutarch's heroes, Agricola is a representative of political integrity, but the genuine admiration of Tacitus for his father-in-law and his personal acquaintance with him give the book a depth of feeling and a quality of intimacy which are not found in Plutarch's *Lives.* The methods of Tacitus in his great historical works the *Annals* and the *Histories* are also to a large extent biographical, and there is no doubt that his powerful studies of character in these books had an important effect on the development of biography in Europe after the Renaissance. *The Lives of the Cæsars* by Suetonius, a contemporary of

---

[1] See *Corneli Taciti de Vita Agricola,* edited by H. Furneaux; second edition, revised by J. G. C. Anderson (Oxford University Press, 1922).

Plutarch and Tacitus, are early examples of the gossipy anecdotal Court memoir, or *chronique scandaleuse*. Unlike Plutarch, Suetonius had no high moral aims, and, unlike Tacitus, he is no profound psychologist; but he was an indefatigable collector of facts, anecdotes, and witty sayings. It is to him that we owe the story of Nero's last utterance, "What an artist dies in me,"[1] and Vespasian's flippant dying remark, "Oh, dear, I think I am turning into a god."[2] Suetonius was also a pioneer in literary biography, and wrote lives of Roman authors, of which only his accounts of Terence and Virgil survive.

One of the results of the rise of Christianity was the development of a new kind of life-record called hagiography, or the writing of lives of saints, for the purpose of edification. The narratives of the New Testament may be considered as the prototypes of this kind of biography, of which enormous quantities were produced all over Europe, from the records of St Polycarp in the second century A.D. to those of St Ignatius Loyola and St Teresa in the sixteenth. Many collections of them were made; the most famous of these is the *Aurea Legenda*, or *Golden Legend*, of the thirteenth-century Italian chronicler Jacobus de Voragine, translated into English in the fifteenth century by William Caxton.

Antiquity may thus be seen to have bequeathed three main types of biography which have influenced the writing of lives in every modern European country. They are the 'ethical' life of the hero, statesman, or soldier as written by Plutarch and Tacitus; the royal or Court biography as found in the lives of the Roman emperors; and the life of the saint or sage, with an account of his teaching and miraculous acts. All these are types of generalized biography. Although the recording of individual characteristics was by no means excluded, the emphasis was always on a central figure, regarded less as a unique individual than as a representative of a class, and the biographer always had a definite purpose, which was usually

---

[1] "Qualis artifex pereo."   [2] "Væ, puto deus fio."

didactic. The saint's life is the perfect type of this sort of life-record, which is admirably described by Professor Stauffer: "The saint is not individualized. He is rarely a breathing creature. The necessary centring upon his holiness, which gives these lives admirable unity, makes characterization impossible."[1]

In Britain, as in other modern European countries, biography begins with the lives of saints. These works are in Latin, and belong to a tradition already well established on the Continent. There was a great flowering of British hagiography in the eighth century. The lives of saints written in this period include the beautiful and touching life of St Columba by Adamnan and the homely, realistic life of St Cuthbert by Bede. Under the Norman kings the writing of the lives of ecclesiastics developed considerably in the monasteries. Eadmer, a monk of Canterbury (1060—? 1124), wrote in Latin a life of St Anselm, the famous Archbishop of Canterbury, which is one of the fullest and most interesting biographies of the Middle Ages. The author of this work is completely untrammelled by the conventions of hagiography, and, like Boswell seven centuries later, uses with great effect records of intimate conversation and Anselm's private correspondence. Other notable English ecclesiastical biographies of the Middle Ages are Adam of Eynsham's powerful and candid life of St Hugh of Lincoln (c. 1212—20) and the remarkably vivid and readable life of Abbot Samson in the *Chronicle of Jocelin of Brakelond* (early thirteenth century), used by Carlyle with great effect in his *Past and Present*.

The earliest English secular biographies are lives of kings. The life of Alfred ascribed to Bishop Asser, written in the ninth century, is a clumsy, ill-constructed Latin work, but it contains some interesting anecdotes, and the author's lack of skill is to some extent compensated by his enthusiasm and reverence. The earliest known English biographies in the

---

[1] *English Biography before 1700* (Oxford University Press, 1930), p. 7.

B

vernacular are Ælfric's Lives of St Oswald and St Edmund, written in the tenth century, which belong partly to the tradition of hagiography and partly to that of royal biography. The contemporary Latin lives of the English medieval kings (sometimes in verse) belong to the tradition of the chronicle rather than that of biography. As Professor Stauffer has written, "Individualization in medieval royal biography is negligible. All kings are alike."[1]

In the late Middle Ages the didactic biography of a monarch embodying a moral was popularized by Boccacio's huge Latin compilation *De Casibus Virorum et Feminarum Illustrium*, which was translated by John Lydgate into English verse from a French version in the middle of the fifteenth century. The conception of the fall of a great man through the vicissitudes of fortune had a considerable influence on the writing of English biography in the sixteenth century. It was in this century that the first biographies of literary value were written in English. The invention of printing, the enthusiasm for the Latin and Greek classics, which led to the study of Plutarch, Tacitus, and Suetonius, and the humanistic interest in the individual mind were among the factors which encouraged the writing of biography both in Latin and in the vernacular. The members of Sir Thomas More's circle were certainly interested in this kind of writing. Erasmus wrote brilliant character sketches in Latin of the members of the group, including one of Colet, which is really a short biography. More's early work *The Life of Picus Earl of Mirandola* (*c.* 1505) is an abridged English version of a Latin biography of the great Italian humanist; in spite of its stiffness and rhetorical style it is a pioneer work of some importance as the first English biography of a man who was neither a monarch nor an ecclesiastic. *The History of Richard the Third* (*c.* 1517) is a more mature work of More, and was probably a fragment of a longer historical study which he planned. It is the first English

[1] *Op. cit.*, p. 31.

biography of real literary merit. Here was an English author capable of learning from the great classical biographers of the first century. The vigorous, flexible style of his work, its masterly characterization and vivid dramatic quality, are More's own, but they certainly owe much to an intelligent study of Tacitus and Suetonius.

The Life of Cardinal Wolsey by his gentleman usher George Cavendish remained in manuscript till 1641, although it is said to have been used by Thomas Storer for a poem published in 1599 and by Shakespeare for his *Henry VIII*. Cavendish's book is perhaps the first attempt at an intimate biography in English; he was an eyewitness of most of the scenes which he describes, and his remarkable visual memory and naive delight in the splendours of Tudor pageantry fill his pages with colour and movement. He was probably unaffected by classical models, but was certainly strongly influenced by the late medieval conception of the falls of princes. The whole of his narrative works up to the climax of Wolsey's fall, which is foretold by omens and premonitions, and is described with real pathos and majestic moralizing.

The Life of Sir Thomas More, by his son-in-law, William Roper (written about 1588, but first published in 1626), is the other notable English biography of the Tudor period. Like Cavendish, Roper writes with the vividness of an eyewitness, and the intimacy and charm of his portrait of his father-in-law have kept his book fresh in spite of the fact that it is, to some extent, a work of religious propaganda, belonging to the old tradition of hagiography. In the books of Cavendish and Roper the English genius for realism and concrete statement is already to be seen breaking through the framework of medieval convention, and anticipating a new kind of biographical art.

No original English biography of importance appeared in the Elizabethan Age. A few lives of ecclesiastics were published, such as Humfrey's Latin life of Bishop Jewel (1573) and John Josselin's short life of Archbishop Parker, an English version of which appeared in 1574. The great biographies of classical antiquity were, however, all rendered into English in this period. North's vivid and racy version of Plutarch's *Lives* (used extensively by Shakespeare) appeared in 1579, Sir Henry Savile's version of the *Agricola* of Tacitus in 1591, and Philemon Holland's of Suetonius's *Lives of the Cæsars* in 1606. These translations unquestionably stimulated interest in biography, and provided attractive, if somewhat dangerous, models for English biographers. However, apart from the works of Cavendish and Roper (which were not published till the seventeenth century), English biography in the sixteenth century was still an exotic, and rarely transcended the conception of the generalized and didactic life-record inherited from classical antiquity and the Middle Ages.

THE CLIMATE OF OPINION

Francis Bacon, in the second book of *The Advancement of Learning* (published in 1605), divides 'history' into three kinds: "it either representeth a time, or a person, or an action. The first we call chronicles, the second lives, and the third narrations or relations." It is to be noticed that 'biography' had not yet been naturalized as an English word. In his review of the deficiencies in 'history' in his time Bacon comments particularly on the scarcity of "lives":

> For lives, I do find strange that these times have so little esteemed the virtues of the times, as that the writings of lives should be no more frequent. For although there be not many sovereign princes or absolute commanders, and that States are most collected into monarchies, yet are there many worthy personages that deserve better than disperst report or barren elogies.

When Bacon wrote these words it must be remembered that neither Cavendish's *Life of Wolsey* nor Roper's *Life of*

More had been published, and the only English biographies in print (apart from the saints' lives in Caxton's *Golden Legend*) were the experiments of Sir Thomas More, some short ecclesiastical biographies, like the "Lives" of Jewell and Parker, and the Elizabethan translations. In spite of Bacon's complaint, no real advance in the art of biography was made in England in the first forty years of the seventeenth century. It was an age of ponderous and pedantic learning and the elaborate literary formality mocked by Swift in *A Tale of A Tub*. If the drama is left out of account, it produced, at its best, the subtle and witty poetry of the metaphysical poets, the stately and learned verse of the young Milton, the sonorous and erudite prose-poetry of Donne's sermons and *The Anatomy of Melancholy*. It was the age of the *précieuses*, of 'Platonic love,' and the vogue of the 'portrait' and the Theophrastan character. Sir Thomas Browne was a true son of his age when he declared, "I love to lose my self in a mystery; to pursue my Reason to an *O altitudo*."[1] This is a state of mind which may produce admirable poetry and meditative prose, but it is not likely to produce good biographies. Literature was mainly an affair of the Court and the universities. The trading and artisan middle class was mainly interested in works of devotion and religious controversy. No Defoe or Richardson had yet appeared to produce a literature of middle-class culture. The best that this class could do in the way of biography is to be found in works that are almost indistinguishable from funeral sermons, like Anthony Nyxon's short *Memoriall of the Life and Death of Maister Robert Dove* (1612), a "Citizen and Merchant-Taylor of London," which consists simply of a catalogue of Dove's charitable deeds, such as "his maintenance of 13 aged men, to whom he gives yearely 20 nobles a peece," with the author's pious reflections, but containing no chronological narrative or recognizable portrait of a human being.

The chief models for literary biography in the early seven-

[1] *Religio Medici*, I, 9.

teenth century were the 'ethical-type' biographies of Plutarch and Tacitus. It is significant that Sir Henry Savile's translation of the *Agricola* went through six editions. The example of these classic biographies was reinforced by the Court fashion for character studies. On the one hand, there were the generalized 'Characters,' based on the Greek ethical characters of Theophrastus, translated into Latin by Casaubon in 1592, and imitated in a host of English collections,[1] such as those of Sir Thomas Overbury (1614) and Nicholas Breton (1615), and John Earle's *Microcosmographie* (1628). On the other, there was the slightly later vogue of the 'portraits,' or character studies of individuals, connected both with the study of Tacitus and with the *roman à clef*, made fashionable by the *précieuses* of the circle of Mlle de Montpensier, and seen at their best in England in the stately and elaborate characters in Clarendon's *History of the Great Rebellion*.[2] These models helped, as Harold Nicolson[3] has remarked, "to give method and unity to psychological investigation." But, as the same critic has pointed out, their influence "led biographers to fix upon a certain quality or type, and subsequently so to adjust details as to fit them into the thesis or frame selected." Their method was static and deductive and hampered the development of the native genius for empirical and inductive realism.

The typical English biographies of the early seventeenth century are described very well by Bacon's phrase "disperst report or barren elogies." They are prolix, learned, and formal, tending to confuse biography either with history or with panegyric.

Bacon's own *Life of Henry VII* is a noble and stately piece of Jacobean prose, and is still readable as the work of an acute political observer and a master of English style; but it is dis-

---

[1] See *A Book of Characters*, edited by R. Aldington (Routledge, 1924).
[2] See *Characters from the Histories and Memoirs of the Seventeenth Century*, edited by D. Nichol Smith (Clarendon Press, 1918), with its valuable Introduction.
[3] *The Development of English Biography* (Hogarth Press, 1928), p. 41.

appointing as a biography. In his dedication of the book to Prince Charles he writes of Henry, "I have not flattered him, but took him to life as well as I could, sitting so far off and having no better light." Bacon depicts the King merely as a ruler and statesman, and his work is modelled rather on the *Annals* of Tacitus than on the *Agricola*. It is, in fact, a history of England from Bosworth Field to the death of Henry VII, with the King as the central figure. We hear nothing of the life of Henry of Richmond before his expedition to England in 1485, and, though there is a shrewd analysis of his character, there are no vivid or intimate personal touches. Bacon's short Latin work *In Felicem Memoriam Elizabethæ Reginæ* is not a biography of the great Queen, but an impressive and penetrating character-study with a certain amount of conventional adulation.

The failure of English biography in the early seventeenth century is exemplified in a striking way by Fulke Greville's *Life of the Renowned Sir Philip Sidney*, written about 1610–12, but not published till 1652. Greville was a man with remarkable literary and intellectual gifts and a powerful imagination. He also had the advantage of intimate and lifelong acquaintance with Sidney. Such a man, one would expect, must have preserved at least some vivid impressions of Sidney's character, appearance, and conversation. The reader, however, will look for these things in vain in Greville's *Life of the Renowned Sir Philip Sidney*. The nearest that Greville gets to portraiture is to be found in such charming but vague eulogy as the following description:

> Though I lived with him, and knew him from a child, yet I never knew him other than a man: with such staiednesse of mind, lovely, and familiar gravity, as carried grace, and reverence above greater years. His talk ever of knowledge, and his very play tending to enrich his mind: So as even his teachers found something in him to observe, and learn above that which they usually read, or taught.

Greville's book contains no dates, no consecutive narrative, no account of Sidney's habits or friends, or the houses where he lived, or his marriage, hardly any description of his life at Court, and, except for some criticism of the *Arcadia* from the viewpoint of the political philosopher, no reference to his writings. It consists mainly of rambling, though sometimes eloquent and impressive, discussions of Elizabeth's policy and the political problems of her reign, with some account of Sidney's views on these subjects. The only vivid biographical passage is the famous account of the last days of Sidney's life, at Zutphen, and even this passage is overlaid with unctuous and long-winded moralizing.

Biography, unlike poetry, was a kind of writing which benefited enormously by the great change in the climate of European opinion which took place about the middle of the seventeenth century. This change had many aspects. The most striking was the scientific revolution of which the great prophet in England was Francis Bacon with his rehabilitation of "Nature," or the material world, as the book of God which men had neglected and which they should now study with the same fervour as that with which they had applied themselves to the study of revealed religion. Bacon insisted on the importance of experiment and the inductive approach to truth; he proclaimed his determination "to dwell among things soberly and to establish for ever a true and legitimate union between the experimental and rational faculty." Man was no longer to look inward upon his own soul, but outward upon Nature with a new humility and a new pride.

For the wit and mind of man, if it work upon matter, which is contemplation of the creatures of God, worketh according to the stuff and is limited thereby; but if it work upon itself, as the spider worketh his web, then it is endless, and bring forth indeed cobwebs of learning, admirable for the fineness of thread and work, but of no substance or profit.

[1] *The Advancement of Learning*, I, iv, 5.

The last words are an allusion to the scholastic philosophers of the Middle Ages, but they apply admirably to the work of such a biographer as Fulke Greville. "To work upon matter, which is the contemplation of the creatures of God" was the new ideal of progressive minds in the seventeenth century. This is what Blake nearly two hundred years later was to call "the single vision and Newton's sleep." In the seventeenth century, however, Bacon and his followers did not think of Nature as dead, colourless matter governed by mechanical laws, but as "the creatures of God" to. be approached both with scientific curiosity and religious awe and veneration.

Abraham Hill, in *Some Account of the Life of Dr Isaac Barrow* (see p. 151), tells how that typical scholar of the mid-seventeenth century when he was at Cambridge "applied himself to the reading and considering the Writings of the *Lord Verulam* [Bacon], *Monsieur Des Cartes, Galileo* and the other great Wits of the last Age." In the writings of René Descartes (1596–1650), the French philosopher and mathematician, the adventurous minds of the age found a more thoroughgoing scepticism than anything which had been known since the days of ancient Greek philosophy. They were exhilarated by what Professor Butterfield has called his "determination to doubt everything and start naked once again without any foothold whatever save the consciousness that I who do the doubting must exist."[1] His search for truth ended with his famous acceptance of clearness and distinctness as the only reliable guides. "Cogito ergo sum (I think and therefore I exist)": that was a clear and distinct idea, and so was the idea of God. From them the whole universe could be deduced. "He established," writes Professor Butterfield, "the great principle of common sense in modern times, for if he insisted on one point more than any other it was his thesis: 'All things which we clearly and distinctly perceive are true.' "[2] It was not the positive teaching of Descartes that influenced his contemporaries so

[1] *The Origins of Modern Science* (G. Bell, 1949), p. 98.   [2] *Ibid.*, p. 97.

much as the spirit of his *Discourse on Method*, that "dramatic rejection of inherited systems and ideas." The *Discourse* was not only significant as philosophy: it is a record of personal experience which provides an admirable model for the biographer in its vividness and clarity and economy of phrase.

All Europe had heard of the revival by the Italian physicist and astronomer Galileo Galilei[1] (1546–1642) of the atomic theory of ancient philosophy, and his rejection of the orthodox Aristotelian doctrines of matter and cosmology. Galileo looked at the moon and other heavenly bodies through his newly invented telescope and confuted the Aristotelians by the evidence of sense impression. In actual fact, he and they were talking a different language. Their kind of 'truth' was metaphysical truth; Galileo's was scientific truth. The new scientific truth was, however, accepted with enthusiasm by progressive minds all over Europe. For a time it gave men a fresh and exciting vision of the material universe as a "brave new world," and a new faith in the power of the human mind to understand it and master it.

The writer who typified the "new philosophy" in England in its most uncompromising, and, to many minds, its most threatening aspects, was Thomas Hobbes of Malmesbury, whose thoroughgoing materialism and hatred of the bookish verbosity of the learned men of his day are expressed in his *Leviathan* (1651) with a force and a cogency which dealt a shattering blow at what he called "the Kingdom of darkness" and the "frequencie of insignificant speech." It is no accident that Hobbes was the friend and admired master of John Aubrey, the most original and revolutionary English writer of biography of the seventeenth century.

About the year 1645, according to John Wallis the mathematician, a group of "divers worthy persons" interested in the "new philosophy" were meeting in London to discuss

---

[1] An English translation of his *Systeme of the World in Four Dialogues* by T. Salisbury appeared in 1661.

scientific matters. Later the group, which was nicknamed the "Invisible College," was transferred to Oxford, where it met in the rooms of Dr Wilkins, the Warden of Wadham, and in those of the Hon. Robert Boyle, the founder of modern chemistry. At the Restoration the meetings in London were resumed, and Charles II took a personal interest in its proceedings. The group now became organized as a regular society, and in 1662 received a Royal Charter. The Royal Society of London soon became famous all over Europe as one of the chief centres of the new experimental science. It is remarkable that of the four biographers whose work is represented in this volume three were early Fellows of the Royal Society, and of these one was its second Treasurer. The aim of the Society, as described by Thomas Sprat its first historian, was to make England "a land of *Experimental Knowledge*." Its motto was *Nullius in Verba*—"on the word of no one"—and for its members the proper study of mankind was the world of "nature" and "sense," to be approached by the empirical method recommended by Bacon. Part of that world was man, conceived no longer primarily as an immortal spirit voyaging between heaven and hell, but "in his proper habit as he lived," a citizen of London, Paris, or Amsterdam with certain physical and mental characteristics, which could be recorded in that "close, naked, natural way of speaking," which Sprat tells us the Society "exacted from all their members."

Already on the Continent a new type of scientific life-record had begun to appear. Such works were not displays of learning or piety or conventional eulogy, but records of fact stated as accurately and as lucidly as possible. A pioneer work of this kind was the *De Vita Propria* (*Book of My Own Life*), by the Italian physician and mathematician Girolamo Cardano, or Jerome Cardan (1501–76), written in Latin, and first published in Paris in 1643 (second edition, Amsterdam, 1654). It was, perhaps, the frankest and most uninhibited study of a single human being which had been published in Europe up to that date. Cardan describes in the greatest detail the circumstances of his birth and childhood, his family, his personal appearance, his habits, his meals, his health, his recreations, his studies, his dreams, his eccentricities, and his religious opinions. Nothing is too trifling or too undignified for him to record. We learn that he had a narrow chest, slender arms, a shrill voice, and "a blotch over his left eyebrow like a small lentil," that he preferred fish to meat, liked especially river crabs, and thought four suits of clothes enough for any man. "My book," he writes in his Preface, "is without any artifice and does not aim at instructing anyone; but is simply a historical record, recounting my life and not sensational events."[1] John Aubrey bought a copy of the 1643 edition of the *De Vita Propria* in 1674,[2] and he must have learnt much from Cardan's detached curiosity and his methodical recording of details.

Pierre Gassendi (1592–1655), a French philosopher and mathematician and a great champion of the "new philosophy" and the experimental method, published in Latin, in 1641, a biography of his elder contemporary and fellow-countryman Nicholas de Peiresc (the "learned Peireskius" of Sterne; see *Tristram Shandy*, Book I, Chapter XXXIX). Gassendi's *Vita Peireskii*, first published in 1641, was a very popular book and was translated into French and English. The English version by W. Rand, Doctor of Physic, appeared in 1657. Gassendi, in his Preface, like Cardan, expressly disclaims elegance of style and prides himself on "the simplicity and plainness" of his narration. He anticipates the criticism that he dwells on "so many petty businesses," and defends himself on the ground that "even the very crums which fall from the Tables of the Gods, seem worthy to be picked up." In a passage which foreshadows Dr Johnson's remarks in *The Rambler* (see above,

---

[1] "Nostra autem sine fuco, et non doctura quemquam sed pura historia contenta, vitam non tumultus habet."
[2] See "John Aubrey's Books," in the *Times Literary Supplement*, January 13, 1950.

p. 11) he argues that for "those who desire to be thoroughly
acquainted with great men," it will not be unpleasant to learn
about "their private transactions, and such as they themselves
would not willingly have the World acquainted with." The
Vita Peireskii is one of the fullest and most detailed of seventeenth-century biographies. It records not only Peireskius's
ancestry, learned friendships, travels, and historical and
scientific researches, but also precise details of his personal
appearance, habits, and health. Dates are given in the margin,
and, though there is a certain amount of conventional adulation, the book presents a remarkably complete picture of a
man who, though of noble birth and distinguished in the
world of learning, was neither a monarch nor an ecclesiastic.

While the growth of the scientific spirit undoubtedly had a
revolutionary and beneficial effect on the writing of biography,
certain religious movements in England in the late seventeenth
century also encouraged the fearless and sincere exploration of
human character and personality. Professor Basil Willey has
drawn attention to the close parallelism between English
Protestantism and the new "experimental philosophy." In the
moral sphere, as Professor Willey has pointed out, the Protes-
tants were experimenters and "had the same disdain for all
that was not 'truth' as the natural philosopher had in his."[1]
On the one hand, there was Anglicanism of various shades,
generally 'Arminian'—*i.e.*, favouring the doctrine of Free
Will—and, after the Restoration especially, inclining more and
more to the tolerant, philosophical, latitudinarian Christianity
taught by the Cambridge Platonists. This was a Christian
humanism, the religion of scholars and gentlemen like John
Donne, George Herbert, Henry More, Jeremy Taylor, and
Isaac Barrow. Its ideal was a combination of spiritual beauty
and sweetness of character with intellectual culture based on
classical learning, which might be combined either with
mystical theology, as in More or Traherne, or with scientific

[1] *The Seventeenth-century Background* (Chatto and Windus, 1934), pp. 226, 227.

interests, as in Sprat and Barrow. On the other hand, there
was Puritanism, the Calvinist religion of the lower-middle and
working class, strongly democratic and inclined to echo the
claim of Colonel Rainsborough: "I think that the poorest he
in England hath a life to live, as the greatest he." For the
Puritan, as the works of John Bunyan show, psychological
analysis and the study of character were of the greatest importance. The 'professor' or converted man had to search his
heart as well as the Scriptures for signs of that Grace by which
alone he could be justified. No priest or Church stood
between the soul and God, and each individual had the awful
responsibility of working out his own salvation under Divine
Providence.

The scientific spirit, Christian humanism, and Puritanism
had produced at the time of the Restoration an intellectual
atmosphere that was favourable to the production of good
biography, but it must not be supposed that the art was
immediately revolutionized. The process was slow, and the
greatest English biographies did not appear till the second
half of the eighteenth century. Some remarkable work was,
indeed, done by English writers in the Restoration period, and
and it will be described in the last section of this Introduction,
but biographies of the old type continued to appear. Thus,
when Peter Heylyn wished to commemorate Archbishop Laud
he produced a ponderous folio[1] which is merely a gigantic
Royalist pamphlet and gives no clear conception of the
character, appearance, or habits of the Archbishop. Thomas
Sprat, the author of the excellent *History of the Royal Society*,
had the chance of writing the biography of one of the most
interesting men of his time, the poet Abraham Cowley. He
was Cowley's intimate friend and literary executor, but out of
mistaken delicacy he refused to print the poet's letters[2] and

[1] *Cyprianus Anglicus* (London, 1668).
[2] On the ground that "In such Letters the Souls of Men should appear
undress'd: And in that negligent Habit, they may be fit to be seen by one or
two in a Chamber, but not to go abroad into the Streets."

prefixed to his works a colourless and discreet *Account of his Life*, which is admirably described by Dr Johnson:

> ... his zeal of friendship, or ambition of eloquence has produced a funeral oration rather than a history: he has given the character, not the life, of Cowley; for he writes with so little detail, that scarcely anything is distinctly known, but all is shown confused and enlarged through the mist of panegyrick.[1]

Nowhere have the typical faults of the old kind of biography been better summarized than in this devastating criticism.

THE NEW BIOGRAPHY

Professor Butterfield, in his *Origins of Modern Science*,[2] has called the decade of the sixteen-eighties "the galvanic period" for the development of the scientific movement in England and France, "the years that came to their peak in 1687 with the publication of Newton's *Principia*." The period from 1660 to 1700 may be called a 'galvanic' period for English biography, when, in spite of the survival of the bad traditions of the discreet official biography and the "mists of panegyric," empirical and inductive methods, closely parallel to those of the 'new science,' were used in a series of works of a kind hitherto unattempted in the English language—life-records which are not only reasonably accurate and detailed, but also vivid and convincing portraits of human beings.

Bacon had demanded that his new scientific investigators should come to their work with "minds washed clean of opinions," and Fontenelle, in his *Éloge du Père Malebranche*, tells how Malebranche after he had started to read Descartes was reproached by his friends for neglecting all his other studies. He replied by asking them if Adam did not possess perfect knowledge. When they agreed that, according to the

---

[1] "Life of Cowley," in *The Lives of the Poets*.   [2] P. 144.

theologians, this was Adam's condition before the Fall Male-branche answered that perfect knowledge was not criticism or history, and that he only wanted to know what Adam had known. This determination to see the world with a fresh vision, unhampered by systems or useless learning, was not confined to the scientists. It is also found in the religious writers and the poets. It is the subject to which Thomas Traherne recurs again and again in his poems and his *Centuries of Meditations*:

> This made me present evermore
>   With whatsoere I saw.
> An object, if it were before
> My Ey, was by Dame Nature's Law,
>   Within my Soul. Her store
> Was all at once within me; all her Treasures
> Were my Immediate and Internal Pleasures.

One of the chief literary results of the new curiosity, the desire to see "the thing as it is" and record it effectively, was the remarkable development of autobiographical writing in seventeenth-century England. Before 1600 few works of this kind had been written, and those that survive from the sixteenth century are bald, impersonal records. The first half of the seventeenth century, however, saw the composition (though not the publication) of such lively and readable autobiographies as those of Robert Cary, Earl of Monmouth, and Lord Herbert of Cherbury, while post-Restoration England produced an unrivalled wealth of personal records of every description, ranging from the colourful diary of Pepys and the decorous memoirs of Evelyn to Clarendon's weighty and dignified *Life* and the great spiritual autobiographies of John Bunyan, George Fox, and Richard Baxter. Autobiography and bio-graphy, as Professor Stauffer has pointed out, were closely related in the seventeenth century. Much of the peculiar flavour of Walton's "Lives" is due to the autobiographical element in them, Burnet's memoir of Rochester is partly autobiographical, and the vivid entries in Pepys's diary clearly belong to the same climate of opinion as the brilliant jottings of Aubrey.

It is highly significant that the words 'biography' and 'biographer' were used for the first time in English in works published in 1661 and 1662.[1] A new word was added to the language to denote a new conception of the writing of lives. The new biographies of the later seventeenth century were 'short lives,' in which the authors tried to avoid unnecessary parades of learning, and, in the spirit of the young Malebranche and the 'new science,' to concentrate on "experimental" knowledge and verifiable facts. A pioneer of the new art was Izaak Walton (1593–1683), a writer whose work forms a bridge between the old poetic world and the new realistic world and between the old 'ethical type' life and the new inductive biography. Walton is generally known as the author of the idyllic *Compleat Angler*, and his memory was enveloped in a haze of sentiment in the nineteenth century. His "Lives" were remembered as works of piety and associated with Wordsworth's famous tribute:

> The feather, whence the pen
> Was shaped that traced the lives of these good men,
> Dropped from an Angel's wing.

Actually Walton, as Professor Butt has shown in an admirable essay,[2] was an extremely conscientious and painstaking biographer with a keen interest in the political and ecclesiastical life of his age. He had certain initial advantages. He was not a professional scholar or ecclesiastic or courtier, but a London shopkeeper. As a tradesman he had a respect for facts and for accurate chronology which was not generally found among the scholars and courtiers of his day. Nevertheless he had opportunities for intercourse with some of the finest minds of

---

[1] Stauffer, *op. cit.*, pp. 217–219.
[2] *Essays and Studies by Members of the English Association* (Oxford University Press, 1934), vol. xix, pp. 67–85.

C

his time, which must have been very rare for men of his class, and he was able to share in that gracious atmosphere of Christian humanism and courtly culture which distinguished the finest English society of the seventeenth century. Like Chaucer, he was able to enjoy the advantages of aristocratic culture without the disadvantages (for an author) of aristocratic birth. He became a biographer late in life, and almost by accident. His house was close to the Church of St Dunstan's-in-the-West, where he held several parish offices. John Donne was vicar of this parish when he was Dean of St Paul's, and Walton seems to have made his acquaintance at this time. He may well have owed his introduction to Donne to his wife —a great-grand-daughter of Archdeacon Cranmer, brother of Archbishop Cranmer, and great-niece of George Cranmer, the favourite pupil of Richard Hooker, the great defender of the Anglican Church settlement in Elizabeth's reign. He thus had personal connexions with some of the most distinguished churchmen of the age. Donne probably introduced him to Sir Henry Wotton and to Henry King, the poet, afterwards Bishop of Chichester.

At an early period in his life Walton seems to have started to make notes about some of the distinguished people with whom he was connected. As early as 1626, the date of his marriage, he was, he tells us, "a diligent inquisitor into many matters that concerned" Richard Hooker, his wife's famous ancestor. It may be noticed that, although Walton's connexions were mainly ecclesiastical, he admired Bacon, whom he described in a memorable phrase as "the great Secretary of Nature, and all learning,"[1] and he may well have been impressed by Bacon's remarks about the lack of English "Lives," as well as by his empirical approach to truth. After Donne's death in 1631 Sir Henry Wotton was asked to write his life

---

[1] The phrase "secretary of Nature" (γραμμάτευς τῆς φύσεως) was originally applied by Suidas to Aristotle. It is significant that Walton transfers it to Bacon.

as an introduction to an edition of his sermons, and he asked
Walton to help him to collect material. Wotton, however,
died on December 9, 1639, and no life of Donne was found
among his papers. The publisher of Donne's sermons resolved
to print them immediately, but Walton was so deeply moved
at the thought that the sermons would appear without a
biographical introduction that, in his own words, he "reviewed
his forsaken collections," and produced a *Life of Donne* in
about six weeks, which was printed as a preface to Donne's
LXXX Sermons, which appeared in 1640. It is significant
that the practice of prefacing a short life of an author to an
edition of his works, which had been common in editions of
classical authors since the Renaissance, was now being adopted
by publishers of English works. Walton's *Life of Donne* was
one of the first English works of this kind, and it was certainly
by far the most artistic and accurate English biography which
had appeared up to 1640.

Walton had been blamed because the Donne whom he shows
in his *Life* is the great preacher and saintly Dean of St Paul
rather than Jack Donne, the "tortured amorist" of the early
poems. It must be remembered, however, that Walton only
knew Donne in the latter part of his life, and his work is, no
doubt, true to the impression which the great Dean made on
the cultivated young tradesman. In writing his "Lives"
Walton certainly had an 'ethical type' at the back of his mind,
and one of his chief objects was to exalt the ideal character
produced by the Christian Humanism of the Church of England,
the combination of gentleman, scholar, and saint, as opposed
to what he considered to be the narrower and harsher type
encouraged by Puritanism. On the other hand, he is not, as
he has sometimes been represented, a mere painter of flat,
idyllic water-colours. He has a strong sense of the importance
of fact and accurate information. He uses Donne's letters and
poems freely and effectively, and enlivens his narrative by

anecdotes such as that of the vision of his wife which Donne saw in Paris, and by the more questionable device of imaginary conversations.

Walton's *Life of Donne* was followed by a *Life of Wotton*, written, like *The Life of Donne*, as a preface to a volume of collected works and first printed in *Reliquiæ Wottonianæ* (1651). Like *The Life of Donne*, this is a straightforward narrative. Just as Walton's eyes in his earlier biography are fixed on the Donne whom he called "a second St Austin," so in *The Life of Wotton* they are fixed on the idyllic picture of the Provost of Eton, who, after a somewhat stormy career as a courtier and diplomat, retired to a haven "where he was freed from all corroding cares and seated on such a rock so the waves of want could not probably shake," and could spend his time in study, prayer, and the indulgence of "his innate pleasure of Angling."

After the Restoration Walton had a chance of using the notes which he had been making on the life of Richard Hooker. An edition of Hooker's *Works* appeared in 1662 with a very inadequate memoir by Bishop Gauden. Walton, who now had a reputation as a biographer, was asked by Archbishop Sheldon to write a new and authoritative Life to correct Gauden's work. Walton's *Life of Hooker* appeared first separately in 1665, and then in a revised form as a preface to an edition of Hooker's *Works* published in 1666, and it is, perhaps, the most elaborate of his biographies. *The Life of Hooker*, as Professor Butt has pointed out, is really a "Life and Times" biography, and the bulk of it is occupied by a history of the controversies in the Elizabethan Church with Hooker, the great Anglican Champion, as its central figure. Nevertheless Walton is at pains to give a clear picture of Hooker as a man, and here for the first time humour appears as an element in an English biography. There is demure, restrained, but unmistakable comedy in the famous pictures of the simple-minded young country clergyman who comes to preach in

London and is lured by his cunning landlady into a marriage with her shrewish daughter, and of the great philosophic theologian who is forced by his wife to mind the sheep and rock the cradle even when his learned friends came to visit him.

Walton's fourth biography, *The Life of George Herbert*, is, perhaps, his artistic masterpiece. It was published separately in 1670, and in a revised version with the "Lives" of Donne and Hooker in 1675. Walton tells us that he did not write it by request, but for his own pleasure. It is not a "Life and Times" biography, like that of Hooker, but the interest is wholly concentrated on the figure of the saintly and aristocratic poet-priest. Walton had no personal acquaintance with Herbert. He saw him on only one occasion, but he was able to draw on a considerable body of reliable material, including much first-hand knowledge. Two previous accounts of Herbert had been published, one by Nicholas Ferrar, in a short preface to the edition of Herbert's poems called *The Temple* (1633), and the other in a brief biography by Barnabas Oley, a clergyman who edited *Herbert's Remains* (1652). Walton uses both these sources and many others, including information which he received from Herbert's intimate friend Arthur Woodnot, academic and diocesan records, and Herbert's own letters and works in verse and prose. Just as in *The Life of Donne* the emphasis is on the Dean of St Paul's, so in *The Life of Herbert* the emphasis is on the saintly Rector of Bemerton, possibly the most perfect embodiment of the spirit of Anglicanism. Too much of the *Life* is perhaps devoted to Herbert's work as a model parish priest, and Walton is obviously holding him up as an example to the clergy of the Restoration period.

It has been said that this biography is Herbert's nearest approach to hagiography. Hagiography is a loose term. Herbert was a saintly priest, and a truthful biographer could not do otherwise than give the reader an impression of the beauty of holiness as displayed in his character. Walton does this with brilliant success by means of such homely and touching anecdotes as the story of the help given to the poor carter by Herbert on his way to the music meeting at Salisbury, and the exquisite idyll of the ploughmen who "let their plow rest when Mr Herbert's Saints-bell rung to Prayers, that they might also offer their devotions to God with him." It is not, however, only the Saint of Bemerton who is to be found in Walton's *Life*. There is a very delicate ironic humour in his portrayal of George Herbert, the aristocratic and academic dandy who "kept himself too much retir'd, and at too great a distance with all his inferiours," and whose "cloathes seemed to prove he put too great a value on his parts and Parentage," and George Herbert, the Public Orator who "enjoyed his genteel humor for cloaths, and seldom look'd towards *Cambridge*, unless the King were there, but then he never fail'd." Walton certainly does not give a very clear impression of the violent struggle which took place in Herbert's mind when he resolved to renounce the pleasure of his courtly and cultivated life in favour of the austere existence of a model parish priest. As in the other "Lives," the biographer compromises between an inductive treatment of carefully compiled factual material and the imaginative presentation of an ideal ethical type. In *The Life of Herbert* Walton's exquisite appreciation of the poetry of Herbert's character has produced the most lyrical of all English biographies.

His fifth biography, *The Life of Bishop Sanderson* (1678), is, like *The Life of Hooker*, a "Life and Times," showing the condition of the Church at the time of its struggle with the Puritans in the mid-seventeenth century. This *Life* is the least poetic and most factual of Walton's biographies. The realism of the scene in which Walton meets Sanderson under a penthouse in Little Britain during a shower and goes with him to "a cleanly house" to eat bread and cheese and drink ale by the fire anticipates the art of Defoe, and he does not think it beneath the dignity of his work to record that the

Bishop was "every winter punished by a diarrhoea, which left not till warm weather returned and removed it."

Gilbert Burnet, the Scottish Whig divine who became Bishop of Salisbury after the Revolution and was caricatured by Dryden as the Buzzard in *The Hind and the Panther*, was a bustling, energetic person, wholly unlike the gentle Walton. He is now ·generally remembered for one great book, the *History of His Own Time*, published after his death in the early eighteenth century (1724–34). Burnet was interested in biography from the beginning of his career, and his earliest literary work was *The Memoirs of the Lives and Actions of James and William Dukes of Hamilton and Castleherald*. This is not a biography in the modern sense of the word, but a "Life and Times" of the Dukes compiled from their papers, and is really, in fact, a History of Scotland from 1625 to 1651, with numerous illustrations from the Hamiltons' correspondence.

The preface shows that Burnet was already thinking seriously about biography. He complains that, in spite of the example of Plutarch, "there is no sort of history worse done" than the writing of the lives of great persons, "they being so full of gross partiality and flattery, and often swelled with trifling and impertinent things." He published three other biographical works before the Revolution. The first of these was inspired by the deep impression made on him by the character of the courtier poet John Wilmot, Earl of Rochester, with whom he had conversations about religion in the winter of 1679–80, and whom he visited again when the Earl was dying in July 1680. The second was a short *Life of Sir Matthew Hale*, an eminent judge who died in 1682, and the third a longer memoir of William Bedell, Bishop of Kilmore. Of these three books by far the most successful is *Some Passages of the Life and Death of John Earl of Rochester* (1680). *The Life of William Bedell* (1685) is a rambling narrative with many digressions on the state of the Church, from which no clear impression of the Bishop's character or personality emerges. *The Life and Death of Sir*

Matthew Hale, Kt. (1682) opens with a preface containing an interesting sketch of the history of biography in which Plutarch and Suetonius are praised, Diogenes Laertius compared to his disadvantage as a biographer with Gassendi, whose *Life of Peireskius* receives high commendation, and the hagiographies of the monks condemned for their "indurable humour of telling incredible and inimitable passages."

Burnet had no personal acquaintance with Hale and had seen him only occasionally in the Rolls Chapel. He writes that he has "endeavoured to set him out in the same simplicity in which he lived." This sounds promising, but the effect is spoilt when Burnet goes on to declare that he has said "little of his Domestick Concerns," and that he will "draw a Vail over all these, and shall avoid saying anything of him but what may afford the Reader some profitable Instruction." This revealing passage points clearly to the two great obstacles to the development of biography in this period—the desire to be dignified and discreet and the desire to impart moral instruction. The great portraits in Burnet's *History* such as that of Lauderdale[1] show what he could do when he was writing without thinking of dignity, discretion, or moral improvement. In *The Life of Hale*, unfortunately, he treats his subject, obviously an interesting man, so reverentially that he hardly ever comes to life, and the biography tends to become a catalogue of his virtues. The most human part of the book is to be found in the passages which describe Hale's generosity to beggars and his love of animals: "he was scarce ever seen more Angry than with one of his Servants for neglecting a Bird that he kept, so that it died for want of Food." Even here, however, we find the dignified vagueness which this work shares with Sprat's *Life of Cowley*. We should like to know if the bird was a magpie, a starling, or a parrot, and something about the servant who neglected it.

[1] See *Characters from the Histories and Memoirs of the Seventeenth Century*, pp. 227-229.

SOME
PASSAGES
OF THE
Life and Death
Of the Right Honourable

JOHN

Earl of *ROCHESTER*,
Who died the 26th of *July*, 1680.

Written by his own Direction on his Death-Bed,
By *Gilbert Burnet*, D. D.

LONDON,
Printed for *Richard Chiswel*, at the
Rose and *Crown* in St. *Pauls Church-*
Yard. 1680.

TITLE-PAGE OF THE FIRST EDITION

The particular charm of Burnet's account of the "Life and Death" of Rochester lies in the fact that it is mainly based on first-hand information, and is much more concrete and dramatic than his other biographies. Dr Johnson, who greatly admired the book, said jokingly to Boswell that it was "a good *Death*; there is not much Life." Actually the opening pages contain not only a concise and vivid narrative of Rochester's short career, but a convincing portrait of a man of great charm, restless intellect, and a hunger for every kind of experience. The central part of the book is occupied with an account of Burnet's discussions with the Earl about religion, in which it is to be noticed that Rochester's point of view is stated very fairly. There is real dramatic power in the presentation of the dialogue between two contrasted characters, and the concluding pages describing the death of the poet are among the best that Burnet ever wrote. Here, fortunately, he does not allow dignity or discretion to prevent him from dwelling on details like Rochester's lapse into his old habits of speech when he spoke of "that damned fellow," one of a number of masterly touches that bring the dying man vividly before our eyes.

In 1683 Jacob Tonson published a new translation of *Plutarch's Lives*, made under the supervision of Dryden, who contributed to it an introduction in the form of a *Life of Plutarch*. This work is a compilation from the sources available to seventeenth-century scholars, but it is written so admirably that it makes us regret that Dryden did not devote more attention to this kind of writing. It contains the most important critical remarks on biography which had hitherto appeared in England (see Appendix, p. 200). In the same year as Dryden's *Plutarch* a folio edition of the *Works* of Isaac Barrow was published with an introductory biography addressed to Archbishop Tillotson by Abraham Hill. Like Walton, Hill was a retired business-man and was self-educated. He had been Treasurer of the Royal Society, and, after the Revolution, he became a Commissioner of Trade. His short *Life of Barrow* is unpretentious, vivid, and lively. He quotes Cardan, and refers to Gassendi's *Life of Peireskius*, and it is clear that he has learned much from these writers. He gives a succinct account of Barrow's career and a clear impression of his character, habits, and appearance; fortunately he is not too dignified to reveal the facts that the famous Master of Trinity was a heavy smoker, loved fruit, and wrote a sarcastic epigram on Charles II. It is a pity that the Royal Society did not commission Hill to write a series of "Lives" of its early Fellows which might have been an English counterpart to Fontenelle's "Lives" (*Éloges*) of the members of the French Académie des Sciences.

The man of genius who could have transformed English biography in the Restoration period and anticipated the triumphs of Johnson and Boswell by a century was John Aubrey, a Wiltshire gentleman, who was educated at Trinity College, Oxford, adopted no profession, but spent his time studying local antiquities, astrology, painting, heraldry, architecture, mineralogy, geology, and ancient history, became one of the first Fellows of the Royal Society in 1663, and lost all his property in a series of disastrous lawsuits. Aubrey had an insatiable appetite for knowledge of every kind, and an all-embracing curiosity. He knew nearly all the most interesting Englishmen of his day and was the lifelong friend of Thomas Hobbes, for whose character and genius he had an immense admiration.

The only book by Aubrey published in his lifetime was his *Miscellanies*, a curious collection of stories and traditions of ghosts and supernatural occurrences, which appeared in 1696. Besides this printed book Aubrey left a number of works in manuscript. Of these by far the most interesting is his famous collection of *Brief Lives* which survive in four folio volumes (now in the Bodleian Library, Oxford) compiled between 1669 and 1696. A selection from them was published in 1813, and a scholarly edition by Andrew Clark in 1898. Aubrey seems to have been interested in biography all his life. As early as 1652, when he was only twenty-five, he promised to compile for Samuel Hartlib "a large and particular account" of Francis Potter, and in 1667 he pledged himself to write a life of his friend Thomas Hobbes, the philosopher. If his financial position had been more secure and if he had been less "shift-less . . . roving and magotie headed,"[1] he might have settled down to produce a biography of Hobbes on a grand scale which would have been a masterpiece to rival Boswell's *Life of Johnson*. His collection of *Brief Lives* was the result of his collaboration with Anthony Wood, the Oxford antiquarian, whom he first met in 1667. Wood, at that time, was collecting material for a biographical dictionary of Oxford men, later published under the title of *Athenæ Oxonienses*, and he employed Aubrey to help him in the work. At his request Aubrey jotted down, during a period of over twenty years, everything he could remember or find out concerning over four hundred persons. He described his method in a letter to Wood written in 1680:

> I have, according to your desire, put in writing these minutes of *Lives* tumultuarily, as they occur'd to my thoughts or as occasionally I had information of them. . . . I heere lay down to you . . . the Trueth; the naked and plain truth: (and as near as I can and that religiously) as a Poenitent to a Confessor, nothing but the truth.

He had the help of some of the most distinguished of his contemporaries. Walton helped him with the life of Ben Jonson, Sir Thomas Browne with that of Dr Dee, and Dryden with much information. Aubrey was an indefatigable collector of gossip and anecdotes of every kind. Nothing was too insignificant or undignified or scandalous for him to report. He has no inhibitions and no desire to teach or moralize. His

---

[1] The phrase is from a description of him by Anthony Wood in his *Journal*.

most ambitious biography is his *Life of Hobbes*, which was originally intended to be published as a commentary on Hobbes's Latin metrical autobiography.

Aubrey was in many ways a representative of the 'new philosophy.' Though he had not the precise mind of the scientist, he had the scientist's respect for facts and the truly scientific quality of completely detached curiosity which even Walton had lacked. Yet in the vividness of his language and his sensuous vision he belongs to the old poetic world. To use the phrases of D. H. Lawrence, "the universe was alive" for him, and he sees "the everlasting wonder of things." He shows us Andrew Marvell in a few words: "pretty strong sett, roundish faced, cherry cheek't, hazell eie." Bacon, he tells us, had "a delicate, lively hazel eie . . . it was like the eie of a viper"; Dr Kettell, President of Trinity, had "a terrible gigantique aspect with his sharp grey eyes." He had a wonderful flair for significant anecdote, such as the stories of Hobbes's discovery of Euclid and his conversation with the Divine after giving alms to the beggar in the Strand. Indeed, the only quality of a supremely great biographer which Aubrey lacked was the power of welding his brilliant notes into a coherent and continuous narrative. Isaac D'Israeli called him "a little Boswell," and he was the first English biographer whose mind was wholly fixed on the Boswellian objective of showing the man "as he really was."

The two great literary inventions of the modern world are the biography and the novel; they are closely related, and perhaps the second could hardly have developed in the way in which it did without the example of the first. It is significant that the new kind of biography had taken root in England before the end of the seventeenth century, whereas the new prose fiction did not come into existence till the first half of the eighteenth, when the form which it commonly took was that of the fictitious biography. Lytton Strachey complained of the lack of an English biographical tradition. He was thinking of the loss of the tradition in the nineteenth century. The work of the English seventeenth-century biographers established a sound tradition based on the native talent for empirical realism. It is true that this tradition did not result immediately in a series of masterpieces like the brilliant *Éloges* of Fontenelle in the France of Louis XIV (1699–1714). Aubrey died in 1697, and no important English biography, with the possible exception of the racy and amusing *Lives of the Norths*, appeared till the publication of Johnson's *Life of Savage* in 1744. However, Johnson had an unbounded admiration for Walton's "Lives" (which he planned to edit), and gave high praise to Burnet's *Rochester*. His biographies, and that of his great disciple James Boswell, may be regarded as the successful continuation of the experiments of the English biographers of the seventeenth century.

IZAAK WALTON

THE LIFE OF MR GEORGE HERBERT

George Herbert was born the third day of *April*, in the Year of our Redemption 1593. The place of his Birth was near to the Town of *Montgomery*, and in that *Castle* that did then bear the name of that Town and County; that *Castle* was then a place of state and strength, and had been successively happy in the Family of the *Herberts*, who had long possest it: and, with it, a plentiful Estate, and hearts as liberal to their poor Neighbours. A Family, that hath been blest with men of remarkable wisdom, and a willingness to serve their Country, and indeed, to do good to all Mankind; for which they are eminent: But alas! this Family did in the late Rebellion suffer extreamly in their Estates; and the Heirs of that *Castle*, saw it laid level with that earth, that was too good to bury those Wretches that were the cause of it.

The Father of our *George* was *Richard Herbert*, the Son of *Edward Herbert*, Knight, the Son of *Richard Herbert*, Knight, the Son of the famous Sir *Richard Herbert of Colebrook* in the County of *Monmouth* Banneret, who was the youngest Brother of that memorable *William Herbert*, Earl of Pembroke, that lived in the reign of our King *Edward* the fourth.

His Mother was *Magdalen Newport*, the youngest Daughter of Sir *Richard*, and sister to Sir *Francis Newport* of *High Arkall*, in the County of *Salop*, Kt., and Grand-father of *Francis* Lord *Newport*, now Comptroller of his Majesties Household. A Family, that for their Loyalty have suffered much in their Estates, and seen the ruine of that excellent Structure, where their Ancestors have long liv'd, and been memorable for their Hospitality.

This Mother of *George Herbert* (of whose person, and wisdom, and vertue, I intend to give a true account in a seasonable place) was the happy Mother of seven Sons and three Daughters, which she would often say was *Job's number*, and *Job's distribution*; and, as often bless God, that they were neither defective in their shapes, or in their reason; and very often reprove them that did not praise God for so great a blessing. I shall give the Reader a short accompt of their names, and not say much of their Fortunes.

Edward the eldest was first made Kt. of the *Bath*, at that glorious time of our late Prince *Henries* being install'd Knight of the Garter; and after many years useful travel, and the attainment of many Languages, he was by King *James* sent Ambassador Resident to the then *French* King, *Lewis* the Thirteenth. There he continued about two Years; but he could not subject himself to a compliance with the humors of the Duke *de Luines*, who was then the great and powerful Favourite at Court: so that upon a complaint to our King, he was call'd back into *England* in some displeasure; but at his return he gave such an honourable account of his employment, and so justified his Comportment to the Duke, and all the Court, that he was suddenly sent back upon the same Embassie, from which he return'd in the beginning of the reign of our good King *Charles* the first, who made him first Baron of *Castle-Island*; and not long after of *Cherbery* in the County of *Salop*: *He was a man of great learning and reason, as appears by his printed Book* de veritate; *and by his History of the reign of K.* Hen. *the Eight, & by several other Tracts.*

The second and third Brothers were *Richard* and *William*, who ventured their lives to purchase Honour in the Wars of the *Low Countries*, and died Officers in that employment. *Charles* was the fourth, and died Fellow of *New-Colledge* in *Oxford*. *Henry* was the sixth, who became a menial servant to the Crown in the daies of King *James*, and hath continued to be so for fifty years; during all which time he hath been

Master of the Revels; a place that requires a diligent wisdom, with which God hath blest him. The seventh Son was *Thomas*, who, being made Captain of a Ship in that Fleet, with which Sir *Robert Mansel* was sent against *Algiers*, did there shew a fortunate and true English valor. Of the three Sisters I need not say more, than that they were all married to persons of worth, and plentiful fortunes; and lived to be examples of *vertue*, and to do good in their generations.

I now come to give my intended account of *George*, who was the fifth of those seven Brothers.

George Herbert spent much of his Childhood in a sweet content under the eye and care of his prudent mother, and the tuition of a Chaplain or Tutor to him, and two of his Brothers, in her own family (for she was then a Widow) where he continued till about the age of twelve years; and being at that time well instructed in the Rules of Grammar, he was not long after commended to the care of Dr *Neale*, who was then Dean of *Westminster*; and by him to the care of Mr *Ireland*, who was then chief Master of that School; where the beauties of his pretty behaviour and wit shin'd, and became so eminent and lovely in this his innocent age, that he seem'd to be marked out for piety, and to become the care of Heaven, and of a particular good Angel to guard and guide him. And thus he continued in that School, till he came to be perfect in the learned Languages, and especially in the Greek tongue, in which he after prov'd an excellent Critick.

About the age of Fifteen he, being then a King's S<c>holar, was elected out of that School for *Trinity Colledge* in *Cambridge*, to which place he was transplanted about the year 1608; and his prudent mother, well knowing that he might easily lose or lessen that virtue and innocence which her advice and example had planted in his mind, did therefore procure the generous and liberal Dr *Nevil*, who was then Dean of *Canterbury*, and Master of that Colledge, to take him into his particular care, and provide him a Tutor; which he did most gladly undertake,

D

for he knew the excellencies of his Mother, and how to value such a friendship.

This was the method of his education, till he was settled in *Cambridge*; where we will leave him in his Study, till I have paid my promis'd account of his excellent Mother; and I will endeavour to make it short.

I have told her birth, her Marriage, and the Number of her Children, and, have given some short account of them: I shall next tell the Reader, that her husband dyed when our *George* was about the Age of four years: I am next to tell, that she continued twelve years a Widow; that she then married happily to a Noble Gentleman, the Brother and Heir of the Lord *Danvers*, Earl of Danby, who did highly value both her person and the most excellent endowments of her mind.

In this time of her widowhood, she being desirous to give *Edward*, her eldest son, such advantages of Learning, and other education, as might suit his birth and fortune: and thereby make him the more fit for the service of his Country, did, at his being of a fit age, remove from *Montgomery Castle* with him, and some of her younger sons to *Oxford*; and having entered Edward into *Queen's Colledge*, and provided him a fit Tutor, she commended him to his Care; yet, she continued there with him, and still kept him in a moderate awe of her self; and, so much under her own eye, as to see and converse with him daily; but she managed this power over him without any such rigid sourness, as might make her company a torment to her Child; but with such a sweetness and compliance with the recreations and pleasures of youth, as did incline him willingly to spend much of his time in the company of his dear and careful Mother; which was to her great content: for she would often say, "That as our bodies take a nourishment sutable to the meat on which we feed: so, our souls do as insensibly take in vice by the example or Conversation with wicked company:" and, would therefore as often say, "That ignorance of Vice was the best preservation

of Vertue; and that the very knowledge of wickedness was as
tinder to inflame and kindle sin, and to keep it burning." For
these reasons she indeared him to her own Company, and
continued with him in *Oxford* four years: in which time her
great and *harmless* wit, her *chearful gravity*, and her *obliging
behaviour*, gain'd her an acquaintance and friendship with most
of any eminent worth or learning, that were at that time in or
near that University; and particularly with Mr *John Donne*,
who then came accidentally to that place, in this time of her
being there: It was that John Donne, who was after *Doctor
Donne*, and Dean of *Saint Pauls*, London: and he, at his
leaving *Oxford*, writ and left there in verse a Character of the
Beauties of her body, and mind; and of the first he saies,

> *No* Spring nor Summer-Beauty, *has such grace*
> *As I have seen in an* Autumnal *face.*

Of the latter he sayes,

> *In all her words to every hearer fit,*
> *You may at* Revels, *or at* Council *sit.*

The rest of her Character may be read in his printed Poems,
in that Elegy which bears the name of the *Autumnal Beauty*.
For both he and she were then past the meridian of mans life.
    This Amity, begun at this time, and place, was not an
Amity that polluted their Souls; but an amity made up of a
chain of sutable inclinations and vertues; an *Amity* like that of
St *Chrysostoms* to his dear and vertuous *Olimpias*; whom, in
his letters, he calls his *Saint*: Or an amity, indeed, more like
that of St *Hierome* to his *Paula*; whose affection to her was
such, that he turn'd poet in his old Age, and then made her
*Epitaph: wishing all his Body were turn'd into Tongues, that he might
declare her just praises to posterity.* And this Amity betwixt her
and Mr *Donne* was begun in a happy time for him, he being
then near to the Fortieth year of his age (which was some years
before he entred into Sacred Orders:) a time when his neces-

sities needed a daily supply for the support of his Wife, seven
Children, and a Family: And in this time she prov'd one of his
most bountiful Benefactors; and he, as grateful an acknowledger
of it. You may take one testimony for what I have said of
these two worthy persons, from this following *Letter*, and
Sonnet.

MADAM,

   Your favours to me are every where: I use them, and have
them. I enjoy them at *London*, and leave them there; and yet find
them at *Micham*. such riddles as these become things unexpressible; and, such is your goodness. I was almost sorry to find your
Servant here this day, because I was loth to have any witness of
my not coming home last Night, and indeed of my coming this
Morning. But, my not coming was excuseable, because earnest
business detein'd me; and my coming this day is by the example
of your St *Mary Magdalen*, who rose early upon *Sunday*, to seek
that which she lov'd most; and so did I. And, from her and my
self, I return such thanks as are due to one to whom we owe all
the good opinion, that they whom we need most, have of us—
by this Messenger, and on this good day, I commit the inclosed
Holy Hymns and *Sonnets* (which, for the matter, not the workmanship, have yet escap'd the fire) to your judgment, and to your
protection too, if you think them worthy of it; and I have
appointed this inclosed *Sonnet* to usher them to your happy hand.

                              Your unworthiest servant,
    Micham   *unless, your accepting him to be so,*
    July 11   *have mended him,*
    1607.   JO. DONNE.

         To the Lady *Magdalen Herbert of* St *Mary Magdalen*

            Her of your name, whose fair inheritance
              Bethina was, and jointure Magdalo:
            An active faith so highly did advance,
              That she once knew, more than the Church did know,

The Resurrection; *so much good there is*
Deliver'd of her, that some Fathers be
Loth to believe one woman could do this:
But, think these Magdalens *were two or three.*
Increase their number, Lady, *and their fame:*
To their Devotion *add your* Innocence:
Take so much of th' example, as of the name;
The latter half; and in some recompence
That they did harbour Christ *himself, a* Guest,
Harbour these Hymns, *to his dear name address.*

                                    J.D.

These *Hymns* are now lost to us; but doubtless they were
such, as they two now sing in *Heaven.*

There might be more demonstrations of the Friendship, and
the many sacred Indearments betwixt these two excellent
persons (for I have many of their Letters in my hand) and
much more might be said of her great prudence and piety:
but, my design was not to write hers, but the Life of her Son;
and therefore I shall only tell my Reader, that about that very
day twenty years that this Letter was dated, and sent her, I
saw and heard this Mr *John Donne* (who was then Dean of St
Pauls) weep, and preach her Funeral Sermon, in the Parish
Church of *Chelsey,* near *London,* where she now rests in her
quiet Grave: and where we must now leave her, and return
to her Son *George,* whom we left in his Study in *Cambridge.*

And in *Cambridge* we may find our *George Herberts* behaviour
to be such, that we may conclude, he consecrated the first-
fruits of his early age to vertue, and a serious study of learning.
And that he did so, this following Letter and Sonnet, which
were, in the first year of his going to *Cambridge,* sent his dear
Mother for a New-year's gift, may appear to be some testimony.

—'But I fear the heat of my late *Ague* hath dried up those
springs, by which Scholars say the Muses use to take up their
habitations. However, I need not their help to reprove the
vanity of those many Love-poems, that are daily writ, and

consecrated to *Venus*; nor to bewail that so few are writ, that look towards *God* and *Heaven*. For my own part, my meaning (dear Mother) is, in these Sonnets, to declare my resolution to be, that my poor abilities in *Poetry*, shall be all and ever consecrated to Gods glory: and I beg you to receive this as one testimony.'

> *My God, where is that antient heat towards thee,*
>   *Wherewith whole showls of* Martyrs *once did burn,*
>   *Besides their other flames? Doth Poetry*
> *Wear* Venus *Livery? only serve her turn?*
> *Why are not* Sonnets *made of thee? and layes*
>   *Upon thine Altar burnt? Cannot thy love*
>   *Heighten a spirit to sound out thy praise*
> *As well as any she? Cannot thy* Dove
> *Outstrip their* Cupid *easily in flight?*
>   *Or, since thy ways are deep, and still the same,*
>   *Will not a verse run smooth that bears thy name?*
> *Why doth that fire, which by thy power and might*
>   *Each breast does feel, no braver fewel choose*
>   *Than that, which one day,* Worms, *may chance refuse?*
> *Sure, Lord, there is enough in thee to dry*
>   *Oceans of* Ink; *for, as the Deluge did*
>   *Cover the Earth, so doth thy Majesty:*
> *Each cloud distils thy praise, and doth forbid*
> *Poets to turn it to another use.*
>   *Roses and Lillies speak thee; and to make*
>   *A pair of Cheeks of them, is thy abuse.*
> *Why should I* Women's *eyes for Chrystal take?*
> *Such poor invention burns in their low mind*
>   *Whose fire is wild, and doth not upward go*
>   *To praise, and on thee, Lord, some Ink bestow.*
> *Open the bones, and you shall nothing find*
>   *In the best face but filth; when Lord, in thee*
>   *The beauty lies, in the discovery.*
>
>   G.H.

This was his resolution at the sending this Letter to his

dear Mother; about which time he was in the Seventeenth
year of his Age; and as he grew older, so he grew in learning,
and more and more in favour both with God and man: insomuch that, in this morning of that short day of his life, he
seem'd to be marked out for vertue, and to become the care
of Heaven; for God still kept his soul in so holy a frame, that
he may, and ought to be a pattern of vertue to all posterity,
and especially to his brethren of the Clergy, of which the
Reader may expect a more exact account in what will follow.

I need not declare that he was a strict Student, because, that
he was so, there will be many testimonies in the future part of
his life. I shall therefore only tell, that he was made *Batchelor
of Art* in the year 1611; *Major Fellow* of the *Colledge, March*
15th, 1615; And, that in that year, he was also made *Master of
Arts*, he being then in the 22d year of his Age; during all which
time, all, or the greatest diversion from his Study, was the
practice of Musick, in which he became a great Master; and of
which he would say, 'That it did relieve his drooping spirits,
compose his distracted thoughts, and raised his weary soul so
far above Earth, that it gave him an earnest of the joys of
Heaven, before he possest them.' And it may be noted, that
from his first entrance into the Colledge, the generous Dr *Nevil*
was a cherisher of his Studies, and such a lover of his person,
his behaviour, and the excellent endowments of his mind, that
he took him often into his own company; by which he confirmed his native gentleness; and, if during this time he exprest
any Error, it was, that he kept himself too much retir'd, and at
too great a distance with all his inferiours; and his cloathes
seemed to prove, that he put too great a value on his parts and
Parentage.

This may be some account of his disposition, and of the
employment of his time till he was Master of Arts, which was
Anno 1615. and in the year 1619. he was chosen Orator for the
University. His two precedent Orators were Sir *Robert
Nanton*, and Sir *Francis Nethersoll*. The first was not long

after made Secretary of State, and Sir Francis, not very long after his being Orator, was made Secretary to the Lady *Elizabeth*, Queen of *Bohemia*. In this place of Orator, our *George Herbert* continued eight years; and manag'd it with as becoming and grave a gaiety, as any had ever before, or since his time. For *he had acquir'd great Learning, and was blessed with a high fancy, a civil and sharp wit; and with a natural elegance, both in his behaviour, his tongue, and his pen.* Of all which there might be very many particular evidences; but I will limit myself to the mention of but three.

And the first notable occasion of shewing his fitness for this employment of *Orator* was manifested in a Letter to King *James*, upon the occasion of his sending that University his Book, called *Basilicon Doron*; and their Orator was to acknowledge this great honour, and return their gratitude to His Majesty for such a condescension; at the close of which letter he writ,

> *Quid Vaticanam Bodleianamque objicis hospes!*
> *Unicus est nobis Bibliotheca Liber.*

This Letter was writ in such excellent Latin, was so full of Conceits, and all the expressions so suited to the *genius* of the King, that he inquired the Orators name, and then ask'd *William* Earl of *Pembroke*, if he knew him? whose answer was, 'That he knew him very well; and, that he was his kinsman; but he lov'd him more for his learning and vertue, than for that he was of his name and family. At which answer the king smil'd, and asked the Earl leave "that he might love him too; for he took him to be the Jewel of that University."

The next occasion he had and took to shew his great Abilities, was, with them, to shew also his great affection to that Church in which he received his *Baptism*, and of which he profest himself a member; and, the occasion was this; There was one *Andrew Melvin*, a Minister of the Scotch Church, and Rector of St *Andrews*; who, by a long and constant

Converse with a discontented part of that Clergy which
oppos'd Episcopacy, became at last to be a chief leader of that
Faction; and, had proudly appear'd to be so to King James,
when he was but King of that Nation, who, the second year
after his Coronation in England, conven'd a part of the
Bishops, and other Learned Divines of his Church, to attend
him at *Hampton-Court*, in order to a friendly Conference with
some Dissenting Brethren, both of this, and the Church of
Scotland: of which Scotch party *Andrew Melvin* was one; and
he being a man of learning, and inclin'd to *Satyrical Poetry*, had
scatter'd many malicious, bitter Verses against our *Liturgy*,
our *Ceremonies*, and our *Church-government*; which were by some
of that party, so magnified for the wit, that they were therefore
brought into *Westminster-School*, where Mr *George Herbert*,
then, and often after, made such answers to them, and such
reflexion on him and his *Kirk*, as might unbeguile any man
that was not too deeply pre-ingaged in such a quarrel.—But to
return to Mr *Melvin* at *Hampton-Court Conference*; he there
appeared to be a man of an unruly wit, of a strange confidence,
of so furious a Zeal, and of so ungovern'd passions, that his
insolence to the King, and others at this Conference, lost him
both his Rectorship of St *Andrews* and his liberty too: for his
former Verses, and his present reproaches there used against
the Church and State, caus'd him to be committed prisoner
to the Tower of *London*; where he remained very angry for
three years. At which time of his commitment, he found the
Lady *Arabella* an innocent prisoner there; and he pleased
himself much in sending, the next day after his Commitment,
these two verses to the good Lady; which I will under-write,
because they may give the Reader a taste of his others, which
were like these.

Causa tibi mecum est communis, Carceris, Ara-
Bella; tibi causa est, Araque sacra mihi.

I shall not trouble my Reader with an account of his enlargement from that Prison, or his Death; but tell him Mr *Herberts* verses were thought so worthy to be preserv'd, that Dr *Duport*, the learned Dean of *Peterborough*, hath lately collected and caus'd many of them to be printed, as an honourable memorial of his friend Mr *George Herbert*, and the Cause he undertook.

And in order to my third and last observation of his great Abilities, it will be needful to declare, that about this time King *James* came very often to hunt at *New-Market* and *Royston*; and was almost as often invited to *Cambridge*, where his entertainment was Comedies suted to his pleasant humor; and, where Mr *George Herbert*, was to welcome him with *Gratulations*, and the *Applauses* of an *Orator*; which he always perform'd so well, that he still grew more into the King's favour, insomuch that he had a particular appointment to attend His Majesty at *Royston*; where, after a Discourse with him, his Majesty declared to his Kinsman, the Earl of *Pembroke*, 'That he found the Orators learning and wisdom, much above his age or wit.' The year following, the King appointed to end His progress at *Cambridge*, and to stay there certain days; at which time he was attended by the great Secretary of Nature, and all Learning, Sir *Francis Bacon* (Lord *Verulam*) and by the ever-memorable and learned Dr *Andrews*, Bishop of *Winchester*, both which did at that time begin a desir'd friendship with our *Orator*. Upon whom, the first put such a value on his judgment, that he usually desir'd his approbation before he would expose any of his Books to be printed; and thought him so worthy of his friendship, that having translated many of the Prophet *Davids* Psalms into English Verse, he made *George Herbert* his Patron, by a publick dedication of them to him, as the best Judge of *Divine Poetry*. And for the learned Bishop, it is observable, that at that time there fell to be a modest debate betwixt them two about *Predestination*, and *Sanctity of life*; of both of which the *Orator* did, not long after, send the Bishop some safe and useful *Aphorisms*, in a long Letter, written in Greek; which Letter was so remarkable for the language and reason of it, that, after the reading it, the Bishop put it into his bosom, and did often shew it to many Scholars, both of this, and forreign Nations; but did alwaies return it back to the place where he first lodg'd it, and continued it so near his heart till the last day of his life.

To this, I might add the long and intire friendship betwixt him and Sir *Henry Wotton*, and Doctor *Donne*; but I have promised to contract my self, and shall therefore only add one testimony to what is also mentioned in the Life of Doctor *Donne*; namely, that a little before his death, he caused many Seals to be made, and in them to be ingraven the figure of *Christ crucified on an Anchor*, (the emblem of hope) and of which Dr *Donne* would often say, *Crux mihi Anchora.*—These Seals he gave or sent to most of those friends, on which he put a value, and, at Mr *Herberts* death, these Verses were found wrapt up with that Seal, which was by the Doctor given to him;

> *When my dear friend could write no more,*
> *He gave this* Seal *and so gave ore.*
>
> *When winds and waves rise highest, I am sure,*
> *This* Anchor *keeps my* faith, *that, me secure.*

At this time of being *Orator*, he had learned to understand the *Italian, Spanish,* and *French* Tongues very perfectly: hoping, that as his Predecessors, so he might in time attain the place of a *Secretary of State*, he being at that time very high in the Kings favour, and not meanly valued and lov'd by the most eminent and most powerful of the Court-Nobility. This, and the love of a Court-conversation, mixed with a laudible ambition to be something more than he then was, drew him often from *Cambridge*, to attend the King wheresoever the Court was, who then gave him a Sine Cure, which fell into His Majesties disposal, I think, by the death of the Bishop of St *Asaph*. It was the same that Queen *Elizabeth* had formerly given to her Favourite Sir *Philip Sidney*; and valued to be worth an hundred and twenty pounds *per Annum*. With this, and his Annuity, and the advantage of his Colledge, and of his Oratorship, he enjoyed his gentile humor for cloaths, and Court-like company, and seldom look'd towards *Cambridge*, unless the King were there, but then he never fail'd; and, at other times, left the manage of his Orators place to his learned friend, Mr *Herbert Thorndike*, who is now Prebend of *Westminster*.

I may not omit to tell, that he had often designed to leave the University, and decline all Study, which he thought did impair his health; for he had a body apt to a *Consumption*, and to *Fevers*, and other infirmities, which he judg'd were increased by his Studies; for he would often say, He had too thoughtful a Wit; a Wit like a Pen-knife in too narrow a sheath, too sharp for his Body. But his Mother would be no means allow him to leave the University, or to travel; and, though he inclin'd very much to both, yet he would by no means satisfy his own desires at so dear a rate, as to prove an undutiful Son to so affectionate a Mother; but did always submit to her wisdom. And what I have now said may partly appear in a Copy of Verses in his printed Poems; 'tis one of those that bear the title of *Affliction*; and it appears to be a pious reflection on God's providence, and some passages of his life, in which he saies,

> *Whereas my birth and spirit rather took*
> *The way that takes the Town;*
> *Thou didst betray me to a lingring Book,*
> *And wrap me in a Gown:*
> *I was intangled in a World of strife,*
> *Before I had the power to change my life.*
>
> *Yet, for I threatned oft the Siege to raise,*
> *Not simpring all mine age;*
> *Thou often didst with Academic praise,*
> *Melt, and dissolve my rage:*

I took the sweetned Pill, till I came where
I could not go away, nor persevere.

Yet, least perchance I should too happy be
    In my unhappiness,
Turning my purge to food, thou throwest me
    Into more sicknesses.
Thus doth thy power, Cross-byass me, not making
Thine own gifts good, yet, me from my ways taking:

Now I am here, what thou wilt do with me
    None of my Books will shew.
I read, and sigh, and I wish I were a Tree,
    For then sure I should grow
To fruit or shade, at least some Bird would trust
Her Houshold with me, and I would be just.

Yet, though thou troublest me, I must be meek;
    In weakness must be stout:
Well, I will change my service, and go seek
    Some other Master out:
Ah my dear God! though I am clean forgot,
Let me not love thee, if I love thee not.

                                G.H.

In this time of Mr *Herberts* attendance and expectation of
some good occasion to remove from *Cambridge* to Court, God,
in whom there is an unseen Chain of Causes, did in a short
time put an end to the lives of two of his most obliging and
most powerful friends, *Lodowick* Duke of *Richmond*, and *James*
Marquis of *Hamilton*; and not long after him King *James* died
also, and with them, all Mr *Herbert's* Court-hopes: so that he
presently betook himself to a Retreat from *London*, to a Friend
in *Kent*, where he lived very privately, and was such a lover of
solitariness, as was judg'd to impair his health, more than his
Study had done. In this time of Retirement, he had many
Conflicts with himself, whether he should return to the
painted pleasures of a Court-life, or betake himself to a study
of Divinity, and enter into Sacred Orders? (to which his dear

Mother had often persuaded him). These were such Conflicts, as they only can know, that have endur'd them; for ambitious Desires, and the outward Glory of this World, are not easily laid aside; but, at last, God inclin'd him to put on a resolution to serve at his Altar.

He did, at his return to *London*, acquaint a Court-friend with his resolution to enter into *Sacred Orders*, who persuaded him to alter it, as too mean an employment, and too much below his birth, and the excellent abilities and endowments of his mind. To whom he replied, 'It hath been formerly judged that the Domestick Servants of the King of Heaven, should be of the noblest Families on Earth: and, though the Iniquity of the late Times have made Clergy-men meanly valued, and the sacred name of *Priest* contemptible; yet, I will labour to make it honourable, by consecrating all my learning, and all my poor abilities to advance the glory of that God that gave them; knowing, that I can never do too much for him, that hath done so much for me, as to make me a Christian. And I will labour to be like my Saviour, by making Humility lovely in the eyes of all men, and by following the merciful and meek example of my *dear Jesus*.'

This was then his resolution; and the God of Constancy, who intended him for a great example of vertue, continued him in it, for within that year he was made Deacon, but the day when, or by whom, I cannot learn; but that he was about that time made Deacon, is most certain; for I find by the Records of *Lincoln*, that he was made Prebend of *Layton Ecclesia*, in the Diocese of *Lincoln*, July 15th, 1626, and that this Prebend was given him by *John*, then *Lord Bishop of that See*. And now he had a fit occasion to shew that Piety and Bounty that was derived from his generous Mother, and his other memorable Ancestors, and the occasion was this.

This *Layton Ecclesia* is a village near to *Spalden*, in the County of *Huntington*, and the greatest part of the Parish Church was fallen down, and that of it which stood was so decayed, so little, and so useless, that the Parishioners could not meet to perform their duty to God in publick prayer and praises; and thus it had been for almost 20 years, in which time there had been some faint endeavours for a publick Collection to enable the Parishioners to rebuild it, but with no success, till Mr *Herbert* undertook it, and he, by his own, and the contribution of many of his Kindred, and other noble Friends, undertook the Re-edification of it; and made it so much his whole business, that he became restless till he saw it finisht as it now stands; being for the workmanship, a costly Mosaick: for the form, an *exact Cross*; and for the decency and beauty, I am assur'd, it is the most remarkable *Parish-church* that this Nation affords. He lived to see it so wainscoated, as to be exceeded by none; and, by his order, the Reading Pew and Pulpit were a littie distant from each other, and both of an equal height; for he would often say, 'They should neither have a precedency or priority of the other; but, that *Prayer* and *Preaching*, being equally useful, might agree like Brethren, and have an equal honour and estimation.'

Before I proceed farther, I must look back to the time of Mr *Herberts* being made Prebend, and tell the Reader, that not long after, his mother being inform'd of his intentions to Re-build that church, and apprehending the great trouble and charge that he was like to draw upon himself, his Relations and Friends, before it could be finisht, sent for him from *London* to *Chelsey* (where she then dwelt) and at his coming, said—'*George*, I sent for you, to persuade you to commit Simony, by giving your patron as good a gift as he has given to you; namely, that you give him back his Prebend; for, *George*, it is not for your weak body, and empty purse, to undertake to build Churches.' Of which, he desired he might have a Days time to consider, and then make her an Answer. And at his return to her the next Day, when he had first desired her blessing, and she given it him, his next request was, 'That she would at the Age of Thirty-Three years, allow

him to become an *undutiful* Son; for, he had made a Vow to
God, that, if he were able, he would Re-build that Church.'
And then, shew'd her such reasons for his resolution, that she
presently subscribed to be one of his Benefactors: and undertook to sollicit *William* Earl of *Pembroke* to become another,
who subscribed for fifty pounds; and not long after, by a
witty and persuasive letter from Mr *Herbert*, made it fifty
pounds more. And in this nomination of some of his benefactors, *James* Duke of *Lenox*, and his brother, Sir *Henry
Herbert*, ought to be remembred; as also the bounty of Mr
Nicholas Farrer, and Mr *Arthur Woodnot*; the one, a Gentleman
in the neighbourhood of Layton, and the other, a Goldsmith
in *Foster Lane*, *London*, ought not to be forgotten: for the
memory of such great men ought to out-live their lives. Of
Master *Farrer*, I shall hereafter give an account in a more
seasonable place; but before I proceed farther, I will give this
short account of Mr *Arthur Woodnot*.

He was a man, that had consider'd, overgrown Estates do
often require more care and watchfulness to preserve than get
them, and considered that there be many Discontents, that
Riches cure not; and did therefore set limits to himself, as to
desire of wealth: And having attain'd so much as to be able to
shew some mercy to the Poor, and preserve a competence for
himself, he dedicated the remaining part of his life to the service of God, and to be useful to his Friends; and he prov'd to
be so to Mr *Herbert*; for beside his own bounty, he collected
and return'd most of the money that was paid for the Rebuilding of that Church; he kept all the account of the charges,
and would often go down to state them, and see all the Work-
men paid. When I have said, that this good man was a useful
friend to Mr *Herberts* Father, and to his Mother, and continued to be so to him, till he clos'd his eyes on his Death-bed;
I will forbear to say more, till I have the next fair occasion to
mention the holy friendship that was betwixt him and Mr
Herbert—From whom Mr *Woodnot* carryed to his mother this

following Letter, and delivered it to her in a sickness which
was not long before that which prov'd to be her last.

A Letter of MR GEORGE HERBERT *to
his Mother, in her Sickness.*

MADAM,

*At my last parting from you, I was the better content, because I was
in hope I should my self carry all sickness out of your family: but, since
I know I did not, and that your share continues; or rather increaseth, I
wish earnestly that I were again with you: and would quickly make good
my wish, but that my employment does fix me here, it being now but a
month to our* Commencement: *wherein, my absence, by how much it
naturally augmenteth suspicion, by so much shall it make my prayers the
more constant and the more earnest for you to the God of all Consolation.
—In the mean time, I beseech you to be chearful, and comfort your self
in the God of all Comfort, who is not willing to behold any sorrow but
for sin.—What hath Affliction grievous in it more than for a moment?
or why should our afflictions here, have so much power or boldness as to
oppose the hope of our Joys hereafter!—Madam! as the Earth is but a
point in respect of the heavens, so are earthly Troubles compared to
heavenly Joys; therefore, if either Age or Sickness lead you to those Joys
consider what advantage you have over* Youth *and* Health, *who are now
so near those true Comforts.—Your last letter gave me Earthly preferment, and I hope kept Heavenly for yourself: but would you divide and
choose too? Our Colledge Customs allow not that: and I shou'd account
myself most happy, if I might change with you; for I have always observed
the thred of Life to be like other threds or skenes of silk, full of snarles
and incumbrances: Happy is he, whose bottom is wound up and laid
ready for work in the* New Jerusalem.—*For myself,* dear Mother,
*I alwaies fear'd sickness more then death, because sickness hath made me
unable to perform those Offices for which I came into the world, and
must yet be kept in it; but, you are freed from that fear, who have already
abundantly discharg'd that part, having both ordered your Family, and
so brought up your Children, that they have attain'd to the years of
Discretion, and competent Maintenance.—So, that now, if they do not
well, the fault cannot be charg'd on you, whose Example and Care of
them, will justifie you both to the world and your own Conscience: insomuch that, whether you turn your thoughts on the life past, or on the*

E

Joys that are to come, you have strong preservatives against all disquiet.—
And, for temporal Afflictions: I beseech you consider all that can happen
to you are either afflictions of Estate, *or* Body, *or* Mind.—*For those of*
Estate? of what poor regard ought they to be, since, if we had Riches,
we are commanded to give them away: so that the best use of them is,
having, not to have them.—But perhaps, being above the Common
people, our Credit and estimation calls on us to live in a more splendid
fashion?—but, O God! how easily is that answered, when we consider that
the blessings in the holy Scripture are never given to the Rich; but to the
poor. I never find ' Blessed be the Rich,' *or* Blessed be the Noble; *but,*
Blessed be the Meek, *and,* 'Blessed be the Poor,' *and* Blessed be the
Mourners, for they shall be comforted.—*And yet, O God! most*
carry themselves so, as if they not only not desir'd, but even fear'd to be
blessed.—And for Afflictions of the Body, dear Madam, *remember the*
holy Martyrs of God, how they have been burned by thousands, and have
endured such other Tortures, as the very mention of them might beget
amazement; but their Fiery-trials have had an end; and yours (which,
praised be God are less) are not like to continue long.—I beseech you,
let such thoughts as these moderate your present fear and sorrow; and
know that if any of yours should prove a Goliah-*like trouble, yet you*
may say with David—That God, who hath delivered me out of the
paws of the Lion and Bear, will also deliver me out of the hands
of this uncircumcised *Philistin.'—Lastly, for those Afflictions of the*
Soul: consider that God intends that to be as a Sacred Temple *for him-*
self to dwell in, and will not allow any room there for such an in-mate as
Grief; or allow that any sadness shall be his Competitor.—And, above all,
If any care of future things molest you? remember those admirable words
of the Psalmist: Cast thy care on the Lord, and he shall nourish
thee.[1] *To which join that of* St *Peter,* Casting all your Care on the
Lord, for he careth for you.[2]—What *an admirable thing is this, that*
God puts his shoulder to our burthen! and entertains our care for us, that
we may the more quietly intend his service.—To Conclude, Let me com-
mend only one place more to you (Philip. 4, 4.) *St* Paul *saith* there,
Rejoice in the Lord alwaies, and again I say, rejoice. *He doubles*
it to take away the scruple of those that might say, What, shall we
rejoice in afflictions? yes, I say again, rejoice; so that it is not left to us
to rejoice, or not rejoice; but, whatsoever befalls us, we must always, at all

---

[1] Psal. 55.   [2] 1 Pet. 5. 7.

times, rejoice in the Lord, who taketh care for us: And it follows in the next verses: Let your moderation appear to all men: the Lord is at hand: be careful for nothing. *What can be said more comfortably?* trouble not yourselves; God *is at hand, to deliver us from all, or, in all.* —Dear Madam, *pardon my boldness, and, accept the good meaning of,*
Your most obedient son,
Trin. Col. May 25, 1622. GEORGE HERBERT

About the year 1629 and the 34th of his Age, Mr *Herbert* was seized with a sharp *Quotidian Ague*, and thought to remove it by the change of Air; to which end, he went to *Woodford* in *Essex*, but thither more chiefly, to enjoy the company of his beloved brother, Sir *Henry Herbert*, and other friends then of that Family. In his House he remained about Twelve Months, and there became his own Physitian, and cur'd himself of his Ague, by forbearing Drink, and not eating any Meat, no not Mutton, nor a Hen, or Pidgeon, unless they were salted; and by such a constant Dyet he remov'd his Ague, but with inconveniencies that were worse; for he brought upon himself a disposition to Rheums, and other weaknesses, and a supposed Consumption. And it is to be Noted, that in the sharpest of his extream Fits, he would often say, *Lord, abate my great affliction, or increase my patience, but Lord, I repine not, I am dumb, Lord, before thee, because thou doest it.* By which, and a sanctified submission to the Will of God, he shewed he was inclinable to bear the sweet yoke of *Christian Discipline*, both then and in the latter part of his life, of which there will be many True testimonies.

And now his care was to recover from his Consumption, by a change from *Woodford* into such an air as was most proper to that end. And his remove was to *Dantsey* in *Wiltshire*, a noble House, which stands in a choice Air; the owner of it then was the Lord *Danvers*, Earl of *Danby*, who lov'd Mr *Herbert* so very much, that he allow'd him such an apartment in it, as might best sute with his accommodation and liking. And, in this place, by a *spare Dyet*, declining all *perplexing*

Studies, moderate exercise, and a *chearful conversation,* his health was apparently improv'd to a good degree of strength and chearfulness. And then, he declar'd his resolution both to marry, and to enter into the Sacred Order of Priesthood. These had long been the desires of his Mother, and his other Relations; but she lived not to see either, for she died in the year 1627. And though he was disobedient to her about *Layton* Church, yet, in conformity to her will, he kept his Orators place, till after her death; and then presently declin'd it: and the more willingly, that he might be succeeded by his friend *Robert Creighton,* who now is Dr *Creighton,* and the worthy Bishop of *Wells.*

I shall now proceed to his Marriage; in order to which, it will be convenient that I first give the Reader a short view of his person, and then an account of his Wife, and of some circumstances concerning both.—*He was for his person of a stature inclining towards Tallness; his Body was very straight, and so far from being cumbred with too much flesh, that he was lean to an extremity. His aspect was chearful, and his speech and motion did both declare him a Gentleman; for they were all so meek and obliging, that they purchased love and respect from all that knew him.*

These, and his other visible vertues, begot him much love from a Gentleman of a Noble fortune, and a near kinsman to his friend the Earl of *Danby*; namely, from Mr *Charles Danvers* of *Bainton,* in the County of *Wilts,* Esq. This Mr *Danvers,* having known him long, and familiarly, did so much affect him, that he often and publicly declared a desire, that Mr *Herbert* would marry any of his Nine Daughters (for he had so many) but rather his daughter *Jane* than any other, because *Jane was his beloved Daughter*: And he had often said the same to Mr *Herbert* himself; and that if he could like her for a Wife, and she him for a Husband, *Jane* should have a *double blessing*: and Mr *Danvers* had so often said the like to *Jane,* and so much commended Mr *Herbert* to her, that *Jane* became so much a Platonick, as to fall in love with Mr *Herbert* unseen.

This was a fair preparation for a Marriage; but, alas, her father died before Mr *Herberts* retirement to *Dantsey*: yet some friends to both parties, procur'd their meeting; at which time a mutual affection entred into both their hearts, as a Conqueror enters into a surprized City; and Love having got such possession, govern'd, and made there such Laws and Resolutions, as neither party was able to resist; insomuch, that she chang'd her name into *Herbert* the third day after this first interview.

This haste might in others be thought a *Love-phrensie*, or worse; but it was not, for they had wooed so like Princes, as to have select Proxies; such as were true friends to both parties; such as well understood Mr *Herberts* and her temper of mind; and also their Estates so well, before this Interview, that the suddenness was justifiable by the strictest Rules of prudence: And, the more, because it prov'd so happy to both parties; for, the eternal lover of mankind, made them happy in each other's mutual and equal affections, and compliance; indeed, so happy, that there never was any opposition betwixt them, unless it were a Contest which should most incline to a compliance with the others desires. And though this begot, and continued in them, such a mutual *love* and *joy* and *content*, as was no way defective: yet this mutual *content* and *love*, and *joy*, did receive a daily augmentation, by such daily obligingness to each other, as still added such new affluences to the former fulness of these divine Souls, as was only improvable in Heaven, where they now enjoy it.

About three months after this Marriage, Dr *Curle*, who was then Rector of *Bemerton*, in *Wiltshire*, was made Bishop of *Bath* and *Wells*, and not long after translated to *Winchester*, and by that means the presentation of a Clerk to *Bemerton*, did not fall to the Earl of Pembroke (who was the undoubted Patron of it) but to the King, by reason of Dr Curles advancement: but *Philip*, then Earl of *Pembroke* (for *William* was lately dead) requested the King to bestow it upon his kinsman *George Herbert*; and the King said, *Most willingly to Mr* Herbert, *if it be worth his acceptance*: and the Earl as willingly and suddenly sent it him, without seeking. But though Mr *Herbert* had formerly put on a resolution for the Clergy: yet, at receiving this presentation, the apprehension of the last great Account, that he was to make for the Cure of so many Souls, made him fast and pray often, and consider for not less than a month: in which time he had some resolutions to decline both the Priesthood, and that Living. And in this time of considering, *He endured* (as he would often say) such spiritual Conflicts, as none can think, but only those that have endur'd them.

In the midst of these Conflicts, his old and dear friend, Mr *Arthur Woodnot*, took a journey to salute him at *Bainton* (where he then was with his wife's friends and relations) and was joyful to be an eye-witness of his Health and happy Marriage. And after they had rejoyc'd together some few days, they took a journey to *Wilton*, the famous seat of the Earls of *Pembroke*; at which time the King, the Earl, and the whole Court were there, or at *Salisbury*, which is near to it. And at this time Mr *Herbert* presented his Thanks to the Earl, for his presentation to *Bemerton*, but had not yet resolv'd to accept it, and told him the reason why; but that night, the Earl acquainted Dr *Laud*, then Bishop of London, and after Archbishop of *Canterbury*, with his Kinsmans irresolution. And the Bishop did the next day so convince Mr *Herbert*, that the *refusal of it was a sin*; that a Taylor was sent for to come speedily from *Salisbury* to *Wilton*, to take measure, and make him Canonical cloaths against next day; which the Taylor did: and Mr *Herbert* being so habited, went with his presentation to the learned Dr *Davenant*, who was then Bishop of *Salisbury*, and he gave him Institution immediately (for Mr Herbert had been made Deacon some years before) and he was also the same day (which was *April* 26th, 1630) inducted into the good, and more pleasant, than healthful, Parsonage of *Bemerton*; which is a Mile from *Salisbury*.

I have now Brought him to the Parsonage of Bemerton, *and to*

*the thirty-sixth Year of his Age, and must stop here, and bespeak
the Reader to prepare for an almost incredible story, of the great
sanctity of the short remainder of his holy life; a life! so full of* Charity,
Humility, *and all Christian vertues,* that it deserves the eloquence
of St Chrysostom *to commend and declare! it a life, that if it were
related by a Pen like his, there would then be no need for this Age to
look back into times past for the examples of primitive piety; for
they might be all found in the life of* George Herbert. *But now,
alas! who is fit to undertake it! I confess I am not; and, am not
pleas'd with my self that I must; and profess myself amaz'd, when I
consider how few of the Clergy liv'd like him then, and how many live so
unlike him now: But it becomes not me to censure: my design is rather
to assure the Reader, that I have used very great diligence to inform
myself, that I might inform him of the truth of what follows; and
though I cannot adorn it with eloquence, yet I will do it with sincerity.*

When at his Induction he was shut into *Bemerton* Church,
being left there alone to Toll the Bell, (as the Law requires
him;) he staid so much longer than an ordinary time, before
he returned to those Friends that staid expecting him at the
Church-door, that his friend, Mr *Woodnot* looked in at the
Church-window, and saw him lie prostrate on the ground
before the Altar: at which time and place (as he after told
Mr *Woodnot*) he set some Rules to himself, for the future
manage of his life; and then and there made a vow to labour
to keep them.

And the same night that he had his Induction, he said to
Mr *Woodnot, I now look back upon my aspiring thoughts, and think
myself more happy than if I had attain'd what then I so ambitiously
thirsted for: And I can now behold the Court with an impartial Eye,
and see plainly that it is made up of* Fraud *and* Titles, *and* Flattery,
*and many other such empty, imaginary, painted Pleasures: Pleasures,
that are so empty, as not to satisfy when they are enjoy'd; but, in
God, and his service, is a fulness of all* joy *and* pleasure, *and no
satiety. And I will now use all my endeavours to bring my Relations
and dependents to a love and relyance on* him, who never fails

those that trust him. *But above all, I will be sure to live well, because the vertuous life of a Clergyman is the most powerful eloquence to perswade all that see it to reverence and love, and at least to desire to live like him. And this I will do, because I know* we live in an Age that hath more need of good examples than precepts. *And I beseech that God, who hath honour'd me so much as to call me to serve him at his Altar: that as by his special grace he hath put into my heart these good desires and resolutions; so he will, by his assisting grace, give me ghostly strength to bring the same to good effect. And I beseech him, that my humble and charitable life may so win upon others, as to bring glory to my* JESUS, whom I have this day taken to be my Master and Governour; *and I am so proud of his service, that I will alwaies observe, and obey, and do his will; and alwaies call him,* Jesus my Master, *and I will always contemn my birth, or any title or dignity that can be conferr'd upon me, when I shall compare them with my title of being a* Priest, *and serving at the* Altar *of* Jesus my Master.

And that he did so, may appear in many parts of his book of *Sacred Poems*: especially in that which he calls *The Odour*. In which he seems to rejoyce in the thoughts of that word *Jesus*, and say, that the adding these words, *my Master*, to it, and the often repetition of them, seem'd to perfume his mind, and leave an oriental fragrancy in his very breath. And for his unforc'd choice to serve at Gods-Altar, he seems in another place of his poems (THE PEARL, *Matth.* 13.), to rejoyce and say—*He knew the waies of Learning; knew, what nature does willingly, and what, when it is forc'd by fire; knew the waies of honour, and when glory inclines the Soul to noble expressions: knew the Court; knew the waies of pleasure, of love, of wit, of musick, and upon what terms he declined all these for the service of his Master* JESUS; and then concludes, saying,

> *That, through these Labyrinths, not my groveling Wit:*
> *But thy Silk-twist, let down from Heaven to me,*
> *Did, both conduct, and teach me, how by it,*
> *To climb to thee.*

The third day after he was made Rector of *Bemerton*, and had chang'd his sword and silk Cloaths into a Canonical Coat, he return'd so habited with his friend Mr *Woodnot* to *Bainton*: And immediately after he had seen and saluted his Wife, he said to her—*You are now a Ministers Wife, and must now so far forget your fathers house, as not to claim a precedence of any of your parishioners; for, you are to know, that a Priest's Wife can challenge no precedence or place, but that which she purchases by her obliging humility; and I am sure, places so purchased do best become them.* And let me tell you, *that I am so good a Herald, as to assure you that this is truth.* And she was so meek a Wife, *as to assure him, it was no vexing News to her, and that he should see her observe it, with a chearful willingness.* And, indeed, her unforc'd humility, that humility that was in her so original, as to be born with her! made her so happy as to do so; and her doing so begot her an unfeigned love, and a serviceable respect from all that converst with her; and this love followed her in all places, as inseparably as shadows follow substances in Sunshine.

It was not many days before he returned back to *Bemerton*, to view the Church, and repair the Chancel: and indeed to rebuild almost three parts of his house, which was fall'n down, or decayed by reason of his Predecessors living at a better Parsonage-house; namely, at *Minal*, 16 or 20 miles from this place. At which time of Mr *Herberts* coming alone to *Bemerton*, there came to him a poor old Woman, with an intent to acquaint him with her necessitous condition, as also, with some troubles of her mind, but after she had spoke some few words to him, she was surpriz'd with a fear, and that begot a shortness of breath, so that her spirits and speech fail'd her; which he perceiving, did so compassionate her, and was so humble, that he took her by the hand, and said, *Speak, good Mother, be not afraid to speak to me; for I am a man that will hear you with patience; and will relieve your necessities too, if I be able: and this I will do willingly; and therefore, Mother, be not afraid to acquaint me with what you desire.* After which comfortable speech, he again took her by the hand, made her sit down by him, & understanding she was of his Parish, he told her, *He would be acquainted with her, and take her into his care.* And having with patience heard and understood her wants (and it is some relief for a poor body to be but hear'd with patience) he, like a Christian Clergyman, comforted her by his meek behaviour and counsel; but because that cost him nothing, he reliev'd her with money too, and so sent her home with a chearful heart, praising God, and praying for him. *Thus worthy, and (like Davids blessed man) thus lowly, was Mr* George Herbert *in his own eyes*; and thus lovely in the eyes of others.

At his return that Night to his Wife at *Bainton*, he gave her an account of the passages betwixt him and the poor Woman; with which she was so affected, that she went next day to *Salisbury*, and there bought a pair of Blankets, and sent them as a Token of her love to the poor Woman; and with them a message, *That she would see and be acquainted with her, when her house was built at* Bemerton.

There be many such passages both of him and his Wife, of which some few will be related; but I shall first tell, that he hasted to get the Parish-Church repaired; then to beautifie the Chappel (which stands near his House) and that at his own great charge. He then proceeded to re-build the greatest part of the Parsonage-house, which he did also very compleatly, and at his own charge; and having done this good work, he caus'd these Verses to be writ upon, or ingraven in, the Mantle of the Chimney in his Hall.

To My Successor

If thou chance for to find
A new House to thy mind,
And built without thy Cost:
Be good to the Poor,
As God gives thee store,
And then, my Labour's not lost.

We will now, by the Reader's favour, suppose him fixed at *Bemerton*, and grant him to have seen the Church repair'd, and the Chappel belonging to it very decently adorned at his own great charge (which is a real Truth) and having now fixt him there, I shall proceed to give an account of the rest of his behaviour, both to his Parishioners, and those many others that knew and convers'd with him.

Doubtless Mr *Herbert* had consider'd, and given Rules to himself for his Christian carriage both to God and man, before he entered into *Holy Orders*. And 'tis not unlike, but that he renewed those resolutions at his prostration before the *Holy Altar*, at his Induction into the Church of *Bemerton*: but as yet he was but a *Deacon*, and therefore long'd for the next *Ember-week*, that he might be ordain'd *Priest*, and made capable of administering both the Sacraments. At which time the Reverend Dr *Humphrey Henchman*, now Lord Bishop of *London* (who does not mention him but with some veneration for his life and excellent learning) tells me, *He laid his hand on Mr* Herbert's *Head, and, (alas!) within less than three years, lent his Shoulder to carry his dear Friend to his Grave.*

And that Mr *Herbert* might the better preserve those holy Rules which such a *Priest* as he intended to be, ought to observe; and that time might not insensibly blot them out of his memory, but that the next year might shew him his variations from this years resolutions; he therefore did set down his rules, then resolv'd upon, in that order as the World now sees them printed in a little Book, called, *The Countrey Parson*, in which some of his Rules are:

The Parsons knowledge.	*The Parson Condescending.*
The Parson on Sundays.	*The Parson in his Journey.*
The Parson Praying.	*The Parson in his Mirth.*
The Parson Preaching.	*The Parson with his Church-*
The Parsons Charity.	*wardens.*
The Parson comforting the Sick.	*The Parson Blessing the People.*
The Parson Arguing.	

And his behaviour toward God and man may be said to be a
practical Comment on these, and the other holy rules set down
in that useful Book. A Book, so full of plain, prudent, and
useful Rules that that *Countrey Parson*, that can spare 12d,
and yet wants it, is scarce excusable; because it will both
direct him what he ought to do, and convince him for not
having done it.

At the Death of Mr *Herbert*, this Book fell into the hands
of his friend Mr *Woodnot*; and he commended it into the trusty
hands of Mr *Barnabas Oly*, who published it with a most
conscientious, and excellent Preface; from which I have had
some of those Truths, that are related in this life of Mr *Herbert*.
The Text for his first Sermon, was taken out of *Solomons
Proverbs* [chap. iv. 23], and the words were, *Keep thy heart with
all diligence.* In which first Sermon he gave his Parishioners
many necessary, holy, safe Rules for the discharge of a good
Conscience, both to God and man. And, deliver'd his Sermon
after a most florid manner; both with great learning and
eloquence; but, at the close of this sermon, told them, *That
should not be his constant way of Preaching; for since Almighty God
does not intend to lead men to Heaven by hard Questions, he would
not therefore fill their heads with unnecessary Notions; but, that, for
their sakes, his language and his expressions should be more plain and
practical in his future Sermons.* And he then made it his humble
request, *That they would be constant to the Afternoons Service, and
Catechising*: and shewed them convincing reasons why he
desir'd it; and his obliging example and perswasions brought
them to a willing conformity to his desires.

The Texts for all his future Sermons (which God knows,
were not many) were constantly taken out of the Gospel for
the day; and he did as constantly declare why the Church did
appoint that portion of Scripture to be that day read: And in
what manner the *Collect* for every Sunday does refer to the
Gospel, or to the *Epistle* then read to them; and, that they
might pray with understanding, he did usually take occasion

to explain, not only the *Collect* for every particular Sunday, but the reasons of all the other *Collects* and *Responses* in our Church-service; and made it appear to them, that the whole *Service of the Church* was a reasonable, and therefore an acceptable Sacrifice to God; as namely, that we begin with *Confession of our selves to be vile, miserable sinners:* and that we begin so, because, till we have confess'd ourselves to be such, we are not capable of that mercy which we acknowledge we need, and pray for: but having, in the prayer of our Lord, begg'd pardon for those sins which we have confest; and hoping, that as the *Priest* hath declar'd our Absolution, so by our public Confession, and real Repentance, we have obtain'd that pardon: Then we dare and do proceed to beg of the Lord, *to open our lips, that our mouths may shew forth his praise*; for, till then we are neither able nor worthy to praise him. But this being suppos'd, we are then fit to say, *Glory be to the Father, and to the Son, and to the Holy Ghost*, and fit to proceed to a further service of our God, in the *Collects*, and *Psalms*, and *Lauds*, that follow in the service.

And as to the *Psalms* and *Lauds*, he proceeded to inform them why they were so often, and some of them daily, repeated in our *Church-service*; namely, the *Psalms* every month, because they be an *Historical* and thankful repetition of mercies past, and such a composition of prayers and praises, as ought to be repeated often, and publickly; for with such *Sacrifices, God is honour'd and well-pleased*. This, for the *Psalms*.

And for the *Hymns* and *Lauds*, appointed to be daily repeated or sung after the first and second Lessons are read to the Congregation; he proceeded to inform them, that it was most reasonable, after they have heard the will and goodness of God declar'd or preach't by the *Priest* in his reading the two Chapters, that it was then a seasonable duty to rise up, and express their gratitude to Almighty God, for those his mercies to them, and to all Mankind; and then to say with the *Blessed Virgin, That their souls do magnifie the Lord, and that* their *spirits do also rejoyce in God their Saviour*; and that it was their duty also to rejoice with *Simeon* in his Song, and say with him, *that their eyes have* also *seen their salvation*; for they have seen that salvation which was but prophesied till his time: and he then broke out into those expressions of joy that he did see it; but they live to see it daily in the History of it, and therefore ought daily to rejoice, and daily to offer up their Sacrifices of praise to their God, for that particular mercy. A service, which is now the constant employment of that *blessed Virgin* and *Simeon*, and all those blessed Saints that are possest of Heaven: and where they are at this time interchangeably, and constantly singing, *Holy, Holy, Holy, Lord God, Glory be to God on High, and on Earth peace.*—And he taught them, that to do this was an acceptable service to God, because the Prophet *David* says in his Psalms, *He that praiseth the Lord honoureth him.*

He made them to understand how happy they be that are freed from the incumbrances of that Law which our Fore-fathers groan'd under: namely, from the *Legal Sacrifices*, and from the many *Ceremonies of the Levitical Law*: freed from *Circumcision*, and from the strict observation of the *Jewish Sabbath*, and the like: And he made them know, that having receiv'd so many and so great blessings, by being born since the days of our Saviour, it must be an acceptable sacrifice to Almighty God, for them to acknowledge those blessings daily, and stand up and worship, and say as *Zacharias* did, *Blessed be the Lord God of* Israel, *for he hath* (in our days) *visited and redeemed his people; and* (he hath in our days) *remembred, and shewed that mercy which by the mouth of the Prophets, he promised to our Fore-fathers;* and this he hath done *according to his holy Covenant made with them.* And he made them to understand that we live to see and enjoy the benefit of it, in his *Birth*, in his *Life*, his *Passion*, his *Resurrection*, and *Ascension* into Heaven, where he now sits sensible of all our temptations and infirmities; and where he is at this present time making intercession, for us, to his and our Father: and therefore they ought daily to express their public gratulations, and say daily with *Zach-arias, Blessed be the Lord God of* Israel, *that hath thus visited, and thus redeemed his people.*—These were some of the reasons, by which Mr *Herbert* instructed his Congregation for the use of the *Psalms* and *Hymns* appointed to be daily sung or said in the Church-service.

He informed them also, when the *Priest* did pray only for the Congregation, and not for himself; and when they did only pray for him; as namely, after the repetition of the *Creed* before he proceeds to pray the Lords Prayer, or any of the appointed Collects, the Priest is directed to kneel down, and pray for them, saying—*The Lord be with you*—and when they pray for him, saying—*And with thy spirit*; and then they join together in the following Collects: and he assur'd them, that when there is such mutual love, and such joint prayers offer'd for each other, then the holy Angels look down from Heaven, and are ready to carry such charitable desires to God Almighty, and he as ready to receive them; and that a Christian Congregation calling thus upon God with one heart, and one voice, and in one reverent and humble posture, looks as beautifully as *Jerusalem*, that is at peace with it self.

He instructed them also why the prayer of our Lord was prayed often in every full service of the Church; namely, at the conclusion of the several parts of that Service; and pray'd then, not only because it was composed and commanded by our *Jesus* that made it, but as a perfect pattern for our less perfect Forms of prayer, and therefore fittest to sum up and conclude all our imperfect Petitions.

He instructed them also, that as by the second Commandment we are required not to bow down, or worship an *Idol*, or *false God*; so, by the contrary Rule, we are to bow down and kneel, or stand up and *worship* the true God. And he instructed them why the Church required the congregation to stand up at the repetition of the Creeds; namely, because they thereby declare both their obedience to the Church, and an assent to that faith into which they had been baptiz'd. And he taught them, that in that shorter Creed, or Doxology, so often repeated daily; they also stood up to testify their belief to be, that *the God that they trusted in was one God, and three persons; the Father, the Son, and the Holy Ghost; to whom they & the Priest gave glory.* And because there had been Heretics that had denied some of those three persons to be God, therefore the Congregation stood up and honour'd him, by confessing and saying, *It was so in the beginning, is now so, and shall ever be so World without end.* And all gave their assent to this belief, by standing up and saying, *Amen.*

He instructed them also, what benefit they had by the Church's appointing the Celebration of Holy-dayes, and the excellent use of them; namely, that they were set apart for particular Commemorations of particular mercies received from Almighty God; and (as Reverend Mr *Hooker* saies) to be the *Landmarks* to distinguish times; for by them we are taught to take notice how time passes by us, and that we ought not to let the Years pass without a Celebration of praise for those mercies which those days give us occasion to remember, & therefore they were to note that the Year is appointed to begin the 25th day of *March*; a day in which we commemorate the *Angels* appearing to the *B. Virgin*, with the joyful tidings that *she should conceive and bear a Son, that should be the Redeemer of Mankind.* And, she did so Forty weeks after this joyful salutation; namely, at our *Christmas*: a day in which we commemorate his Birth with joy and praise: and that eight days after this happy Birth we celebrate his *Circumcision*; namely, in that which we call *New-years day.* And that, upon that day which we call *Twelfth-day*, we commemorate the manifestation of the unsearchable riches of Jesus to the Gentiles: and that that day we also celebrate the memory of his goodness in sending a *Star* to guide the *three wise men* from the *East* to *Bethlem*, that they might there worship, and present him with their oblations of *Gold, Frankincense,* and *Myrrh*. And he (Mr *Herbert*) instructed them, that *Jesus* was Forty days after his Birth, presented by his blessed mother in the *Temple*; namely, on that day which we call, *The Purification of the Blessed Virgin, Saint* Mary. And he instructed them, that by the *Lent-fast* we imitate and commemorate our Saviours humiliation in fasting Forty days; and that we ought to endeavour to be like him in purity. And, that on *Good-friday* we commemorate and condole his *Crucifixion*; and at *Easter* commemorate his *glorious Resurrection*. And he taught them, that after Jesus had manifested himself to his Disciples to be *that Christ that was crucified, dead and buried*; and by his appearing and conversing with his Disciples for the space of Forty days after his *Resurrection*, he then, and not till then, *ascended into Heaven*, in the sight of those Disciples; namely, on that day which we call the *Ascension*, or *Holy Thursday*. And that we then celebrate the performance of the promise which he made to his Disciples, at or before his Ascension: namely, *that though he left them, yet he would send them the Holy Ghost to be their Comforter*; and that he did so on that day which the Church calls *Whitsunday*.—Thus the Church keeps an Historical and circular Commemoration of times, as they pass by us; of such times as ought to incline us to occasional praises, for the particular blessings which we do, or might receive, by those holy Commemorations.

He made them know also, why the Church hath appointed *Ember-weeks*; and to know the reason why the *Commandements*, and the *Epistles* and *Gospels*, were to be read at the *Altar* or *Communion Table*: why the Priest was to pray the *Litany* kneeling; and why to pray some *Collects* standing: and he gave them many other observations, fit for his plain Congregation, but not fit for me now to mention; for I must set limits to my Pen, and not make that a Treatise, which I intended to be a much shorter account than I have made it;—but I have done, when I have told the Reader, that he was constant in *Catechising* every *Sunday* in the After-noon, and that his catechising was

F

after his second lesson, and in the Pulpit; and that he never exceeded his half-hour, and was always so happy as to have an obedient, and a full Congregation.

And to this I must add, that if he were at any time too zealous in his Sermons, it was in reproving the indecencies of the peoples behaviour in the time of Divine Service; and of those Ministers that huddled up the Church-prayers, without a visible reverence and affection; namely, *such as seem'd to say the Lords prayer, or a Collect, in a breath.* But for himself, his custom was, to stop betwixt every Collect, and give the people time to consider what they had pray'd, and to force their desires affectionately to God, before he engag'd them into new Petitions.

And by this account of his diligence to make his Parishioners understand what they prayed, and why they praised and adored their Creator, I hope I shall the more easily obtain the Readers belief to the following account of Mr *Herberts* own practice; which was to appear constantly with his Wife and three Neeces (the daughters of a deceased Sister) and his whole Family, twice every day at the Church-prayers, in the Chappel, which does almost joyn to his Parsonage-house. And for the time of his appearing, it was strictly at the Canonical hours of 10 and 4: and then, and there he lifted up pure and charitable hands to God in the midst of the Congregation. And he would joy to have spent that time in that place, where the honour of his *Master Jesus* dwelleth; and there, by that inward devotion which he testified constantly by an humble behaviour and visible adoration, he, like *Josua*, brought not only *his own Houshold thus to serve the Lord*; but brought most of his Parishioners, and many Gentlemen in the Neighbourhood, constantly to make a part of his Congregation twice a day: and some of the meaner sort of his Parish did so love and reverence Mr *Herbert*, that they would let their Plow rest when Mr. *Herberts Saints-Bell* rung to Prayers, that they might also offer their devotions to God with him: and would then return back to their Plow. And his most holy life was such, that it begot such reverence to God, and to him, that they thought themselves the happier, when they carried Mr *Herberts* blessing back with them to their labour. Thus powerful was his reason and example, to perswade others to a practical piety, and devotion.

And his constant publick prayers did never make him to neglect his own private devotions, nor those prayers that he thought himself bound to perform with his Family, which always were a Set-form, and not long; and he did alwaies conclude them with that Collect which the Church hath appointed for the day or week.—*Thus he made every days sanctity a step towards that Kingdom, where Impurity cannot enter.*

His chiefest recreation was Musick, in which heavenly Art he was a most excellent Master, and did himself compose many *divine Hymns* and *Anthems*, which he set and sung to his *Lute* or *Viol*: and though he was a lover of retiredness, yet his love to *Musick* was such, that he went usually twice every week, on certain appointed days, to the *Cathedral Church* in *Salisbury*; and at his return would say *That his time spent in Prayer, and Cathedral-Musick elevated his Soul, and was his Heaven upon Earth.* But before his return thence to *Bemerton*, he would usually sing and play his part at an appointed private Musick-meeting; and, to justifie this practice, he would often say, *Religion does not banish mirth, but only moderates, and sets rules to it.*

And as his desire to enjoy his *Heaven upon Earth* drew him twice every week to *Salisbury*, so, his walks thither were the occasion of many happy accidents to others; of which I will mention some few.

In one of his walks to *Salisbury*, he overtook a Gentleman, that is still living in that city; and in their walk together, Mr *Herbert* took a fair occasion to talk with him, and humbly begg'd to be excus'd, if he ask'd him some account of his faith; and said, *I do this the rather, because though you are not of my Parish, yet I receive Tythe from you by the hand of your Tenant; and, Sir, I am the bolder to do it, because I know there be some*

Sermon-hearers that be like those fishes, that always live in salt water, and yet are always fresh.

After which expression, Mr *Herbert* asked him some needful Questions, and having received his answer, gave him such Rules for the trial of his sincerity, and for a practical piety, and in so loving and meek a manner, that the Gentleman did so fall in love with him, and his discourse, that he would often contrive to meet him in his walk to *Salisbury*, or to attend him back to *Bemerton*; and still mentions the name of Mr *George Herbert* with veneration, and still praiseth God for the occasion of knowing him.

In another of his *Salisbury* walks, he met with a neighbour Minister; and after some friendly discourse betwixt them, and some Condolement for the decay of Piety, and too general contempt of the Clergy, Mr *Herbert* took occasion to say,

One cure for these distempers would be, for the Clergy themselves to keep the Ember-weeks *strictly, and beg of their Parishioners to ioyn with them in* Fasting *and* Prayers *for a more Religious Clergy.*

And another Cure would be, *for themselves to restore the great and neglected duty of* Catechising, *on which the salvation of so many of the poor and ignorant Lay-people does depend;* but *principally, that the Clergy themselves would be sure to live unblameably; and that the dignifi'd Clergy especially which preach Temperance, would avoid Surfeiting and take all occasions to express a visible humility, and charity in their lives; for this would force a love & an imitation, and an unfeigned reverence from all that knew them to be such.* (And for proof of this, we need no other testimony than the life and death of Dr *Lake*, late Lord Bishop of *Bath* and *Wells*.) *This* (said Mr *Herbert*) *would be a cure for the wickedness and growing Atheism of our* Age. *And*, my dear Brother, *till this be done by us, and done in earnest, let no man expect a reformation of the manners of the* Laity; *for 'tis not learning, but this, this only that must do it; and, till then, the fault must lye at our doors.*

In another walk to *Salisbury*, he saw a poor man with a poorer horse, that was fall'n under his Load; they were both

in distress, and needed present help; which Mr *Herbert* perceiving, put off his Canonical Coat, and help'd the poor man
to unload, and after to load, his horse: The poor man blest
him for it, and he blest the poor man; and was so like the
good Samaritan, that he gave him money to refresh both
himself and his horse; and told him, *That if he lov'd himself, he
should be merciful to his Beast.*—Thus he left the poor man:
and at his coming to his musical friends at *Salisbury*, they began
to wonder that Mr *George Herbert*, which us'd to be so trim
and clean, came into that company so soyl'd and discompos'd:
but he told them the occasion: And when one of the company
told him, *He had disparag'd himself by so dirty an employment;* his
answer was, *That the thought of what he had done would prove
Musick to him at Midnight; and that the omission of it would have
upbraided and made discord in his Conscience, whensoever he should
pass by that place; for if I be bound to pray for all that be in distress,
I am sure that I am bound, so far as it is in my power, to practise
what I pray for. And though I do not wish for the like occasion
every day, yet let me tell you, I would not willingly pass one day of my
life without comforting a sad soul, or shewing mercy; and I praise God
for this occasion.* And now let's tune our Instruments.

Thus, as our blessed Saviour, after his Resurrection, did take
occasion to interpret the Scripture to *Cleopas*, and that other
Disciple, which he met with and accompanied in their journey to
Emmaus; so Mr *Herbert*, in his path toward Heaven, did daily take
any fair occasion to instruct the ignorant, or comfort any that
were in affliction; and did alwaies confirm his precepts, by shewing humility and mercy, and ministring grace to the hearers.

And he was most happy in his Wives unforc'd compliance
with his acts of Charity, whom he made his *Almoner*, and paid
constantly into her hand, a *tenth penny* of what money he
receiv'd for Tythe, and gave her power to dispose that to the
poor of his Parish, and with it a power to dispose a tenth part
of the Corn that came yearly into his Barn; which trust she did
most faithfully perform, and would often offer to him *an*

account of her stewardship, and as often beg an inlargement of his bounty; for she rejoyced in the employment: and this was usually laid out by her in *Blankets* and *Shooes* for some such poor people, as she knew to stand in most need of them. This as to her Charity.—And for his own, he set no limits to it: nor did ever turn his face from any that he saw in want, but would relieve them; especially his poor Neighbours; to the meanest of whose Houses he would go, and inform himself of their wants, and relieve them chearfully, if they were in distress; and would alwaies praise God, as much for being willing, as for being able to do it.—And when he was advis'd by a friend to be more frugal, because he might have Children, his answer was, *He would not see the danger of want so far off: but, being the Scripture does so commend Charity, as to tell us that* Charity *is the top of Christian* vertues, *the covering of sins, the fulfilling of the* Law, *the Life of* Faith; *And that* Charity *hath a promise of the blessings of this life, and of a reward in that life which is to come, being these, and more excellent things are in Scripture spoke of thee,* O Charity! *and that, being all my Tythes and Church-dues are a* Deodate *from thee, O my God, O my God, make me, O my God! so far to trust thy promise, as to return them back to thee; and by thy grace I will do so, in distributing them to any of thy poor members that are in distress, or do but bear the image of* Jesus my Master. *Sir* (said he to his friend) *my Wife hath a competent maintenance secur'd her after my death; and therefore, as this is my prayer, so this my resolution shall, by Gods grace, be unalterable.*

This may be some account of the excellencies of the active part of his life; and thus he continued, till a Consumption so weakened him, as to confine him to his House, or to the Chappel, which does almost joyn to it; in which he continued to read Prayers constantly twice every day, though he were very weak; in one of which times of his reading, his Wife observ'd him to read in pain, and told him so, and that it wasted his spirits, and weakned him: and he confess'd it did, but said, *His life could not be better spent, than in the service of his*

Master Jesus, *who had done and suffered so much for him. But,* said he, *I will not be wilful; for though my spirit be willing, yet I find my flesh is weak; and therefore Mr* Bostock shall be *appointed to read Prayers for me to-morrow; and I will now be only a hearer of them, till this mortal shall put on immortality.* And Mr *Bostock* did the next day undertake and continue this happy employment, till Mr *Herberts* death. This Mr *Bostock* was a learned and vertuous man, an old friend of Mr Herberts, and then his Curate to the Church of *Fulston,* which is a mile from Bemerton to which Church, Bemerton is but a *Chappel of ease.*—And this Mr *Bostock* did also constantly supply the *Church-service* for Mr *Herbert* in that Chappel, when the Musick meeting at *Salisbury,* caus'd his absence from it.

About one month before his death, his friend Mr *Farrer* (for an account of whom I am by promise indebted to the Reader, and intend to make him sudden payment) hearing of Mr *Herberts* sickness, sent Mr *Edmund Duncon* (who is now Rector of *Frier Barnet* in the County of *Middlesex*) from his house of *Gidden Hall,* which is near to *Huntington,* to see Mr *Herbert,* and to assure him, he wanted not his daily prayers for his recovery; and, Mr *Duncon* was to return back to *Gidden,* with an account of Mr *Herberts* condition. Mr *Duncon* found him weak, and at that time lying on his Bed, or on a Pallat; but at his seeing Mr *Duncon* he raised himself vigorously, saluted him, and with some earnestness *inquir'd the health of his brother* Farrer? of which Mr *Duncon* satisfied him; and after some discourse of Mr *Farrers* holy life, and the manner of his constant serving God, he said to Mr *Duncon—Sir, I see by your habit that you are a Priest, and I desire you to pray with me*; which being granted, Mr *Duncon* asked him, *what Prayers?* To which Mr *Herberts* answer was, *O, Sir, the Prayers of my Mother, the Church of* England; *no other prayers are equal to them! But, at this time, I beg of you to pray only the* Litany, *for I am weak and faint;* and Mr *Duncon* did so. After which, and some other discourse of Mr *Farrer,* Mrs *Herbert* provided Mr *Duncon* a plain Supper, and a clean Lodging, and he betook himself to rest.—*This Mr* Duncon *tells me;* and tells me, that, at his first view of Mr *Herbert*, he saw *majesty* and *humility* so reconcil'd in his looks and behaviour, as begot in him an awful reverence for his person: and saies, *his discourse was so pious, and his motion so gentile and meek, that after almost forty years, yet they remain still fresh in his memory.*

The next morning Mr *Duncon* left him, and betook himself to a Journey to *Bath*, but with a promise to return back to him within five days; and he did so; but before I shall say any thing of what discourse then fell betwixt them two, I will pay my promis'd account of Mr *Farrer*.

Mr Nicholas Farrer (who got the reputation of being call'd Saint *Nicholas* at the age of six years) was born in *London*, and doubtless had good education in his youth; but certainly was, at an early age, made Fellow of *Clare-Hall* in *Cambridge*; where he continued to be eminent for his *piety, temperance,* and *learning.*—About the 26th year of his Age, he betook himself to Travel: in which he added, to his *Latin* and *Greek*, a perfect knowledge of all the languages spoken in the Western parts of our Christian world; and, understood well the principles of their Religion, and of their manner, and the reasons of their worship.—In this his Travel he met with many perswasions to come into a communion with that Church which calls itself *Catholick*: but, he return'd from his Travels as he went, eminent for his obedience to his Mother, *the Church of England.* In his absence from England, Mr *Farrers* father, (who was a Merchant) allow'd him a liberal maintenance; and, not long after his return into *England*, Mr *Farrer* had, by the death of his father, or an elder brother, or both, an Estate left him, that enabled him to purchase Land to the value of 4 or 500 l. a year; the greatest part of which Land was at *Little Glidden*, 4 or 6 miles from *Huntington*, and about 18 from *Cambridge*: which place he chose for the privacy of it, and for the Hall, which had the Parish-Church or Chappel, belonging and adjoining near to it; for Mr *Farrer*, having seen the manners and vanities of the World, and found them to be, as Mr *Herbert* says, *a nothing between two Dishes*; did so contemn it, that he resolv'd to spend the remainder of his life in mortifications, and in devotion, and charity, and to be alwaies prepared for Death:—And his life was spent thus:

He and his Family, which were like a little Colledge, and about Thirty in number, did most of them keep *Lent*, and all *Ember-weeks* strictly, both in fasting and using all those mortifications and prayers that the Church hath appointed to be then used: and he and they did the like constantly on *Fridays*, and on the *Vigils* or Eves appointed to be fasted before the Saints-days; and, this frugality and abstinence turn'd to the relief of the poor: but this was but a part of his charity: none but God and he knew the rest.

This Family, which I have said to be in number about Thirty, were a part of them his Kindred, and the rest chosen to be of a temper fit to be moulded into a devout life; and all of them were for their dispositions *serviceable* and *quiet* and *humble* and *free from scandal*. Having thus fitted himself for his Family, he did, about the year 1630, betake himself to a constant and methodical service of God; and it was in this manner. —He, being accompanied with most of his Family, did himself use to read the Common prayers (for he was a Deacon) every day, at the appointed hours of Ten and Four, in the Parish Church, which was very near his House, and which he had both repair'd and adorn'd; for it was fallen into a great ruine, by reason of a depopulation of the Village before Mr *Farrer* bought the Mannor. And, he did also constantly read the Mattins every Morning at the hour of six, either in the Church, or in an Oratory, which was within his own House. And many of the Family did there continue with him after the Prayers were ended, and there they spent some hours in singing *Hymns*, or *Anthems*, sometimes in the Church, and often to an Organ in the Oratory. And there they sometimes betook

themselves to meditate, or to pray privately, or to read a part
of the New Testament to themselves, or to continue their
praying or reading the Psalms; and in case the Psalms were
not always read in the day, then Mr *Farrer*, and others of the
Congregation, did at Night, at the ringing of a Watch-bell,
repair to the Church or Oratory, and there betake themselves
to prayers and lauding God, and reading the Psalms that had
not been read in the day: and, when these, or any part of the
Congregation, grew weary, or faint, the Watch-bell was Rung,
sometimes before, and sometimes after Midnight; and then
another part of the Family rose, and maintained the Watch,
sometimes by praying, or singing Lauds to God, or reading
the Psalms: and when, after some hours, they also grew weary
or faint, then they rung the Watch-bell and were also reliev'd
by some of the former, or by a new part of the Society, which
continued their devotions (as hath been mentioned) until
morning.—And it is to be noted, that in this continued serving
of God, the Psalter or the whole Book of Psalms, was in every
four and twenty hours, sung or read over, from the first to
the last verse: and this was done as constantly as the Sun runs
his Circle every day about the World, and then begins again
the same instant that it ended.

Thus did Mr *Farrer* and his happy Family serve God day
and night; thus did they alwaies behave thsemselves as in his
presence. And they did alwaies eat and drink by the strictest
rules of Temperance; eat and drink so, as to be ready to rise
at midnight, or at the call of a Watch-bell, and perform their
devotions to God.—And 'tis fit to tell the Reader, that many
of the Clergy, that were more inclin'd to *practical piety* and
devotion, than to doubtful and needless Disputations, did often
come to *Gidden Hall*, and make themselves a part of that
happy Society, and stay a week or more, and then join with
Mr *Farrer*, and the Family in these Devotions, and assist and
ease him or them in their Watch by Night. And, these various
Devotions had never less than two of the Domestick Family

in the night; and the Watch was alwaies kept in the Church or Oratory, unless in extream cold Winter nights, and then it was maintain'd in a Parlour, which had a fire in it: and the Parlour was fitted for that purpose; and this course of Piety, and great liberality to his poor Neighbours, Mr *Farrer* maintain'd till his death, which was in the year 1639.

Mr *Farrers*, and Mr *Herberts* devout lives, were both so noted, that the general report of their sanctity, gave them occasion to renew that slight acquaintance which was begun at their being Contemporaries in *Cambridge*; and this new holy friendship was long maintain'd without any interview, but only by loving and endearing Letters. And, one testimony of their friendship and pious designs, may appear by Mr *Farrers* commending the considerations of *John Valdesso* (a Book which he had met with in his Travels, and translated out of *Spanish* into *English*) to be examined and censur'd by Mr *Herbert* before it was made publick; which excellent book Mr *Herbert* did read, and return back with many marginal Notes, as they be now printed with it: And with them, Mr *Herberts* affectionate Letter to Mr *Farrer*.

This *John Valdesso* was a *Spaniard*, and was for his learning and virtue much valued and loved by the great Emperour *Charles the Fifth*, whom *Valdesso* had followed as a *Cavalier* all the time of his long and dangerous Wars: and when *Valdesso* grew old, and grew weary both of War and the World, he took his fair opportunity to declare to the Emperour, that his resolution was to decline his Majesties service, and betake himself to a quiet and contemplative life, *because there ought to be a vacancy of time, betwixt fighting and dying.*—The Emperor had himself, for the same, or other like reasons, put on the same resolution: but God and himself did, till then, only know them; and he did therefore desire *Valdesso* to consider well of what he had said, and to keep his purpose within his own breast, till they two might have a second opportunity of a friendly Discourse: which *Valdesso* promised to do.

In the mean time the Emperour appoints privately a day for him and *Valdesso* to meet again; and, after a pious and free discourse, they both agreed on a certain day to receive the blessed Sacrament publickly; and appointed an eloquent and devout Fryer to preach a Sermon of *contempt of the World*, and of the happiness and benefit of a quiet and contemplative life; which the Fryer did most affectionately.—After which Sermon, the Emperor took occasion to declare openly, *That the preacher had begot in him a resolution to lay down his Dignities, and to forsake the World, and betake himself to a Monastical life.* And, he pretended, he had perswaded *John Valdesso* to do the like: but this is most certain, that after the Emperor had called his son *Philip* out of *England*, and resign'd to him all his Kingdoms, that then the Emperor, and John Valdesso, did perform their resolutions.

This account of *John Valdesso* I receiv'd from a friend, that had it from the mouth of Mr *Farrer*. And the Reader may note that in this retirement, *John Valdesso* writ his 110 Considerations, and many other Treatises of worth, which want a second Mr *Farrer* to procure and Translate them.

After this account of Mr *Farrer* and *John Valdesso*, I proceed to my account of Mr *Herbert*, and Mr *Duncon*, who, according to his promise, return'd from the Bath the fifth day, and then found Mr *Herbert* much weaker than he left him; and therefore their Discourse could not be long: but at Mr Duncon's parting with him, Mr Herbert spoke to this purpose: *Sir, I pray you give my brother* Farrer *an account of the decaying condition of my body, and tell him I beg him to continue his daily prayers for me, and, let him know, that I have consider'd,* that God only is what he would bee; *and that I am, by his grace, become now so like him, as to be pleas'd with what pleaseth him; and tell him, that I do not repine, but am pleas'd with my want of health: and tell him, my heart is fixed on that place where true joy is only to be found; and that I long to be there, and do wait for my appointed change with* hope and patience. Having said this, he did, with so sweet a humility as seem'd to exalt him, bow down to Mr *Duncon*, and with a thoughtful and contented look, say to him, *Sir, I pray deliver this little Book to my dear brother* Farrer, *and tell him, he shall find in it a picture of the many spiritual Conflicts that have past betwixt God and my Soul, before I could subject mine to the will* of Jesus my Master: *in whose service I have now found perfect freedom; desire him to read it; and then, if he can think it may turn to the advantage of any dejected poor Soul? let it be made publick: if not? let him burn it: for,* I and it are less than the least of Gods mercies.—Thus meanly did this humble man think of this excellent Book, which now bears the name of *The TEMPLE! Or, Sacred Poems and Private Ejaculations;* of which Mr *Farrer* would say, *There was in it the picture of a divine Soul in every page: and, that the whole book was such a harmony of holy passions, as would enrich the World with pleasure and piety.* And, it appears to have done so; for there have been more than Twenty thousand of them sold since the first Impression.

And this ought to be noted, that when Mr *Farrer* sent this book to *Cambridge* to be Licensed for the Press, the *Vice-Chancellor* would by no means allow the two so much noted Verses,

> *Religion stands a Tip-toe in our Land,*
> *Ready to pass to the* American *Strand,*

to be printed; and Mr *Farrer* would by no means allow the Book to be printed, and want them: But after some time, and some arguments, for and against their being made publick, the *Vice-Chancellor* said, *I knew Mr* Herbert *well, and know that he had many heavenly Speculations, and was a Divine Poet; but I hope the World will not take him to be an inspired Prophet, and therefore I License the whole Book.* So that it came to be printed without the diminution or addition of a syllable, since it was delivered into the hands of Mr *Duncon*, save only, that Mr Farrer hath added that excellent Preface that is printed before it.

At the time of Mr *Duncons* leaving Mr *Herbert* (which was

about three weeks before his death) his old and dear friend
Mr *Woodnot* came from *London* to *Bemerton*, and never left him
till he had seen him draw his last breath, and clos'd his Eyes
on his Death-bed. In this time of his decay, he was often
visited and pray'd for by all the Clergy that liv'd near to him,
especially by his friends the Bishop and Prebends of the
Cathedral Church in *Salisbury*; but by none more devoutly
than his Wife, his three Neeces (then a part of his Family)
and Mr *Woodnot*, who were the sad witnesses of his daily
decay; to whom he would often speak to this purpose.—
*I now look back upon the pleasures of my life past, and see the content
I have taken in* beauty, *in* wit, *in* musick, *and* pleasant Conversation, *are now all past by me like a dream, or as a shadow that
returns not, and are now all become dead to me, or I to them; and
I see, that as my father and generation hath done before me, so I also
shall now suddenly (with* Job) *make* my Bed also in the dark;
*and I praise God I am prepared for it; and I praise him that I am
not to learn patience, now I stand in such need of it; and that I have
practised Mortification, and endeavoured to dye daily, that I might
not dye eternally; and my hope is, that I shall shortly leave this valley
of tears, and be free from all fevers and pain; and, which will be a
more happy condition, I shall be free from sin, and all the temptations
and anxieties that attend it; and this being past, I shall dwell in the
new* Jerusalem; *dwell there with men made perfect; dwell where these
eyes shall see my Master and Saviour* Jesus; *and with him see my
dear Mother, and all my Relations and Friends—But I must dye,
or not come to that happy place: And, this is my content, that I am
going daily towards it: and, that every day which I have lived, hath
taken a part of my appointed time from me; and that I shall live the
less time, for having liv'd this, and the day past.*—These, and the
like expressions, which he utter'd often, may be said to *be* his
enjoyment of Heaven before he enjoy'd it.—The *Sunday* before
his death, he rose suddenly from his Bed or Couch, call'd for
one of his Instruments, took it into his hand, and said—

My God, my God,
My Musick shall find thee,
And every string
shall have his attribute to sing.

And having tun'd it, he played and sung:

The Sundays of Mans life,
Thredded together on time's string,
Make Bracelets to adorn the Wife
Of the eternal glorious King:
On Sundays, Heavens dore stands ope;
Blessings are plentiful and rife,
More plentiful than hope.

Thus he sung on Earth such Hymns and Anthems, as the Angels, and he, and Mr *Farrer*, now sing in Heaven.

Thus, he continued meditating, and praying, and rejoicing till the day of his death; and on that day said to Mr *Woodnot*, *My dear friend, I am sorry I have nothing to present to my merciful God but sin and misery; but the first is pardoned, and a few hours will now put a period to the latter;* for I shall suddenly go hence, and be no more seen. Upon which expression Mr *Woodnot* took occasion to remember him of the Re-edifying *Layton* Church and his many acts of mercy; To which he made answer, saying, *They be good works, if they be sprinkled with the blood of Christ, and not otherwise.* After this Discourse he became more restless, and his Soul seem'd to be weary of her earthly Tabernacle; and this uneasiness became so visible, that his Wife, his three Neeces, and Mr *Woodnot*, stood constantly about his bed, beholding him with sorrow, and an unwillingness to lose the sight of him, whom they could not hope to see much longer.— As they stood thus beholding him, his Wife observ'd him to breath faintly, and with much trouble: and, observ'd him to fall into a sudden Agony; which so surpriz'd her, that she fell into a sudden passion, and requir'd of him to know *how he did?* to which his answer was, *That he had passed a Conflict with his last Enemy, and had overcome him by the merits of his Master Jesus.* After which answer, he look'd up, and saw his Wife and Neeces, weeping to an extremity, and charg'd them, *If they lov'd him, to withdraw into the next room, and there pray every one alone for him, for nothing but their lamentations could make his death uncomfortable.* To which request their sighs and tears would not suffer them to make any reply: but they yielded him a sad obedience, leaving only with him Mr *Woodnot*, and Mr *Bostock*. Immediately after they had left him, he said to Mr *Bostock, Pray Sir, open that door, then look into that Cabinet, in which you may easily find my last Will, and give it into my hand;* which being done Mr *Herbert* deliver'd it into the hand of Mr *Woodnot*, and said, *My old Friend, I here deliver you my last Will, in which you will find that I have made you my sole Executor for the good of my Wife and Neeces; and I desire you to shew kindness to them, as they shall need it: I do not desire you to be just: for I know you will be so for your own sake; but I charge you, by the Religion of our friendship, to be careful of them.* And having obtain'd Mr *Woodnots* promise to be so, he said, *I am now ready to dye:* after which words, he said, *Lord, forsake me not now my strength faileth me: but grant me mercy for the merits of my Jesus: And now Lord, Lord, now receive my Soul.* And with those words he breath'd forth his Divine Soul, without any apparent disturbance: Mr *Woodnot* and Mr *Bostock* attending his last breath, and closing his eyes.

Thus he liv'd, and thus he dy'd, like a Saint, unspotted of the World, and full of Alms-deeds, full of Humility, and all the examples of a vertuous life; which I cannot conclude better, than with this borrowed observation:

> ——*All must to their cold Graves;*
> *But the religious actions of the just,*
> *Smell sweet in death, and blossom in the dust.*

Mr *George Herberts* have done so to this, and will doubtless do so to succeeding Generations.—I have but this to say more of him: that if *Andrew Melvin* dyed before him, then *George Herbert* dyed without an enemy—I wish (if God shall be so pleased) that I may be so happy as to dye like him.

There is a debt justly due to the memory of Mr Herberts *vertuous Wife; a part of which I will endeavour to pay, by a very short account of the remainder of her life, which shall follow.*

She continu'd his disconsolate Widow, about six years, bemoaning her self, and complaining, That she had lost the delight of her eyes; *but more,* that she had lost the spiritual guide for her poor soul; *and would often say,* O that I had, like holy *Mary,* the Mother of Jesus, treasur'd up all his sayings in my heart! But since I have not been able to do that, I will labour to live like him, that where he now is, I may be also. *And she would often say,* (*as the Prophet* David *for his son* Absolon) —O that I had dyed for him! *Thus she continued mourning, till time and conversation had so moderated her sorrows, that she became the happy Wife of* Sir Robert Cook, *of* Highnam, *in the County of* Gloucester, *Knight. And though he put a high value on the excellent accomplishments of her mind and body, and was so like Mr* Herbert, *as not to govern like a Master, but as an affectionate Husband; yet, she would even to him often take occasion to mention the name of* Mr George Herbert, *and say,* That name must live in her memory, till she put off mortality.—*By* Sir Robert, *she had only one Child, a Daughter, whose parts and plentiful estate make her happy in this world, and her well using of them gives a fair testimony, that she will be so in that which is to come.*

Mrs Herbert *was the Wife of* Sir Robert *eight years,* and *liv'd his Widow about fifteen; all which time, she took a pleasure in mentioning, and commending the excellencies of Mr* George Herbert. *She dyed in the year* 1663, *and lies buried at* Highnam: *Mr* Herbert *in his own Church, under the Altar, and cover'd with a Grave-stone without any inscription.*

This Lady Cook *had preserv'd many of Mr* Herberts *private Writings, which she intended to make publick; but they, and* Highnam *house, were burnt together, by the late Rebels, and so lost to posterity.*

G

GILBERT BURNET

SOME PASSAGES OF THE LIFE AND DEATH OF JOHN EARL OF ROCHESTER

John Wilmot Earl of *Rochester* was born in *April, Anno Dom.*
1648. his Father was *Henry* Earl of *Rochester*, but best known
by the Title of the Lord *Wilmot*, who bore so great a part in
all the late Wars, that mention is often made of him in the
History: And had the chief share in the Honour of the preservation of his Majesty that now Reigns, after *Worcester* Fight,
and the Conveying him from Place to Place, till he happily
escaped into *France*: But dying before the King's Return, he
left his Son little other Inheritance, but the Honour and Title
derived to him, with the pretensions such eminent Services
gave him to the Kings favour: These were carefully managed
by the great prudence and discretion of his Mother, a Daughter
of that Noble and ancient Family of the *St Johns of Wiltshire*,
so that his Education was carried on in all things sutably to
his Quality.

When he was at School he was an extraordinary Proficient
at his Book: and those shining parts which have since appeared
with so much lustre; began then to shew themselves: He
acquired the *Latin* to such perfection, that to his dying-day
he retained a great rellish of the fineness and Beauty of that
Tongue: and was exactly versed in the incomparable Authors
that writ about *Augustus's* time, whom he read often with that
peculiar delight which the greatest Wits have ever found in
those Studies.

When he went to the *University* the general Joy which over-
ran the whole Nation upon his Majesties Restauration, but

was not regulated with that Sobriety and Temperance that became a serious gratitude to God for so great a Blessing, produced some of it's ill effects on him: He began to love these disorders too much; His Tutor was that Eminent and Pious Divine Dr *Blanford*, afterwards promoted to the Sees of *Oxford* and *Worcester*: And under his Inspection, he was committed to the more immediate care of Mr *Phineas Berry*, a Fellow of *Wadham*-Colledge, a very learned and good natured man; whom he afterwards ever used with much respect, and rewarded him as became a great man. But the humour of that time wrought so much on him, that he broke off the Course of his Studies; to which no means could ever effectually recall him; till when he was in *Italy* his Governor Dr *Balfour* a learned and worthy man, now a Celebrated Physitian in *Scotland* his Native Country; drew him to read such Books, as were most likely to bring him back to love Learning and Study: and he often acknowledged to me, in particular three days before his Death, how much he was obliged to Love and Honour this his Governour, to whom he thought he owed more than to all the World, next after his Parents, for his great Fidelity and Care of him, while he was under his trust. But no part of it affected him more sensibly, than that he engaged him by many tricks (so he expressed it) to delight in Books and reading; So that ever after he took occasion in the Intervals of those woful Extravagancies that consumed most of his time to read much: and though the time was generally but indifferently employed, for the choice of the Subjects of his Studies was not always good, yet the habitual Love of Knowledge together with these fits of study, had much awakened his Understanding, and prepared him for better things, when his mind should be so far changed as to rellish them.

He came from his Travels in the 18*th* Year of his Age, and appeared at Court with as great Advantages as most ever had. He was a Graceful and well shaped Person, tall and well made, if not a little too slender: He was exactly well bred, and what by a modest behaviour natural to him, what by a Civility become almost as natural, his Conversation was easie and obliging. He had a strange Vivacity of thought, and vigour of expression: His Wit had a subtility and sublimity both, that were scarce imitable. His Style was clear and strong: When he used Figures they were very lively, and yet far enough out of the Common Road: he had made himself Master of the Ancient and Modern Wit, and of the Modern *French* and *Italian* as well as the *English*. He loved to talk and write of Speculative Matters, and did it with so fine a thread, that even those who hated the Subjects that his Fancy ran upon, yet could not but be charmed with his way of treating of them. *Boileau* among the *French*, and *Cowley* among the *English* Wits, were those he admired most. Sometimes other mens thoughts mixed with his Composures, but that flowed rather from the Impressions they made on him when he read them, by which they came to return upon him as his own thoughts; than that he servilely copied from any. For few men ever had a bolder flight of fancy, more steddily governed by Judgment than he had. No wonder a young man so made, and so improved was very acceptable in a Court.

Soon after his coming thither he laid hold on the first Occasion that offered to shew his readiness to hazard his life in the Defence and Service of his Country. In *Winter* 1665. he went with the Earl of *Sandwich* to Sea, when he was sent to lie for the *Dutch East-India Fleet*; and was in the *Revenge*, Commanded by Sir *Thomas Tiddiman*, when the Attack was made on the Port of *Bergen* in *Norway*, the *Dutch* ships having got into that *Port*. It was as desperate an attempt as ever was made: during the whole Action, the Earl of *Rochester* shewed as brave and as resolute a Courage as was possible: A Person of Honour told me he heard the Lord *Clifford*, who was in the same Ship, often magnifie his Courage at that time very highly. Nor did the Rigours of the Season, the hardness of the Voyage, and the extream danger he had been in, deter him from running the like on the very next Occasion; For the *Summer* following he went to Sea again, without communicating his design to his nearest Relations. He went aboard the Ship Commanded by Sir *Edward Spragge* the day before the great Sea-fight of that Year: Almost all the Volunteers that were in the same Ship were killed. Mr *Middleton* (brother of Sir *Hugh Middleton*) was shot in his Arms. During the Action, Sir *Edward Spragge* not being satisfied with the behaviour of one of the Captains, could not easily find a Person that would chearfully venture through so much danger, to carry his Commands to that Captain. This Lord offered himself to the Service; and went in a little Boat, through all the shot, and delivered his Message, and returned back to Sir *Edward*: which was much commended by all that saw it. He thought it necessary to begin his life with these Demonstrations of his Courage in an Element and way of fighting, which is acknowledged to be the greatest trial of clear and undaunted Valour.

He had so entirely laid down the Intemperance that was growing on him before his Travels, that at his Return he hated nothing more. But falling into Company that loved these Excesses, he was, though not without difficulty, and by many steps, brought back to it again. And the natural heat of his fancy, being inflamed by Wine, made him so extravagantly pleasant, that many to be more diverted by that humor, studied to engage him deeper and deeper in Intemperance: which at length did so entirely subdue him; that, as he told me, for five years together he was continually Drunk: not all the while under the visible effect of it, but his blood was so inflamed, that he was not in all that time cool enough to be perfectly Master of himself. This led him to say and do many wild and unaccountable things: By this, he said, he had broke the firm constitution of his Health, that seemed so strong, that nothing was too hard for it; and he had suffered so much in his Reputation, that he almost despaired to recover it. There were two Principles in his natural temper, that being heighten'd by that heat carried him to great excess: a violent love of Pleasure and a disposition to extravagant Mirth. The one involved him in great sensuality: the other led him to many odd Adventures and Frollicks, in which he was oft in hazard of his life. The one being the same irregular appetite in his Mind, that the other was in his Body, which made him think nothing diverting that was not extravagant. And though in cold blood he was a generous and good natured man, yet he would go far in his heats, after any thing that might turn to a Jest or matter of Diversion: He said to me, He never improved his Interest at Court, to do a premeditated Mischief to other persons. Yet he laid out his Wit very freely in *Libels* and *Satyrs*, in which he had a peculiar Talent of mixing his Wit with his Malice, and fitting both with such apt words, that Men were tempted to be pleased with them: from thence his Composures came to be easily known, for few had such a way of tempering these together as he had; So that when any thing extraordinary that way came out, as a Child is fathered sometimes by its Resemblance, so was it laid at his Door as its Parent and Author.

These Exercises in the course of his life were not always equally pleasant to him; he had often sad Intervals and severe Reflections on them: and though then he had not these awakened in him from any deep Principle of Religion, yet the horrour that Nature raised in him, especially in some Sicknesses, made him too easie to receive some ill Principles, which others endeavoured to possess him with; so that he was too soon brought to set himself to secure, and fortify his Mind against that, by dispossessing it all he could of the belief or apprehensions of Religion. The Licentiousness of his temper, with the briskness of his Wit, disposed him to love the Conversation of those who divided their time between lewd Actions and irregular Mirth. And so he came to bend his Wit, and direct his Studies and Endeavours to support and strengthen these ill Principles both in himself and others.

An accident fell out after this, which confirmed him more in these Courses: when he went to Sea in the Year 1665, there happened to be in the same Ship with him Mr *Mountague* and another Gentleman of Quality, these two, the former especially, seemed perswaded that they should never return into *England*. Mr *Mountague* said, He was sure of it: the other was not so positive. The Earl of *Rochester*, and the last of these, entered into a formal Engagement, not without Ceremonies of Religion, that if either of them died, he should appear, and give the other notice of the future State, if there was any. But Mr *Mountague* would not enter into the Bond. When the day came that they thought to have taken the *Dutch*-Fleet in the Port of *Bergen*, Mr *Mountague* though he had such a strong Presage in his Mind of his approaching death, yet he generously stayed all the while in the place of greatest danger: The other Gentleman signalized his Courage in a most undaunted manner, till near the end of the Action; when he fell on a sudden into such a trembling that he could scarce stand: and Mr *Mountague* going to him to hold him up, as they were in each others Arms, a Cannon Ball killed him outright, and carried away Mr *Mountague's* Belly, so that he died within an hour after. The Earl of *Rochester* told me that these presages they had in their minds made some impression on him, that there were separated Beings: and that the Soul either by a natural sagacity, or some secret Notice communicated to it, had a sort of Divination: But that Gentlemans never appearing was a great snare to him, during the rest of his life. Though when he told me this, he could not but acknowledge, it was an unreasonable thing for him, to think, that Beings in another State were not under such Laws and Limits, that they could not command their own motions, but as the Supream Power should order them: and that one who had so corrupted the Natural Principles of Truth, as he had, had no reason to expect that such an extraordinary thing should be done for his Conviction.

He told me of another odd Presage that one had of his approaching Death in the Lady *Warre*, his Mother in Laws house: The Chaplain had dream't that such a day he should die, but being by all the Family put out of the belief of it, he had almost forgot it: till the Evening before at Supper, there being Thirteen at Table; according to a fond conceit that one of these must soon die, One of the young Ladies pointed to him, that he was to die. He remembering his Dream fell into some disorder, and the Lady *Warre* reproving him for his Superstition, he said, He was confident he was to die before Morning, but he being in perfect health, it was not much minded. It was *Saturday* Night, and he was to Preach next day. He went to his Chamber and sate up late, as appeared by the burning of his Candle, and he had been preparing his Notes for his Sermon, but was found dead in his Bed the next Morning: These things he said made him inclined to believe, the Soul was a substance distinct from matter: and this often returned into his thoughts. But that which perfected his perswasion about it, was, that in the Sickness which brought him so near death before I first knew him, when his Spirits were so low and spent, that he could not move nor stir, and he did not think to live an hour; He said, His Reason and Judgment were so clear and strong, that from thence he was fully persuaded that Death was not the spending or dissolution of the Soul; but only the separation of it from matter. He had in that Sickness great Remorses for his past Life, but he afterwards told me, They were rather general and dark Horrours, than any Convictions of sinning against God. He was sorry he had lived so as to wast his strength so soon, or that he had brought such an ill name upon himself, and had an Agony in his Mind about it, which he knew not well how to express; But at such times, though he complied with his Friends in suffering Divines to be sent for, he said, He had no great mind to it: and that it was but a piece of his breeding, to desire them to pray by him, in which he joyned little himself.

As to the Supream Being, he had always some Impression of one: and professed often to me, That he had never known an entire *Atheist*, who fully believed there was no God. Yet when he explained his Notion of this Being, it amounted to no more than a vast power, that had none of the Attributes of Goodness or Justice, we ascribe to the Deity: These were his thoughts about Religion, as himself told me. For Morality, he freely own'd to me, that though he talked of it, as a fine thing, yet this was only because he thought it a decent way of speaking, and that as they went always in Clothes, though in their Frollicks they would have chosen sometimes to have gone naked, if they had not feared the people: So though some of them found it necessary for humane life to talk of Morality, yet he confessed they cared not for it, further than the reputation of it was necessary for their credit, and affairs: of which he gave me many Instances, as their professing and swearing Friendship, where they hated mortally; their Oaths and Imprecations in their Addresses to Women, which they intended never to make good; the pleasure they took in defaming innocent Persons, and spreading false Reports of some, perhaps in Revenge, because they could not engage them to comply with their ill Designs: The delight they had in making people quarrel; their unjust usage of their Creditors, and putting them off by any deceitful Promise they could invent, that might deliver them from present Importunity. So that in detestation of these Courses he would often break forth into such hard Expressions concerning himself as would be indecent for another to repeat.

Such had been his Principles and Practices in a Course of many years which had almost quite extinguish't the natural Propensities in him to Justice and Vertue: He would often go into the Country, and be for some months wholly employed in Study, or the Sallies of his Wit: Which he came to direct chiefly to *Satyre*. And this he often defended to me, by saying there were some people that could not be kept in Order, or admonished but in this way. I replied, That it might be granted that a grave way of *Satyre* was sometimes no improfitable way of Reproof. Yet they who used it only out of spite, and mixed Lyes with Truth, sparing nothing that might adorn their *Poems*, or gratifie their Revenge, could not excuse that way of Reproach, by which the Innocent often suffer: since the most malicious things, if wittily expressed, might stick to and blemish the best men in the World, and the malice of a Libel could hardly consist with the Charity of an Admonition. To this he answered, A man could not write with life, unless he were heated by Revenge: For to make a *Satyre* without Resentments, upon the cold Notions of Phylosophy, was as if a man would in cold blood cut mens throats who had never offended him: And he said, The lyes in these Libels came often in as Ornaments that could not be spared without spoiling the beauty of the *Poem*.

For his other Studies, they were divided between the Comical and witty Writings of the Ancients and Moderns, the *Roman* Authors, and Books of Physick: which the ill state of health he was fallen into, made more necessary to himself: and which qualified him for an odd adventure, which I shall but just mention. Being under an unlucky Accident, which obliged him to keep out of the way; He disguised himself, so that his nearest Friends could not have known him, and set up in *Tower-street* for an *Italian Mountebank*, where he practised Physic for some Weeks not without success. In his later years, he read Books of History more. He took pleasure to disguise himself, as a *Porter*, or as a *Beggar*; sometimes to follow some mean Amours, which, for the variety of them, he affected; At other times, meerly for diversion, he would go about in odd shapes, in which he acted his part so naturally, that even those who were on the secret, and saw him in these shapes, could perceive nothing by which he might be discovered.

I have now made the Description of his former Life and Principles, as fully as I thought necessary, to answer my End in writing: And yet with those reserves, that I hope I have given no just cause of offence to any. I have said nothing but what I had from his own mouth, and have avoided the mentioning of the more particular Passages of his life, of which he told me not a few: But since others were concerned in them, whose good only I design, I will say nothing that may either provoke or blemish them. It is their Reformation, and not their Disgrace, I desire: This tender consideration of others has made me suppress many remarkable and useful things, he told me: But finding that though I should name none, yet I must at least Relate such Circumstances as would give too great Occasion for the *Reader* to conjecture concerning the Persons intended, right or wrong, either of which were inconvenient enough, I have chosen to pass them quite over. But I hope those that know how much they were engaged with him in his ill Courses, will be somewhat touched with this tenderness I express towards them: and be thereby the rather induced to reflect on their Ways, and to consider without prejudice or passion what sense this Noble Lord had of their case, when he came at last seriously to reflect upon his own.

I now turn to those parts of this *Narrative*, wherein I myself bore some share, and which I am to deliver upon the Observations I made, after a long and free Conversation with him for some months. I was not long in his Company, when he told me, He should treat me with more freedom than he had ever used to men of my Profession. He would conceal none of his Principles from me, but lay his thoughts open without any Disguise; nor would he do it to maintain Debate, or shew his Wit, but plainly tell me what stuck with him, and protested to me, That he was not so engaged to his old Maxims, as to resolve not to change, but that if he could be convinc'd, he would choose rather to be of another mind: He said, He would impartially Weigh what I should lay before him, and tell me freely when it did convince him, and when it did not. He expressed this disposition of mind to me in a manner so frank, that I could not but believe him, and be much taken with his way of Discourse: So we entred into almost all the parts of Natural and Revealed Religion, and of Morality. He seemed pleased, and in a great measure satisfied, with what I said upon many of these Heads: And though our freest Conversation was when we were alone, yet upon several Occasions, other Persons were Witnesses to it. I understood from many hands that my Company was not distastful to him, and that the Subjects about which we talked most were not unacceptable: and he expressed himself often, not ill pleased with many things I said to him, and particularly when I visited him in his last Sickness, so that I hope it may not be altogether unprofitable to publish the substance of those matters about which We argued so freely, with our reasoning upon them: And perhaps what had some effects on him, may be not altogether ineffectual upon others. I followed him with such Arguments as I saw were most likely to prevail with him: and my not urging other Reasons, proceeded not from any distrust I had of their force, but from the necessity of using those that were most proper for him. He was then in a low state of health, and seemed to be slowly recovering of a great Disease: He was in the Milk-Diet, and apt to fall into Hectical-Fits: any accident weakened him; so that he thought he could not live long; And when he went from *London*, he said, He believed he should never come to Town more. Yet during his being in Town he was so well, that he went often abroad, and had great Vivacity of Spirit. So that he was under no such decay, as either darkened or weakened his Understanding; Nor was he any way troubled with the Spleen, or Vapours, or under the power of Melancholy. What he was then, compared to what he had been formerly, I could not so well judge, who had seen him but twice before. Others have told me they perceived no difference in his parts. This I mention more particularly, that it may not be thought that Melancholy, or the want of Spirits, made him more inclined to receive any Impressions: for indeed I never discovered any such thing in him.

Having thus opened the way to the Heads of our Discourse, I shall next mention them. The *three* chief things We talked about, were *Morality*, *Natural Religion* and *Revealed Religion*, *Christianity* in particular. For *Morality*, he confessed, He saw the necessity of it, both for the Government of the World, and for the preservation of Health, Life and Friendship; and was very much ashamed of his former Practices, rather because he had made himself a Beast, and had brought pain and sickness on his Body, and had suffered much in his Reputation, than from any deep sense of a Supream being, or another State: But so far this went with him, that he resolved firmly to change the Course of his Life; which he thought he should effect by the study of *Philosophy*, and had not a few no less solid than pleasant Notions concerning the folly and madness of Vice: but he confessed he had no remorse for his past Actions, as Offences against God, but only as Injuries to himself and to Mankind.

Upon this Subject I shewed him the Defects of *Philosophy*, for reforming the World: That it was a matter of Speculation, which but few either had the leisure, or the capacity to enquire into. But the Principle that must reform Mankind, must be obvious to every Mans Understanding. That *Philosophy* in matters of Morality, beyond the great lines of our Duty, had no very certain fixed Rule, but in the lesser Offices and Instances of our Duty went much by the Fancies of Men, and Customs of Nations; and consequently could not have Authority enough to bear down the Propensities of Nature, Appetite or Passion: For which I instanced in these two Points; The *One* was, About that *Maxim* of the *Stoicks*, to extirpate all sort of Passion and concern for any thing. That, take it by one hand, seemed desireable, because if it could be accomplish'd, it would make all the accidents of life easie; but I think it cannot, because Nature after all our striving against it, will still return to it self: Yet on the other hand it dissolved the Bonds of Nature and Friendship, and slackened Industry which will move but dully, without an inward heat: And if it delivered a man from many Troubles, it deprived him of the chief pleasures of Life, which rise from Friendship. The *other* was concerning the restraint of pleasure, how far that was to go. Upon this he told me the two *Maxims* of his *Morality* then were, that he should do nothing to the hurt of any other, or that might prejudice his own health: And he thought that all pleasure, when it did not interfere with these, was to be indulged as the gratification of our natural Appetites. It seemed unreasonable to imagine these were put into a man only to be restrained, or curbed to such a narrowness: This he applied to the free use of Wine and Women.

To this I answered, That if Appetites being Natural, was an Argument for the indulging them, then the revengeful might as well alledge it for Murder, and the Covetous for stealing; whose Appetites are no less keen on those Objects; and yet it is acknowledged that these Appetites ought to be curb'd. If the difference is urged from the Injury that another Person receives, the Injury is as great, if a Mans Wife is defiled, or his Daughter corrupted: and it is impossible for a man to let his Appetites loose to Vagrant Lusts, and not to transgress in these particulars: So there was no curing the Disorders, that must rise from thence, but by regulating these Appetites: And why should we not as well think that God intended our bruitish and sensual Appetites should be governed by our Reason, as that the fierceness of Beasts should be managed and tamed, by the Wisdom, and for the use of Man?· So that it is no real absurdity to grant that Appetites were put into Men, on purpose to exercise their Reason in the Restraint and Government of them: which to be able to do, Ministers a higher and more lasting pleasure to a Man, than to give them their full scope and range. And if other Rules of *Philosophy* be observed, such as the avoiding those Objects that stir Passion; Nothing raises higher Passions than ungovern'd Lust, nothing darkens the Understanding, and depresses a mans mind more, nor is any thing managed with more frequent Returns of other Immoralities, such as Oaths and Imprecations which are only intended to compass what is desired: The expence that is necessary to maintain these Irregularities makes a man false in his other dealings. All this he freely confessed was true. Upon which I urged, that if it was reasonable for a man to regulate his Appetite in things which he knew were hurtful to him; Was it not as reasonable for God to prescribe a Regulating of those Appetites, whose unrestrained Course did produce such mischievous effects. That it could not be denied, but doing to others what we would have others do unto us, was a just Rule: Those men then that knew how extream sensible they themselves would be of the dishonour of their Families in the case of their Wives or Daughters, must needs condemn themselves, for doing that which they could not bear from another: And if the peace of Mankind, and the entire satisfaction of our whole life, ought to be one of the chief measures of our Actions, then let all the World judge Whether a Man that confines his Appetite, and lives contented at home, is not much happier, than those that let their Desires run after forbidden Objects. The thing being granted to be better in itself, than the question falls between the restraint of Appetite in some Instances, and the freedom of a mans thoughts, the soundness of his health, his application to Affairs, with the easiness of his whole life. Whether the one is not to be done before the other? As to the difficulty of such a restraint, though it is not easy to be done, when a man allows himself many liberties, in which it is not possible to stop; Yet those who avoid the Occasions that may kindle these impure Flames, and keep themselves well employed, find the Victory and Dominion over them no such impossible, or hard matter, as may seem at first view. So that

though the *Philosophy* and *Morality* of this Point were plain;
Yet there is not strength enough in the Principle to subdue
Nature, and Appetite. Upon this I urged, that *Morality*
could not be a strong thing, unless a man were determined
by a Law within himself: for if he only measured himself by
Decency, or the Laws of the Land, this would teach him only
to use such caution in his ill Practices, that they should not
break out too visibly: but would never carry him to an inward
and universal probity: That Vertue was of so complicated a
Nature, that unless a man came entirely within its discipline,
he could not adhere stedfastly to any one Precept: for Vices
are often made necessary supports to one another. That this
cannot be done, either steddily, or with any satisfaction, unless
the Mind does inwardly comply with, and delight in the
Dictates of Virtue. And that could not be effected, except a
mans nature were internally regenerated, and changed by
a higher Principle: Till that came about, corrupt Nature
would be strong, and *Philosophy* but feeble: especially when it
struggled with such Appetites or Passions as were much
kindled, or deeply rooted in the Constitution of ones Body.
This, he said, sounded to him like *Enthusiasme*, or *Canting*:
He had no notion of it, and so could not understand it: He
comprehended the Dictates of *Reason* and *Philosophy*, in which
as the Mind became much conversant, there would soon
follow as he believed, a greater easiness in obeying its precepts: I told him on the other hand, that all his Speculations
of *Philosophy* would not serve him in any stead, to the reforming
of his Nature and Life, till he applied himself to God for
inward assistances. It was certain, that the Impressions made
in his Reason governed him, as they were lively presented to
him: but these are so apt to slip out of our Memory, and we so
apt to turn our thoughts from them, and at some times the
contrary Impressions are so strong, that let a man set up a
reasoning in his Mind against them, he finds that Celebrated
saying of the Poet,

Video meliora proboq; deteriora sequor.
I feel what is better and approve it: but
follow what is worse.

to be all that *Philosophy* will amount to. Whereas those who
upon such Occasions apply themselves to God, by earnest
Prayer, feel a disengagement from such Impressions, and
themselves endued with a power to resist them. So that those
bonds which formerly held them, fall off.

This he said must be the effect of a heat in Nature: it was
only the strong diversion of the thoughts, that gave the
seeming Victory, and he did not doubt but if one could turn
to a *Problem* in *Euclid*, or to Write a Copy of Verses, it would
have the same effect. To this I answered, That if such Methods
did only divert the thoughts, there might be some force in
what he said: but if they not only drove out such Inclinations,
but begat Impressions contrary to them, and brought men
into a new disposition and habit of mind; then he must confess
there was somewhat more than a diversion, in these changes,
which were brought on our minds by true Devotion. I added
that Reason and Experience were the things that determined
our perswasions: that Experience without Reason may be
thought the delusion of our Fancy, so Reason without Experience had not so convincing an Operation: But these two
meeting together, must needs give a man all the satisfaction
he can desire. He could not say, It was unreasonable to believe
that the Supream Being might make some thoughts stir in our
Minds with more or less force, as it pleased: Especially the
force of these motions, being, for most part, according to the
Impression that was made on our Brains: which that power
that directed the whole frame of Nature, could make grow
deeper as it pleased. It was also reasonable to suppose God
a Being of such goodness that he would give his assistance to
such as desired it: For though he might upon some great
Occasions in an extraordinary manner turn some peoples
minds; Yet since he had endued Man with a faculty of Reason,

H

it is fit that men should employ that, as far as they could; and beg his assistance; which certainly they can do. All this seemed reasonable, and at least probable: Now good men who felt upon their frequent Applications to God in prayer, a freedom from those ill Impressions, that formerly subdued them, an inward love to Vertue and true Goodness, an easiness and delight in all the parts of Holiness, which was fed and cherished in them by a seriousness in Prayer, and did languish as that went off, had as real a perception of an inward strength in their Minds that did rise and fall with true Devotion, as they perceived the strength of their Bodies increased or abated, according as they had or wanted good nourishment.

After many Discourses upon this Subject, he still continued to think all was the effect of Fancy: He said, That he understood nothing of it, but acknowledged that he thought they were very happy whose Fancies were under the power of such Impressions; since they had somewhat on which their thoughts rested and centred: But when I saw him in his last Sickness, he then told me, He had another sense of what we had talked concerning prayer and inward assistances.

This Subject led us to discourse of God, and of the Notion of Religion in general. He believed there was a Supream Being: He could not think the World was made by chance, and the regular Course of Nature seemed to demonstrate the Eternal Power of its Author. This, he said, he could never shake off; but when he came to explain his Notion of the Deity, he said, He looked on it as a vast Power that wrought every thing by the necessity of its Nature: and thought that God had none of those Affections of Love or Hatred, which breed perturbation in us, and by consequence he could not see that there was to be either reward or punishment. He thought our Conceptions of God were so low, that we had better not think much of him: And to love God seemed to him a presumptuous thing, and the heat of fanciful men. Therefore he believed there should be no other Religious

Worship, but a general Celebration of that Being, in some short Hymn: All the other parts of Worship he esteemed the Inventions of Priests, to make the World believe they had a Secret of Incensing and Appeasing God as they pleased. In a word, he was neither perswaded that there was a special Providence about humane affairs; Nor that Prayers were of much use, since that was to look on God as a weak Being, that would be overcome with Importunities. And for the state after death, though he thought the Soul did not dissolve at death; Yet he doubted much of Rewards or Punishments: the one he thought too high for us to attain, by our slight Services; and the other was too extreme to be inflicted for Sin. This was the substance of his Speculations about God and Religion.

I told him his Notion of God was so low, that the Supream Being seemed to be nothing but Nature. For if that being had no freedom, nor choice of its own Actions, nor operated by Wisdom or Goodness, all those Reasons which lead him to acknowledge a God, were contrary to this Conceit; for if the Order of the Universe persuaded him to think there was a God, He must at the same time conceive him to be both Wise and Good, as well as powerful, since these all appeared equally in the Creation: though his Wisdom and Goodness had ways of exerting themselves, that were far beyond our Notions or Measures. If God was Wise and Good, he would naturally love, and be pleased with those that resembled him in these Perfections, and dislike those that were opposite to him. Every Rational Being naturally loves it self, and is delighted in others like it self, and is averse from what is not so. Truth is a Rational Natures acting in conformity to it self in all things, and Goodness is an Inclination to promote the happiness of other Beings: So Truth and Goodness were the essential perfections of every reasonable Being, and certainly most eminently in the Deity: nor does his Mercy or Love raise Passion or Perturbation in Him; for we feel that to be a weakness in our selves, which indeed only flows from our want of power, or skill to do what we wish or desire: It is also reasonable to believe God would assist the Endeavours of the Good, with some helps suitable to their Nature. And that it could not be imagined, that those who imitated him, should not be specially favoured by him: and therefore since this did not appear in this State, it was most reasonable to think it should be in another, where the Rewards shall be an admission to a more perfect State of Conformity to God, with the felicity that follows it, and the Punishments should be a total exclusion from him, with all the horrour and darkness that must follow that. These seemed to be the natural Results of such several Courses of life, as well as the Effects of Divine Justice, Rewarding or punishing. For since he believed the Soul had a distinct subsistance, separated from the Body; Upon its dissolution there was no reason to think it passed into a State of utter Oblivion, of what it had been in formerly: but that as the reflections on the good or evil it had done, must raise joy or horrour in it; So these good or ill Dispositions accompanying the departed Souls, they must either rise up to a higher Perfection, or sink to a more depraved, and miserable State. In this life variety of Affairs and objects do much cool and divert our Minds; and are on the one hand often great temptations to the good, and give the bad some ease in their trouble; but in a State wherein the Soul shall be separated from sensible things, and employed on a more quick and sublime way of Operation, this must very much exalt the Joys and Improvements of the good, and as much heighten the horrour and rage of the Wicked. So that it seemed a vain thing to pretend to believe a Supream Being, that is Wise and Good as well as great, and not to think a discrimination will be made between the Good and Bad, which, it is manifest, is not fully done in this life.

As for the Government of the World, if We believe the Supream Power made it, there is no reason to think he does not govern it: For all that we can fancy against it, is the distraction which that Infinite Variety of Second Causes, and the care of their Concernments, must give to the first, if it inspects them all. But as among men, those of weaker Capacities are wholly taken up with some one thing, whereas those of more enlarged powers can, without distraction, have many things within their care, as the Eye can at one view receive a great Variety of Objects, in that narrow Compass, without confusion; So if we conceive the Divine Understanding to be as far above ours, as his Power of creating and framing the whole Universe, is above our limited activity; We will no more think the Government of the World a distraction to him: and if we have once overcome this prejudice, We shall be ready to acknowledge a Providence directing all Affairs; a care well becoming the Great Creator.

As for Worshipping Him, if we imagine Our Worship is a thing that adds to his happiness, or gives him such a fond Pleasure as weak people have to hear themselves commended; or that our repeated Addresses do overcome Him through our mere Importunity, We have certainly very unworthy thoughts of him. The true ends of Worship come within another consideration: which is this, A man is never entirely Reformed, till a new Principle governs his thoughts: Nothing makes that Principle so strong, as deep and frequent Meditations of God; whose Nature though it be far above our Comprehension, yet his Goodness and Wisdom are such Perfections as fall within our Imagination: And he that thinks of God, and considers him as governing the World, and as ever observing all his Actions, will feel a very sensible effect of such Meditations, as they grow more lively and frequent with him; so the end of Religious Worship either publick or private, is to make the Apprehensions of God, have a deeper root and a stronger influence on us. The frequent returns of these are necessary: Lest if we allow of too long intervals between them, these Impressions may grow feebler, and other

Suggestions may come in their room: And the Returns of Prayer are not to be considered as Favours extorted by meer Importunity, but as Rewards conferred on men so well disposed, and prepared for them: according to the Promises that God has made, for answering our Prayers: thereby to engage and nourish a devout temper in us, which is the chief root of all true Holiness and Vertue.

It is true we cannot have suitable Notions of the Divine Essence; as indeed we have no just *Idea* of any Essence whatsoever: Since we commonly consider all things, either by their outward Figure, or by their Effects: and from thence make Inferences what their Nature must be. So though we cannot frame any perfect Image in our Minds of the Divinity, Yet we may from the Discoveries God has made of Himself, form such Conceptions of Him, as may possess our Minds with great Reverence for Him, and beget in us such a Love of those Perfections as to engage us to imitate them. For when we say we love God; the meaning is, We love that Being that is Holy, Just, Good, Wise; and infinitely perfect: And loving these Attributes in that Object, will certainly carry us to desire them in ourselves. For whatever We love in another, We naturally, according to the degree of our love, endeavour to resemble it. In sum, the Loving and Worshipping God, though they are just and reasonable returns and expressions of the sense we have of his Goodness to us: Yet they are exacted of us not only as a Tribute to God, but as a means to beget in us a Conformity to his Nature, which is the chief end of pure and undefiled Religion.

If some Men, have at several times, found out Inventions to Corrupt this, and cheat the World; It is nothing but what occurs in every sort of Employment, to which men betake themselves. *Mountebanks* Corrupt Physic; *Petty-Foggers* have entangled the matters of Property, and all Professions have been vitiated by the Knaveries of a number of their Calling.

With all these Discourses he was not equally satisfied:

He seemed convinced that the Impressions of God being much in Men's minds, would be a powerful means to reform the World: and did not seem determined against Providence; But for the next State, he thought it more likely that the Soul began anew, and that her sense of what she had done in this Body, lying in the figures that are made in the Brain, as soon as she dislodged, all these perished, and that the Soul went into some other State to begin a new Course. But I said on this Head, That this was at best a conjecture, raised in him by his fancy: for he could give no reason to prove it true; Nor was all the remembrance our Souls had of past things seated in some material figure lodged in the Brain: Though it could not be denied but a great deal of it lay in the Brain. That we have many abstracted Notions and *Idea's* of immaterial things which depends not on bodily Figures: Some Sins, such as Falsehood, and ill Nature were seated in the Mind, as Lust and Appetite were in the Body: And as the whole Body was the Receptacle of the Soul, and the Eyes and Ears were the Organs of Seeing and Hearing, so was the Brain the Seat of Memory: Yet the power and faculty of Memory, as well as of Seeing and Hearing, lay in the Mind: and so it was no unconceivable thing that either the Soul by its own strength, or by the means of some subtiler Organs, which might be fitted for it in another state, should still remember as well as think. But indeed We know so little of the Nature of our Souls, that it is a vain thing for us to raise an *Hypothesis* out of the conjectures We have about it, or to reject one, because of some difficulties that occur to us; since it is as hard to understand how we remember things now, as how We shall do it in another State; only we are sure we do it now, and so we shall be then, when we do it.

When I pressed him with the secret Joys that a good Man felt, particularly as he drew near Death, and the Horrours of ill men especially at that time; He was willing to ascribe it to the Impressions they had from their Education: But he

often confessed, that whether the business of Religion was
true or not, he thought those who had the perswasions of it,
and lived so that they had quiet in their Consciences, and
believed God governed the World, and acquiesced in his
Providence, and had the hope of an endless blessedness in
another State, the happiest men in the World: And said, He
would give all that he was Master of, to be under those Perswasions, and to have the Supports and Joys that must needs
flow from them. I told him the main Root of all Corruptions
in Mens Principles was their ill life: Which as it darkened
their Minds, and disabled them from discerning better things;
so it made it necessary for them to seek out such Opinions
as might give them ease from those Clamours, that would
otherwise have been raised within them: He did not deny but
that after the doing of some things he felt great and severe
Challenges within himself; But he said, He felt not these after
some others which I would perhaps call far greater Sins,
than those that affected him more sensibly: This I said, might
flow from the Disorders he had cast himself into, which had
corrupted his judgment, and vitiated his tast of things; and
by his long continuance in, and frequent repeating of some
Immoralities, he had made them so familiar to him, that they
were become as it were natural: And then it was no wonder
if he had not so exact a sense of what was Good or Evil: as a
Feaverish man cannot judge of Tasts.

He did acknowledge the whole Systeme of Religion, if
believed, was a greater foundation of quiet than any other
thing whatsoever: for all the quiet he had in his mind, was
that he could not think so good a Being as the Deity would
make him miserable. I asked if when by the ill course of his
life he had brought so many Diseases on his Body, he could
blame God for it: or expect that he should deliver him from
them by a Miracle. He confessed there was no reason for
that: I then urged, that if Sin should cast the mind by a natural
Effect, into endless Horrours and Agonies, which being seated

in a Being not subject to Death, must last for ever, unless some Miraculous Power interposed, could he accuse God for that which was the effect of his own choice and ill life.

He said, They were happy that believed: for it was not in every mans power.

And upon this we discoursed long about *Revealed Religion*. He said, He did not understand that business of Inspiration; He believed the Pen-men of the Scriptures had heats and honesty, and so writ; but could not comprehend how God should reveal his Secrets to Mankind. Why was not Man made a Creature more disposed for Religion, and better illuminated? He could not apprehend how there should be any corruption in the Nature of Man, or a Lapse derived from *Adam*. Gods communicating his Mind to one Man, was the putting it in his power to cheat the World: For Prophesies and Miracles, the World had been always full of strange Stories; for the boldness and cunning of Contrivers meeting with the Simplicity and Credulity of the People, things were easily received; and being once received passed down without contradiction. The Incoherences of Stile in the Scriptures, the odd Transitions, the seeming Contradictions, chiefly about the Order of time, the Cruelties enjoyned the *Israelites* in destroying the *Canaanites*, Circumcision, and many other Rites of the *Jewish* Worship; seemed to him insutable to the Divine Nature: And the first three Chapters of *Genesis*, he thought could not be true, unless they were Parables. This was the substance of what he Excepted to *Revealed Religion* in general, and to the Old Testament in particular.

I answerd to all this, that believing a thing upon the testimony of another, in other matters where there was no reason to suspect the testimony, chiefly where it was confirmed by other Circumstances, was not only a reasonable thing, but it was the hinge on which all the Government and Justice in the World depended: Since all Courts of Justice proceed upon the Evidence given by Witnesses; for the use of Writings is but a thing more lately brought into the World. So then if the credibility of the thing, the innocence and disinterestedness of the Witnesses, the number of them, and the publickest Confirmations that could possibly be given, do concur to perswade us of any matter of Fact, it is a vain thing to say, because it is possible for so many men to agree in a Lye, that therefore these have done it. In all other things a man gives his assent when the credibility is strong on the one side, and there appears nothing on the other side to ballance it. So such numbers agreeing in their Testimony to these Miracles; for instance of our Saviours calling *Lazarus* out of the Grave the fourth day after he was buried, and his own rising again after he was certainly dead; If there had been never so many Impostures in the World, no man can with any reasonable colour pretend this was one. We find both by the *Jewish* and *Roman* Writers that lived in that time, that our Saviour was Crucified: and that all his Disciples and Followers believed certainly that he rose again. They believed this upon the Testimony of the Apostles, and of many hundreds who saw it, and died confirming it: They went about to perswade the World of it, with great Zeal, though they knew they were to get nothing by it, but Reproach and Sufferings: and by many wonders which they wrought they confirmed their Testimony. Now to avoid all this, by saying it is possible this might be a Contrivance, and to give no presumption to make it so much as probable, that it was so, is in plain *English* to say, *We are resolved let the Evidence be what it will, We will not believe it.*

He said, If a man says he can not believe, what help is there? for he was not master of his own Belief, and believing was at highest but a probable Opinion. To this I Answered, That if a man will let a wanton conceit possess his fancy against these things, and never consider the Evidence for Religion on the other hand, but reject it upon a slight view of it, he ought not to say he cannot, but he will not believe: and while a man lives an ill course of life, he is not fitly qualified to examine the matter aright. Let him grow calm and vertuous, and upon due application examine things fairly, and then let him pronounce according to his Conscience, if to take it at its lowest, the Reasons on the one hand are not much stronger than they are on the other. For I found he was so possessed with the general conceit that a mixture of Knaves and Fools had made all extraordinary things be easily believed, that it carried him away to determine the matter, without so much as looking on the Historical Evidence for the truth of *Christianity*, which he had not enquired into, but had bent all his Wit and Study to the support of the other side. As for that, that believing is at best but an Opinion; if the Evidence be but probable, it is so: but if it be such that it cannot be questioned, it grows as certain as knowledge: For we are no less certain that there is a great Town called *Constantinople*, the Seat of the *Ottoman* Empire, than that there is another called *London*. We as little doubt that Queen *Elizabeth* once Reigned, as that King *Charles* now Reigns in *England*. So that believing may be as certain, and as little subject to doubting as seeing or knowing.

There are two sorts of believing Divine matters; the one is wrought in us by our comparing all the evidences of matter of Fact, for the confirmation of *Revealed Religion*; with the Prophesies in the Scripture; where things were punctually predicted, some Ages before their completion; not in dark and doubtful words, uttered like Oracles, which might bend to any Event: But in plain terms, as the foretelling that *Cyrus* by name should send the *Jews* back from the Captivity, after the fixed period of seventy years: The History of the *Syrian* and *Egyptian* Kings so punctually foretold by *Daniel*, and the Prediction of the destruction of *Jerusalem*, with many Circumstances relating to it, made by our *Saviour*: joyning these to the excellent Rule and Design of the Scripture in matters of *Morality*, it is at least as reasonable to believe this as any thing else in the World. Yet such a believing as this, is only a general perswasion in the Mind, which has not that effect, till a man applying himself to the Directions set down in the Scriptures (which upon such Evidence cannot be denied to be as reasonable, as for a man to follow the Prescriptions of a learned Physitian, and when the Rules are both good and easie, to submit to them for the recovering of his health) and by following these, finds a power entring within him, that frees him from the slavery of his Appetites and Passions; that exalts his Mind above the accidents of life, and spreads an inward purity in his Heart, from which a serene and calm Joy arises within him: And good men by the efficacy these Methods have upon them, and from the returns of their prayers, and other endeavours, grow assured that these things are true, and answerable to the Promises they find registred in Scripture. All this, he said, might be fancy: But to this I answered. That as it were unreasonable to tell a man that is abroad, and knows he is awake, that perhaps he is in a dream, and in his Bed, and only thinks he is abroad, or that as some go about in their sleep, so he may be asleep still; So good and religious men know, though others may be abused, by their fancies, that they are under no such deception; and find they are neither hot nor *Enthusiastical*, but under the power of calm and clear Principles. All this he said he did not understand, and that it was to assert or beg the thing in Question, which he could not comprehend.

As for the possibility of Revelation, it was a vain thing to deny it: For as God gives us the sense of feeling material Objects by our Eyes, and opened in some a capacity of apprehending high and sublime things, of which other men seemed utterly incapable: So it was a weak assertion that God cannot awaken a power in some mens Minds, to apprehend and know some things, in such a manner that others are not capable of it. This is not half so incredible to us as sight is to a blind man, who yet may be convinced there is a strange power of seeing that governs men, of which he finds himself deprived.

As for the capacity put into such mens hands to deceive the World, We are at the same time to consider, that besides the probity of their tempers, it cannot be thought but God can so forcibly bind up a man in some things, that it should not be in his power to deliver them otherwise then as he gives him in Commission: besides the Confirmation of Miracles are a divine Credential to warrant such persons in what they deliver to the World: which cannot be imagined can be joyned to a Lye, since this were to put the Omnipotence of God, to attest that which no honest man will do. For the business of the Fall of Man, and other things of which we cannot perhaps give our selves a perfect account: We who cannot fathome the Secrets of the Councel of God, do very unreasonably to take on us to reject an excellent Systeme of good and holy Rules, because we cannot satisfie ourselves about some difficulties in them. Common Experience tells us, There is a great disorder in our Natures, which is not easily rectified; All *Philosophers* were sensible of it, and every man that designs to govern himself by Reason, feels the struggle between it and nature: So that it is plain, there is a Lapse of the high powers of the Soul.

But why, said he, could not this be rectified, by some plain Rules given; but men must come and shew a trick to perswade the World they speak to them in the Name of God? I Answered, That Religion being a design to recover and save Mankind, was to be so opened as to awaken and work upon all sorts of people; and generally men of a simplicity of Mind, were those that were the fittest Objects for God to shew his favour to; Therefore it was necessary that Messengers sent from Heaven should appear with such allarming Evidences, as might awaken the World, and prepare them by some astonishing Signs, to listen to the Doctrine they were to deliver. *Philosophy*, that was only a matter of fine Speculation, had few Votaries: And as there was no Authority in it to bind the World to believe its Dictates, so they were only received by some of nobler and refined Natures, who could apply themselves to, and delight in such Notions. But true Religion was to be built on a Foundation, that should carry more weight on it, and to have such Convictions, as might not only reach those who were already disposed to receive them, but rouse up such as without great and sensible excitation would have otherwise slept on in their ill Courses.

Upon this and some such Occasions, I told him, I saw the ill use he made of his Wit, by which he slurred the gravest things with a slight dash of his Fancy: and the pleasure he found in such wanton Expressions, as calling the doing of Miracles, *the shewing of a trick*, did really keep him from examining them, with that care which such things required.

For the *Old Testament*, We are so remote from that time, We have so little knowledge of the Language in which it was writ, have so imperfect an account of the History of those Ages, know nothing of their Customs, Forms of Speech, and the several Periods they might have, by which they reckoned their time, that it is rather a wonder We should understand so much of it, than that many passages in it should be so dark to us. The chief use it has to us *Christians*, is, that from Writings which the *Jews* acknowledge to be divinely inspired, it is manifest the *Messias* was promised before the destruction of their Temple: which being done long ago; and these Prophesies agreeing to our Saviour, and to no other, Here is a great Confirmation given to the Gospel. But though many things in these Books could not be understood by us, who live above 3000 years after the chief of them were written, it is no such extraordinary matter.

For that of the Destruction of the *Canaanites* by the *Israelites*, It is to be considered, that if God had sent a Plague among them all, that could not have been found fault with. If then God had a Right to take away their Lives, without Injustice or Cruelty, he had a Right to appoint others to do it, as well to execute it by a more immediate way: And the taking away people by the Sword, is a much gentler way of dying, than to be smitten with a Plague or a Famine. And for the Children that were Innocent of their Fathers faults, God could in another State make that up to them. So all the difficulty is, Why were the *Israelites* commanded to execute a thing of such Barbarity? But this will not seem so hard, if we consider that this was to be no Precedent, for future times: since they did not do it but upon special Warrant and Commission from Heaven, evidenced to all the World by such mighty Miracles as did plainly shew, That they were particularly design'd by God to be the Executioners of his Justice. And God by imploying them in so severe a Service, intended to possess them with great horrour of Idolatry, which was punished in so extream a manner.

For the Rites of their Religion, We can ill judge of them, Except We perfectly understood the Idolatries round about them: To which we find they were much inclined: So they were to be bent by other Rites to an extream aversion from them: And yet by the pomp of many of their Ceremonies and Sacrifices, great Indulgences were given to a people naturally fond of a visible splendor in Religious Worship. In all which, if we cannot descend to such satisfactory Answers in every particular, as a curious man would desire, it is no wonder. The long interval of time, and other accidents, have worn out those things which were necessary to give us a clearer light into the meaning of them. And for the story of the Creation, how far some things in it may be Parabolical, and how far Historical, has been much disputed: there is nothing in it that may not be historically true. For if it be acknowledged that Spirits can form Voices in the Air, for which we have as good Authority as for any thing in History; Then it is no wonder that *Eve* being so lately created, might be deceived, and think a *Serpent* spake to her, when the Evil Spirit framed the Voice.

But in all these things I told him he was in the wrong way, when he examined the business of Religion, by some dark parts of Scripture: Therefore I desired him to consider the whole Contexture of the *Christian Religion*, the Rules it gives, and the Methods it prescribes. Nothing can conduce more to the peace, order and happiness of the World, than to be governed by its Rules. Nothing is more for the Interests of every man in particular: The Rules of Sobriety, Temperance and Moderation, were the best Preservers of life, and which was perhaps more, of Health. Humility, Contempt of the Vanities of the World, and the being well employed, raised a mans Mind to a freedom from the Follies and Temptations that haunted the greatest part. Nothing was so Generous and Great as to supply the Necessities of the Poor, and to forgive Injuries: Nothing raised and maintained a mans Reputation so much, as to be exactly just, and merciful; Kind, Charitable and Compassionate: Nothing opened the powers of a mans Soul so much as a calm Temper, a serene Mind, free of Passion and Disorder: Nothing made Societies, Families, and Neighbourhoods so happy, as when these Rules which the Gospel prescribes took place, *Of doing as we would have others do to us, and loving our Neighbours as our selves.*

The *Christian Worship* was also plain and simple; suitable to so pure a Doctrine. The Ceremonies of it were few and significant, as the admission to it by a washing with Water, and the Memorial of our Saviour's Death in *Bread* and *Wine*; The Motives in it to perswade to this Purity, were strong: That God sees us, and will Judge us for all our Actions: That we shall be for ever happy or miserable, as we pass our Lives here: The Example of our Saviour's Life, and the great expressions of his Love in Dying for us, are mighty Engagements to Obey and Imitate him. The plain way of Expression used by our Saviour and his Apostles, shews there was no Artifice, where there was so much Simplicity used: There were no Secrets kept only among the Priests, but every thing was open to all *Christians*: The Rewards of Holiness are not entirely put over to another State, but good men are specially blest with peace in their Consciences, great Joy in the Confidence they have of the Love of God, and of seeing Him for ever: And often a signal Course of Blessings follows them in their whole Lives: But if at other times Calamities fell on them, these were so much mitigated by the Patience they were taught, and the inward Assistances, with which they were furnished, that even those Crosses were converted to Blessings.

I desired he would lay all these things together, and see what he could except to them, to make him think this was a Contrivance. Interest appears in all Humane contrivances: Our Saviour plainly had none: He avoided Applause, withdrew Himself from the Offers of a Crown: He submitted to Poverty and Reproach, and much Contradiction in his Life, and to a most ignominious and painful Death. His Apostles had none neither. They did not pretend either to Power or Wealth, But delivered a Doctrine that must needs condemn them, if they ever made such use of it: They declared their Commission fully without reserves till other times: They Recorded their own Weakness: Some of them wrought with their own hands; and when they received the Charities of their Converts, it was not so much to supply their own Necessities, as to distribute to others: They knew they were to suffer much for giving their Testimonies, to what they had seen and heard: In which so many in a thing so visible, as Christ's Resurrection and Ascension, and the Effusion of the Holy Ghost which He had promised, could not be deceived: And they gave such public Confirmations of it by the Wonders they themselves wrought, that great multitudes were converted to a Doctrine, which, besides the opposition it gave to Lust and Passion, was born down and Persecuted for 300 years: and yet its force was such, that it not only weathered out all those Storms, but even grew and spread vastly under them. *Pliny* about threescore years after, found their Numbers great and their Lives Innocent: and even *Lucian* amidst all his Raillery, gives a high Testimony to their Charity and Con-

I

tempt of Life, and the other Vertues of the *Christians*; which is likewise more than once done by Malice it self, *Julian* the Apostate.

If a man will lay all this in one Ballance, and compare with it the few Exceptions brought to it, he will soon find how strong the one, and how slight the other are. Therefore it was an improper way, to begin at some Cavils about some Passages in the *New Testament*, or the *Old*, and from thence to prepossess one's Mind against the whole. The right method had been first to consider the whole matter, and from so general a view to descend to more particular Enquiries: whereas they suffered their Minds to be forestalled with Prejudices, so that they never examined the matter impartially.

To the greatest part of this he seemed to assent, only he excepted to the belief of Mysteries in the *Christian Religion*; which he thought no man could do, since it is not in a mans power to believe that which he cannot comprehend: and of which He can have no Notion. The believing Mysteries, he said, made way for all the Juglings of Priests, for they getting the people under them in that Point, set out to them what they pleased; and giving it a hard Name, and calling it a *Mystery*, The people were tamed, and easily believed it. The restraining a man from the use of Women, Except one in the way of Marriage, and denying the remedy of Divorce, he thought unreasonable Impositions on the Freedom of Mankind: And the business of the Clergy, and their Maintenance, with the belief of some Authority and Power conveyed in their Orders, lookt, as he thought, like a piece of Contrivance: And why, said he, must a man tell me, I cannot be saved, unless I believe things against my Reason, and that I must pay him for telling me of them? These were all the Exceptions which at any time I heard from him to *Christianity*. To which I made these Answers.

For Mysteries it is plain there is in every thing somewhat that is unaccountable. How Animals or Men are formed in their Mothers bellies, how Seeds grow in the Earth, how the Soul dwells in the Body, and acts and moves it; How we retain the Figures of so many words or things in our Memories, and how we draw them out so easily and orderly in our Thoughts or Discourses? How Sight and Hearing were so quick and distinct, how we move, and how Bodies were compounded and united? These things if we follow them into all the Difficulties, that we may raise about them, will appear every whit as unaccountable as any Mystery of Religion: And a blind or deaf man would judge Sight or Hearing as incredible, as any Mystery may be judged by us: For our Reason is not equal to them. In the same rank, different degrees of Age or Capacity raise some far above others: So that Children cannot fathome the Learning, nor weak persons the Councels of more illuminated Minds: Therefore it was no wonder if we could not understand the Divine Essence: We cannot imagine how two such different Natures as a Soul and a Body should so unite together, and be mutually affected with one anothers Concerns, and how the Soul has one Principle of Reason, by which it acts Intellectually, and another of life by which it joyns to the Body and acts Vitally; two Principles so widely differing both in their Nature and Operation, and yet united in one and the same Person. There might be as many hard Arguments brought against the possibility of these things, which yet every one knows to be true, from Speculative Notions, as against the Mysteries mentioned in the Scriptures. As that of the *Trinity*, That in one Essence there are three different Principles of Operation, which, for want of terms fit to express them by, We call *Persons*, and are called in Scripture *The Father, Son, and Holy Ghost*, and that the Second of these did unite Himself in a most intimate manner with the Humane Nature of Jesus Christ: And that the Sufferings he underwent, were accepted of God as a Sacrifice for our Sins: Who thereupon conferred on Him a Power of granting Eternal Life to all that submit to the Terms on which He offers it; And that

the matter of which our Bodies once consisted, which may be
as justly called the Bodies we laid down at our Deaths, as
these can be said to be the Bodies which we formerly lived in,
being refined and made more spiritual, shall be reunited to our
Souls, and become a fit Instrument for them in a more perfect
Estate: And that God inwardly bends and moves our Wills,
by such Impressions, as he can make on our Bodies and Minds.

These, which are the chief Mysteries of our Religion, are
neither so unreasonable, that any other Objection lies against
them, but this, that they agree not with our Common Notions,
nor so unaccountable that somewhat like them, cannot be
assigned in other things, which are believed really to be,
though the manner of them cannot be apprehended: So this
ought not to be any just Objection to the submission of our
Reason to what we cannot so well conceive, provided our
belief of it be well grounded. There have been too many
Niceties brought in indeed, rather to darken then explain
these: They have been defended by weak Arguments, and
illustrated by Similies not always so very apt and pertinent.
And new subtilties have been added, which have rather per-
plexed than cleared them. All this cannot be denied; the
Opposition of *Hereticks* anciently, occasioned too much
Curiosity among the *Fathers*: Which the *School-men* have
wonderfully advanced of late times. But if Mysteries were
received, rather in the simplicity in which they are delivered
in the Scriptures, than according to the descantings of fanciful
men upon them, they would not appear much more incredible,
than some of the common Objects of sense and perception.
And it is a needless fear that if some Mysteries are acknowledged
which are plainly mentioned in the *New Testament*, it will
then be in the power of the Priests to add more at their pleasure. For it is an absurd Inference from our being bound to
assent to some Truths about the Divine Essence, of which
the manner is not understood, to argue that therefore in an
Object presented duly to our Senses, such as *Bread* and *Wine*,

We should be bound to believe against their Testimony, that it is not what our Senses perceived it to be, but the whole *Flesh* and *Blood* of *Christ*; an entire Body being in every Crumb and drop of it. It is not indeed in a man's power to believe thus against his Sense and Reason, where the Object is proportioned to them, and fitly applied, and the Organs are under no indisposition or disorder. It is certain that no Mystery is to be admitted, but upon very clear and express Authorities from Scripture, which could not reasonably be understood in any other sense. And though a man cannot form an explicit Notion of a Mystery, for then it would be no longer a Mystery, Yet in general he may believe a thing to be, though he cannot give himself a particular account of the way of it: or rather though he cannot Answer some Objections which lie against it. We know We believe many such in Humane matters, which are more within our reach: and it is very unreasonable to say, We may not do it in Divine things, which are much more above our Apprehensions.

For the severe Restraint of the use of Women, it is hard to deny that Priviledge to Jesus Christ as a Law-Giver, to lay such Restraints, as all inferiour Legislators do; who when they find the Liberties their Subjects take, prove hurtful to them, set such Limits, and make such Regulations, as they judge necessary and expedient. It cannot be said but the Restraint of Appetite is necessary in some Instances: and if it is necessary in these, perhaps other Restraints are no less necessary to fortifie and secure these. For if it be acknowledged that Men have a property in their Wives and Daughters, so that to defile the one, or corrupt the other, is an unjust and injurious thing; It is certain, that except a man carefully governs his Appetites, he will break through these Restraints: and therefore our Saviour knowing that nothing could so effectually deliver the World from the mischief of unrestrained Appetite, as such a Confinement, might very reasonably enjoyn it. And in all such Cases We are to ballance the Inconveniences on

both hands, and where we find they are heaviest, We are to
acknowledge the Equity of the Law. On the one hand there
is no prejudice, but the restraint of Appetite; On the other,
are the mischiefs of being given up to pleasure, of running
inordinately into it, of breaking the quiet of our own Family
at home, and of others abroad: the ingaging into much
Passion, the doing many false and impious things to compass
what is desired, the Waste of men's Estates, time, and health.
Now let any man judge, Whether the prejudices on this side,
are not greater, than that single one of the other side, of being
denied some pleasure? For *Polygamy*, it is but reasonable since
Women are equally concerned in the Laws of Marriage, that
they should be considered as well as Men. But in a State of
Polygamy they are under great misery and jealousie, and are
indeed barbarously used. Man being also of a sociable Nature,
Friendship and Converse were among the primitive Intend-
ments of Marriage, in which as far as the man may excel the
Wife in greatness of Mind, and height of Knowledge, the
Wife someway makes that up with her Affection and tender
Care. So that from both happily mixed, there arises a Harmony,
which is to virtuous Minds one of the greatest joys of life:
But all this is gone in a state of *Polygamy*, which occasions
perpetual Jarrings and Jealousies. And the Variety does but
engage men to a freer Range of pleasure, which is not to be
put in the Ballance with the far greater Mischiefs that must
follow the other course. So that it is plain, Our Saviour considered the Nature of Man, what it could bear, and what was
fit for it, when he so restrained us in these our Liberties. And
for Divorce, a power to break that Bond would too much
encourage married persons in the little quarrellings that may
rise between them; If it were in their power to depart one
from another. For when they know that cannot be, and that
they must live and die together, it does naturally incline them
to lay down their Resentments, and to endeavour to live as
well together as they can. So the Law of the Gospel being a

Law of Love, designed to engage *Christians* to mutual love; It was fit that all such Provisions should be made, as might advance and maintain it: and all such Liberties be taken away, as are apt to enkindle or foment strife. This might fall in some instances to be uneasie and hard enough, but Laws consider what falls out most commonly, and cannot provide for all particular Cases. The best Laws are in some instances very great grievances. But the Advantages being ballanced with the Inconveniences, Measures are to be taken accordingly. Upon this whole matter I said, That pleasure stood in opposition to other Considerations of great Weight, and so the decision was easie. And since our Saviour offers us so great Rewards, It is but reasonable He gave a Priviledge of loading these Promises with such Conditions, as are not in themselves grateful to our natural Inclinations: For all that propose high Rewards, have thereby a right to exact difficult performances.

To this he said, We are sure the terms are difficult, but are not so sure of the Rewards. Upon this I told him, That we have the same assurance of the Rewards, that we have of the other parts of *Christian Religion*. We have the Promises of God made to us by Christ, confirmed by many Miracles: We have the Earnests of these, in the quiet and peace which follows a good Conscience: and in the Resurrection of Him from the dead, who hath promised to raise us up. So that the Reward is sufficiently assured to us: And there is no reason it should be given to us, before the Conditions are performed, on which the Promises are made. It is but reasonable that we should trust God, and do our Duty, *In hopes of that eternal Life, which God who cannot lie, hath promised.* The Difficulties are not so great, as those which sometimes the commonest concerns of Life bring upon us: The learning some Trades or Sciences, the governing our Health and Affairs, bring us often under as great straights. So that it ought to be no just prejudice, that there are some things in Religion that are uneasie, since this is rather the effect of our corrupt Natures, which are farther deprav'd by vitious habits, and can hardly turn to any new course of life, without some pain, than of the Dictates of *Christianity*, which are in themselves just and reasonable, and will be easie to us when renew'd, and in a good measure restor'd to our Primitive Integrity.

As for the Exceptions, he had to the Maintenance of the Clergy, and the Authority to which they pretended; if they stretched their Designs too far, The Gospel did plainly reprove them for it: So that it was very suitable to that Church, which was so grosly faulty this way, to take the Scriptures out of the hands of the people, since they do so manifestly disclaim all such practices. The Priests of the true *Christian Religion* have no secrets among them, which the World must not know, but are only an Order of Men dedicated to God, to attend on Sacred things, who ought to be holy in a more peculiar manner, since they are to handle the things of God. It was necessary that such persons should have a due Esteem paid them, and a fit Maintenance appointed for them: That so they might be preserved from the Contempt that follows Poverty, and the Distractions which the providing against it might otherways involve them in: And as in the Order of the World, it was necessary for the support of Magistracy and Government, and for preserving its esteem, that some state be used (though it is a happiness when Great Men have Philosophical Minds, to despise the Pageantry of it.) So the plentiful supply of the Clergy, if well used and applied by them, will certainly turn to the Advantage of Religion. And if some men either through Ambition or Covetousness used indirect means, or servile Compliances to aspire to such Dignities, and being possessed of them, applied their Wealth either to Luxury or Vain Pomp, or made great Fortunes out of it for their Families; these were personal failings in which the Doctrine of Christ was not concerned.

He upon that told me plainly, There was nothing that gave him, and many others, a more secret encouragement in their ill ways, than that those who pretended to believe, lived so that they could not be thought to be in earnest, when they said it; For he was sure *Religion* was either a meer Contrivance, or the most important thing that could be: So that if he once believed, he would set himself in great earnest to live suitably to it. The aspirings that he had observed at Court, of some of the Clergy, with the servile ways they took to attain to Preferment, and the Animosities among those of several Parties, about Trifles, made him often think they suspected the things were not true, which in their Sermons and Discourses they so earnestly recommended. Of this he had gathered many Instances; I knew some of them were Mistakes and Calumnies; Yet I could not deny but something of them might be too true: And I publish this the more freely, to put all that pretend to Religion, chiefly those that are dedicated to holy Functions, in mind of the great Obligation that lies on them to live, sutably to their Profession: Since otherwise a great deal of the Irreligion and Atheism that is among us, may too justly be charged on them: for wicked men are delighted out of measure when they discover ill things in them, and conclude from thence not only that they are Hypocrites, but that Religion itself is a cheat.

But I said to him upon this Head, that though no good man could continue in the practice of any known sin, yet such might, by the violence or surprise of a Temptation, to which they are liable as much as others, be of a sudden overcome to do an ill thing, to their great grief all their life after. And then it was a very unjust Inference, Upon some few failings, to conclude that such men do not believe themselves. But how bad soever many are, it cannot be denied but there are also many both of the Clergy and Laity, who give great and real Demonstrations of the power Religion has over them; in their Contempt of the World, the strictness of their Lives, their readiness to forgive Injuries, to relieve the Poor, and to do good on all Occasions: and yet even these may have their failings, either in such things wherein their Constitutions are weak, or their Temptations strong and sudden: And in all such cases We are to judge of men, rather by the course of their Lives, than by the Errors, that they through infirmity or surprize may have slipt into.

These were the chief Heads we discoursed on; and as far as I can remember, I have faithfully repeated the substance of our Arguments: I have not concealed the strongest things he said to me, but though I have not enlarged on all the Excursions of his Wit in setting them off, Yet I have given them their full strength, as he expressed them; and as far as I could recollect, have used his own words: So that I am afraid some may censure me for setting down these things so largely, which Impious Men may make an ill use of, and gather together to encourage and defend themselves in their Vices: But if they will compare them with the Answers made to them, and the sense that so great and refined a Wit had of them afterwards, I hope they may through the blessing of God be not altogether ineffectual.

The issue of all our Discourses was this, He told me, He saw Vice and Impiety were as contrary to Humane Society, as wild Beasts let loose would be; and therefore he firmly resolved to change the whole method of his Life: to become strictly just and true, to be Chast and Temperate, to forbear Swearing and Irreligious Discourse, to Worship and Pray to his Maker: And that though he was not arrived at a full perswasion of *Christianity*, he would never employ his Wit more to run it down, or to corrupt others.

Of which I have since a further assurance, from a person of Quality, who conversed much with him, the last year of his life; to whom he would often say, That he was happy if he did believe, and that he would never endeavour to draw him from it.

To all this I Answered, That a Vertuous Life would be very uneasie to him, unless Vicious Inclinations were removed: it would otherwise be a perpetual constraint. Nor could it be effected without an inward Principle to change him: and that was only to be had by applying himself to God for it in frequent and earnest Prayers: And I was sure if his Mind were once cleared of these Disorders, and cured of those Distempers, which Vice brought on it, so great an Understanding would soon see through all those flights of Wit, that do feed Atheism and Irreligion: which have a false glittering in them, that dazles some weak sighted Minds, who have not capacity enough to penetrate further than the Surfaces of things: and so they stick in these Toyls, which the strength of his Mind would soon break through, if it were once freed from those things that depressed and darkened it.

At this pass he was when he went from *London*, about the beginning of *April*: He had not been long in the Country when he thought he was so well, that being to go to his Estate in *Somersetshire* he rode thither Post. This heat and violent motion did so inflame an Ulcer, that was in his Bladder, that it raised a very great pain in those parts: Yet he with much difficulty came back by Coach to the Lodge at *Woodstock Park*. He was then wounded both in Body and Mind: He understood Physick and his own Constitution and Distemper so well, that he concluded he could hardly recover: For the Ulcer broke and vast quantities of purulent matter past with his Urine. But now the hand of God touched him, and as he told me, It was not only a general dark Melancholy over his Mind, such as he had formerly felt; but a most penetrating cutting Sorrow. So that, though in his Body he suffered extream pain, for some weeks, Yet the Agonies of his Mind sometimes swallowed up the sense of what he felt in his Body. He told me, and gave it me in charge, to tell it to one for whom he was much concern'd, that though there were nothing to come after this life, Yet all the Pleasures he had ever known in Sin, were not worth that torture he had felt in his Mind: He considered he had not only neglected and dishonoured, but had openly defied his Maker, and had drawn many others into the like Impieties: So that he looked on himself as one that was in great danger of being damn'd. He then set himself wholly to turn to God unfeignedly, and to do all that was possible in that little remainder of his life which was before him, to redeem those great portions of it, that he had formerly so ill employed. The Minister that attended constantly on him, was that good and worthy man Mr *Parsons*, his Mothers Chaplain, who hath since his death Preached, according to the Directions he received from him, his Funeral Sermon: in which there are so many remarkable Passages, that I shall refer my *Reader* to them, and will repeat none of them here, that I may not thereby lessen his desire to edify himself by that excellent Discourse, which has given so great and so general a satisfaction to all good and judicious *Readers*. I shall speak cursorily of every thing, but that which I had immediately from himself: He was visited every Week of his sickness by his *Diocesan*, that truly Primitive Prelate, the Lord Bishop of *Oxford*; who though he lived six miles from him, yet looked on this as so important a piece of his Pastoral Care, that he went often to him; and treated him with that decent plainness and freedom which is so natural to him; and took care also that he might not on terms more easie than safe, be at peace with himself. Dr *Marshal* the Learned and Worthy *Rector* of *Lincoln*-Colledge in *Oxford*, being the Minister of the Parish, was also frequently with him: and by these helps he was so directed and supported, that he might not on the one hand satisfie himself with too superficial a Repentance, nor on the other hand be out of measure oppressed with a Sorrow without hope. As soon as I heard he was ill, but yet in such a condition that I might write to him, I wrote a Letter to the best purpose I could. He ordered one that was then with him, to assure me it was very welcome to him: but not satisfied with that, he sent me an Answer, which, as the Countess of *Rochester* his Mother told me, he dictated every word, and then signed it. I was once unwilling to have publish'd it, because of a Complement in it to myself, far above my merit, and not very well suiting with his Condition.

But the sense he expresses in it of the Change then wrought on him, hath upon second thoughts prevail'd with me to publish it, leaving out what concerns myself.

WOODSTOCK-PARK

June 25. 1680. Oxfordshire.

My most Honoured Dr. Burnett,

My Spirits and Body decay so equally together, that I shall write You a Letter as weak as I am in person. I begin to value Church-men above all men in the World, Etc. If God be yet pleased to spare me longer in this World, I hope in your Conversation to be exalted to that degree of Piety, that the World may see how much I abhor what I so long loved, and how much I glory in Repentance, and in Gods Service. Bestow your Prayers upon me, that God would spare me (if it be his good Will) to shew a true Repentance and Amendment of life for the time to come: Or else if the Lord pleaseth to put an end to my worldly being now, that He would mercifully accept of my Death-Bed Repentance, and perform that Promise that He hath been pleased to make, That at what time soever a Sinner doth Repent, He would receive him. *Put up these Prayers, most dear Doctor, to Almighty God for your most Obedient and Languishing Servant.*

ROCHESTER

He told me when I saw him, That he hoped I would come to him upon that general insinuation of the desire he had of my Company; and he was loth to write more plainly: not knowing whether I could easily spare so much time. I told him, That on the other hand, I looked on it as a presumption to come so far, when he was in such excellent hands, and though perhaps the freedom formerly between us, might have excused it with those to whom it was known; yet it might have the appearance of so much Vanity, to such as were strangers to it; So that till I received his Letter, I did not think it convenient to come to him: And then not hearing that there was any danger of a sudden change, I delayed going to him till the Twentieth of *July*. At my coming to his House an accident fell out not worth mentioning, but that some have made a story of it. His Servant being a *French-man* carried up my Name wrong, so that he mistook it for another, who had sent to him, that he would undertake his Cure, and he being resolved not to meddle with him, did not care to see him: This mistake lasted some hours, with which I was the better contented, because he was not then in such a condition, that my being about him could have been of any use to him: for that Night was like to have been his last. He had a *Convulsion-Fit* and raved, but *Opiates* being given him; after some hours rest, his raving left him so entirely, that it never again returned to him.

I cannot easily express the Transport he was in, when he awoke and saw me by him: He brake out in the tenderest Expressions concerning my kindness in coming so far to see *such a One*, using terms of great abhorrence concerning himself, which I forbear to relate. He told me, as his strength served him at several snatches, for he was then so low, that he could not hold up discourse long at once, what sense he had of his past life; what sad apprehension for having so offended his Maker, and dishonoured his Redeemer: What Horrours he had gone through, and how much his Mind was turned to call on God, and on his Crucified Saviour: So that he hoped he should obtain Mercy, for he believed he had sincerely repented; and had now a calm in his Mind after that storm that he had been in for some Weeks. He had strong Apprehensions and Perswasions of his admittance to Heaven: of which he spake once not without some extraordinary Emotion. It was indeed the only time that he spake with any great warmth to me: For his Spirits were then low, and so far spent, that though those about him told me, He had expressed formerly great fervor in his Devotions; Yet Nature was so much sunk, that these were in a great measure fallen off. But he made me pray often with him; and spoke of his Conversion to God as a thing now grown up in him to a setled and calm serenity. He was very anxious to know my Opinion of a Death-Bed Repentance. I told him, That before I gave any Resolution in that, it would be convenient that I should be acquainted more particularly with the Circumstances and Progress of his Repentance.

Upon this he satisfied me in many particulars. He said, He was now perswaded both of the truth of *Christianity*, and of the power of inward Grace, of which he gave me this strange account. He said, Mr *Parsons* in order to his Conviction, read to him the 53.*Chapter* of the Prophesie of *Isaiah*, and compared *that* with the History of our Saviour's Passion, that he might there see a Prophesie concerning it, written many Ages before it was done; which the *Jews* that blasphemed Jesus Christ still kept in their hands, as a Book divinely inspired. He said to me, *That as he heard it read, he felt an inward force upon him, which did so enlighten his Mind, and convince him, that he could resist it no longer: For the words had an authority which did shoot like Raies or Beams in his Mind; So that he was not only convinced by the Reasonings he had about it, which satisfied his Understanding, but by a power which did so effectually constrain him, that he did ever after as firmly believe in his Saviour as if he had seen him in the Clouds.* He had made it be read so often to him, that he had got it by heart: and went through a great part of it in Discourse with me, with a sort of heavenly Pleasure, giving me his Reflections on it. Some few I remember, *Who hath believed our Report?* Here, he said, *was foretold the Opposition the Gospel was to meet with from such Wretches as he was. He had no Form nor Comliness, and when we shall see Him, there is no beauty that we should desire him. On this he said, The meanness of his appearance and Person has made vain and foolish people disparage Him, because he came not in such a Fools-Coat as they delight in.* What he said on the other parts I do not well remember: and indeed I was so affected with what he said then to me, that the general transport

I was under during the whole Discourse, made me less capable to remember these Particulars, as I wish I had done.

He told me, That he had thereupon received the Sacrament with great satisfaction, and that was encreased by the pleasure he had in his Ladies receiving it with him: who had been for some years misled into the Communion of the Church of *Rome*, and he himself had been not a little Instrumental in procuring it, as he freely acknowledged. So that it was one of the joyfullest things that befel him in his Sickness, that he had seen that Mischief removed, in which he had so great a Hand: and during his whole Sickness, he expressed so much tenderness and true kindness to his Lady, that as it easily defaced the remembrance of every thing wherein he had been in fault formerly, so it drew from her the most passionate care and concern for him that was possible: which indeed deserves a higher Character than is decent to give of a Person yet alive. But I shall confine my Discourse to the Dead.

He told me, He had overcome all his Resentments to all the World; So that he bore ill-will to no Person, nor hated any upon personal accounts. He had given a true state of his Debts, and had ordered to pay them all, as far as his Estate that was not setled, could go: and was confident that if all that was owing to him were paid to his Executors, his Creditors would be all satisfied. He said, He found his Mind now possessed with another sense of things, than ever he had formerly: He did not repine under all his pain, and in one of the sharpest Fits he was under while I was with him; He said, *He did willingly submit*; and looking up to Heaven, said, *God's holy Will be done, I bless Him for all He does to me*. He professed he was contented either to die or live, as should please God: And though it was a foolish thing for a man to pretend to choose, Whether he would die or live, yet he wished rather to die. He knew he could never be so well, that life should be comfortable to him. He was confident he should be happy if he died, but he feared if he lived he might Relapse: And then said he to me, *In what a condition shall I be, if I Relapse after all this? But*, he said, *he trusted in the Grace and Goodness of God, and was resolved to avoid all those Temptations, that Course of Life, and Company, that was likely to insnare him: and he desired to live on no other account, but that he might by the change of his Manners some way take off the high Scandal his former Behaviour had given.* All these things at several times I had from him, besides some Messages which very well became a dying Penitent to some of his former Friends, and a Charge to publish any thing concerning him, that might be a mean to reclaim others. *Praying God, that as his life had done much hurt, so his death might do some good.*

Having understood all these things from him, and being pressed to give him my Opinion plainly about his Eternal State; I told him, That though the Promises of the Gospel did all depend upon a real change of Heart and Life, as the indispensable condition upon which they were made; and that it was scarce possible to know certainly whether our Hearts are changed, unless it appeared in our lives; and the Repentance of most dying men, being like the howlings of condemned Prisoners for Pardon, which flowed from no sense of their Crimes, but from the horrour of approaching Death; there was little reason to encourage any to hope much from such Sorrowings: Yet certainly if the Mind of a Sinner, even on a Death-Bed, be truly renewed and turned to God, so great is His Mercy, that He will receive him, even in that extremity. He said, *He was sure his Mind was entirely turned, and though Horrour had given him his first awaking, yet that was now grown up into a setled Faith and Conversion.*

There is but one prejudice lies against all this, to defeat the good Ends of Divine Providence by it upon others, as well as on himself: and that is that it was a part of his Disease, and that the lowness of his Spirits made such an alteration in him, that he was not what he had formerly been and this some have carried so far as to say, That he died mad: These Reports

K

are raised by those who are unwilling that the last Thoughts or Words of a Person, every way so extraordinary, should have any effect either on themselves or others: And it is to be fear'd, that some may have so far feared their consciences, and exceeded the common Measures of Sin and Infidelity, that neither this Testimony, nor one coming from the Dead, would signify much towards their Conviction. That this Lord was either mad or stupid, is a thing so notoriously untrue, that it is the greatest Impudence for any that were about him, to Report it; and a very unreasonable Credulity in others to believe it. All the while I was with him, after he had slept out the disorders of the Fit he was in the first Night, he was not only without Ravings; but had a clearness in his Thoughts, in his Memory, in his reflections on Things and Persons, far beyond what I ever saw in a Person so low in his strength. He was not able to hold out long in Discourse, for his Spirits failed: but once for half an hour, and often for a quarter of an hour, after he awakened, he had a Vivacity in his Discourse that was extraordinary, and in all things like himself. He called often for his Children, his Son the now Earl of *Rochester*, and his three Daughters, and spake to them with a sense and feeling that cannot be expressed in Writing. He called me once to look on them all, and said, *See how Good God has been to me, in giving me so many Blessings, and I have carried myself to Him like an ungracious and unthankful Dog.* He once talked a great deal to me of Publick Affairs, and of many Persons and things, with the same clearness of thought and expression, that he had ever done before. So that by no sign, but his Weakness of Body, and giving over Discourse so soon, could I perceive a difference between what his Parts formerly were, and what they were then.

And that wherein the presence of his Mind appeared most, was in the total change of an ill habit grown so much upon him, that he could hardly govern himself, when he was any ways heated, three Minutes without falling into it; I mean

Swearing. He had acknowledged to me the former Winter, that he abhorred it as a base and indecent thing, and had set himself much to break it off: but he confessed that he was over-power'd by that ill Custom, that he could not speak with any warmth, without repeated Oaths, which, upon any sort of provocation came almost naturally from him: But in his last Remorses this did so sensibly affect him, that by a resolute and constant watchfulness, the habit of it was perfectly master'd; So that upon the returns of pain which were very severe and frequent upon him, the last day I was with him; or upon such displeasures as people sick or in pain are apt to take of a sudden at those about them; On all these Occasions he never swore on Oath all the while I was there.

Once he was offended with the delay of one that he thought made not hast enough, with somewhat he called for, and said in a little heat, *That damned Fellow*: Soon after I told him, I was glad to find his Style so reformed, and that he had so entirely overcome that ill habit of Swearing; Only that word of calling any *damned*, which had returned upon him, was not decent. His Answer was, *Oh that Language of Fiends which was so familiar to me, hangs yet about me: Sure none has deserved more to be damned than I have done.* And after he had humbly asked God Pardon for it, he desired me to call the Person to him, that he might ask him forgiveness: but I told him that was needless, for he had said it of one that did not hear it, and so could not be offended by it.

In this disposition of Mind did he continue all the while I was with him, four days together; He was then brought so low that all hope of Recovery was gone. Much purulent matter came from him with his Urine, which he passed always with some pain; But one day with unexpressible torment: Yet he bore it decently, without breaking out into Repinings, or impatient Complaints. He imagined he had a Stone in his Passage, but it being searched, none was found. The whole substance of his Body was drained by the Ulcer, and nothing was left but Skin and Bone: and by lying much on his Back, the parts there began to mortifie. But he had been formerly so low, that he seemed as much past all hopes of life as now; which made him one Morning after a full and sweet Nights rest procured by *Laudanum*, given him without his knowledge, to fancy it was an effort of Nature, and to begin to entertain some hopes of Recovery: For he said, He felt himself perfectly well, and that he had nothing ailing him, but an extream weakness, which might go off in time: and then he entertained me with the Scheme he had laid down for the rest of his life, how retired, how strict, and how studious he intended to be: But this was soon over, for he quickly felt that it was only the effect of a good sleep, and that he was still in a very desperate state.

I thought to have left him on *Friday*, but not without some Passion, he desired me to stay that day: there appeared no symptome of present death; and a Worthy Physitian then with him, told me, That though he was so low that an accident might carry him away on a suddain; Yet without that, he thought he might live yet some Weeks. So on *Saturday* at Four of the Clock in the Morning I left him, being the 24*th* of *July*. But I durst not take leave of him; for he had expressed so great an unwillingness to part with me the day before, that if I had not presently yielded to one days stay, it was like to have given him some trouble, therefore I thought it better to leave him without any Formality. Some hours after he asked for me, and when it was told him, I was gone, he seem'd to be troubled, and said, *Has my Friend left me, then I shall die shortly*. After that he spake but once or twice till he died: He lay much silent: Once they heard him praying very devoutly. And on *Monday* about Two of the Clock in the Morning, he died, without any *Convulsion*, or so much as a groan.

ABRAHAM HILL

SOME ACCOUNT OF THE LIFE OF
DR ISAAC BARROW

TO THE REVEREND DR TILLOTSON,
DEAN OF CANTERBURY

DR ISAAC BARROW was the son of Mr *Thomas Barrow* (a Citizen
of *London* of good reputation yet living, Brother to *Isaac
Barrow*, late L. Bishop of St *Asaph*) Son of *Isaac Barrow*, Esq.
of *Spiny Abby* in *Cambridge-shire* (where he was a Justice of the
Peace for 40 years), Son of *Philip Barrogh*, who has in Print a
Method of Physick, and had a brother *Isaac Barrow*, Doctour
of Physick, a Benefactour to *Trinity College*, and there Tutor
to *Robert Cecil* Earl of *Salisbury* and Lord Treasurer.

He was born in *London October* 1630, his Mother was *Ann*,
Daughter of *William Buggin* of *North Cray* in *Kent*, Esq.;
whose tenderness he did not long enjoy, she dying when he
was about four years old.

His first schooling was at the *Charterhouse* for two or three
years when his greatest recreation was in such sports as
brought on fighting among the Boys; in his after-time a very
great courage remained, whereof many instances might be set
down, yet he had perfectly subdued all inclination to quarrel-
ling, but a negligence of his Cloaths did always continue with
him. For his Book he minded it not, and his Father had little
hope of success in the profession of a Scholar, to which he
had designed him. Nay, there was then so little appearance
of that comfort which his Father afterward received from
him, that he often solemnly wisht, that if it pleased God to

take away one of his Children it might be his son *Isaac*, so vain a thing is man's judgment, and our providence unfit to guide our own affairs.

Removing thence to *Felsted* in *Essex*, he quickly made so great a progress in Learning, and all things praise-worthy, that his master appointed him a little Tutour to the Lord Viscount *Fairfax* of *Emely* in *Ireland*. While he stayed there he was admitted in *Peter-house* his Uncle the Bishop's College; but when he removed to (and was fit for) the University of *Cambridge, Feb*. 1645 he was planted in *Trinity* College; His condition was very low, his Father having suffered much in his Estate on account of adhering to the King's Cause, and being gone away from *London* to *Oxford*, his chief support at first was from the liberality of the famous and reverend Dr *Hammond*, to whose memory he paid his thanks in an excellent Epitaph (among his Poems) wherein he describes the Doctour and himself too; for the most, and most noble parts of the character do exactly agree to them both. Being now as it were without Relations, he abused not the opportunity to negligence in his studies, or licentiousness in his manners, but seasoned his tender years with the principles and the exercise of diligence, learning and piety, the best preparatives for the succeeding varieties of life.

The Young-man continued such a Royalist that he would never take the *Covenant*; yet carrying himself with fairness, candour and prudence he gained the goodwill of the chief Governours of the University. One day Dr *Hill*, Master of the College, laying his hand on his head, said *thou art a good Lad, 'tis pitty thou art a Cavilier*: and when in an Oration on the *Gun-powder-treason* he had so celebrated the former times as to reflect much on the present, some Fellows were provok'd to move for his expulsion, but the Master silenced them with this; *Barrow is a better man than any of us*. Afterward when the *Ingagement* was imposed, he subscribed it, but upon second thoughts, repenting of what he had done, he went back to the Commissioners and declared his dissatisfaction, and got his name rased out of the List.

For the Juniours, he was always ready to give them his help and very freely, though for all the Exercises he made for them in verse and prose he never received any recompense but one pair of Gloves.

While he was yet a young Scholar his judgment was too great to rest satisfied with the shallow and superficial Physiology then commonly taught and received in the Universities, wherewith Students of meaner abilities contentedly took up, but he applied himself to the reading and considering the Writings of the Lord *Verulam*, *Monsieur des Cartes*, *Galileo* and the other great Wits of the last Age, who seemed to offer something more solid and substantial.

When the time came he could be chosen Fellow of his College. *Ann. Dom.* 1649, he obtained by his merit, nothing else could recommend him who was accounted of the contrary Party. After his Election, finding the times not favourable to men of his opinions in the affairs of Church and State, to qualify him (as he then thought) to do most good, he designed the Profession of Physick, and for some years bent his studies that way, and particularly made a great progress in the knowledge of Anatomy, Botanicks and Chymistry. But afterwards upon deliberation with himself and conference with his Uncle the late Lord Bishop of St *Asaph*, thinking that profession not well consistent with the Oath he had taken when admitted Fellow, to make Divinity the end of his studies, he quitted Medicine and apply'd himself chiefly to what his Oath seemed to oblige him.

He was upon all opportunities so open and communicative that many of his friends (for out of it he had few acquaintances) in the College can, and I hope some one will report frequent instance of his calm temper in a factious time, his large charity in a mean estate, his facetious talk upon fit occasions, his indefatigable industry in various studies, his clear judgment on all arguments, his steady virtue in all difficulties which they must often have observed and can better describe.

Of his way of discourse I shall here note one thing, that when his opinion was demanded, he did usually speak to the importance as well as to the truth of the question; this was an excellent advantage, and to be met with in few mens conversation.

Tractare res multi norunt, aestimare pauci. (Cardan).

When he read *Scaliger* on *Eusebius* he perceived the dependence of Chronology on Astronomy, which put him on the study of *Ptolomy's Almagest,* and finding that Book and all Astronomy to depend on Geometry, he applied himself to *Euclide's Elements,* not satisfied till he had laid firm foundations; and so he made his first entry into the Mathematicks, having the Learned Mr *John Ray* then for his *socius studiorum,* [and sometimes his Fellow-Traveller in simpling] and always for his [very much] esteemed friend: he proceeded to the demonstration of the other ancient Mathematicians, and published his *Euclide* in a less form and a clearer method than any had done before him; at the end of his demonstration of *Apollonius* he has writ

April 14
       intra haec temporis intervalla peractum hoc opus;
May 16

to so much diligence nothing was impossible: and in all his studies his way was not to leave off his design till he brought it to effect, only in the Arabick Language he made an Essay for a little while and then deserted it. In the same place having also writ, *Labore et constantia,* he adds, *Bonae si conjungantur humilitati et subministrent charitati.* With these speculations the largeness of his mind could joyn Poetry, to which he was always addicted and very much valued that part thereof which consists of description, but the Hyperboles of some modern Poets he as much slighted; for our Plays he was an enemy to them as a principal cause of the debauchery of these times, (the other causes he thought to be the French education and the ill examples of great Persons;) for Satyrs he writ none; his Wit was pure and peaceable.

When Dr *Duport* resigned the Chair of Greek Professour, he recommended this his Pupill for his Successour, who justified his Tutour's opinion by an excellent performance of his Probation exercise, but being thought inclined to Arminianism he obtained it not; however he always acknowledged the favour which Dr *Whichcote* shewed him on that as on all occasions. The partiality of others against him in that affair some thought might help forward his desire to see Foreign Countrys. I make no doubt that he, who in lesser occurrences did very judiciously consider all circumstances, had on good grounds made this resolution, and wish we now knew them; for the reasons and counsels of action would take off from the driness of this Narration, and more strongly recommend him to imitation.

To provide for his Voyage, *Ann. Dom.* 1654, he sold his Books and went first into *France*; at *Paris* he found his Father attending the English Court, and out of his small *viaticum* made him a seasonable present; he gave his College an account of his Voyage thither, which will be found among his Poems; and some farther observations in a Letter, which will show his piercing judgment in Political affairs when he applied his thoughts that way.

After some months he went to *Italy*, and made a stay at *Florence*, where he had the favour and neglected not the advantage to peruse many Books in the Great Duke's Library and ten thousand of his Medals, and discourse thereon with Mr *Fitton*, the fame of whose extraordinary abilities in that sort of learning had caused the Duke to invite him to the charge of that great treasury of Antiquity.

Florence was too dear a place for him to remain in long, his desire was to see *Rome* rather than any other place, but the

Plague then raging there, he took ship at *Livorn* (Nov. 1657) for *Smyrna*. [In this Voyage they were attack'd by a Pirate; and though he had never seen any thing like a sea-fight, he stood to the Gun appointed him with great Courage, for he was not so much afraid of Death as Slavery—*Vitali charior aura Libertas* &c. as he expresses himself. At Smyrna] where he made himself most welcome to Consul *Bretton*, and the Merchants; and so at *Constantinople*, to Sir *Thomas Bendish* the English Embassadour, and Sir *Jonathan Daws*, from whose civility he received many favours, and there ever after continued between them an intimate friendship.

As he could presently learn to play at all Games, so he could accommodate his Discourse to all Capacities, that it should be gratefull and profitable; he could argue a point without arrogance or passion to convince the Learned and could talk pleasantly to the entertainment of easier minds, yet still maintaining his own character, which had some such authority as is insinuated in these words of *Cicero* to *Atticus; Non te Bruti nostri vulticulus ab ista oratione deterret?* (Ep. 20.1.14)

At *Constantinople*, the see of St *Chrysostome*, he read over all the Works of that Father, whom he much preferred before any of the others, and remained in *Turkey* above a year; returning thence to *Venice*, as soon as he landed the Ship took fire, and with all the goods was burnt, but none of the People had any harm: he came thence home through *Germany* and *Holland*, and some part of these Travels and Observations are also related in his Poems.

The term of time was now somewhat past before which all Fellows of *Trinity* College are by Oath obliged to take priestly Orders, or quit the College; he had no rest in his mind till he got himself ordained, notwithstanding the times were then very unsetled, the Church of *England* at a very low ebb, and circumstances very much altered from what they were when he took that Oath wherewith others satisfied themselves in the neglect of Orders.

When the Church and state flourished upon the King's restauration, his Friends expected great things for him who had suffered and deserved so much, yet nothing came, so that he was sensible enough to say, (which he has not among his Poems).

Te magis optavit rediturum, Carole, nemo,
Et nemo sensit te rediisse minus.

1660. He was without a Competitour chosen to the Greek Professourship in *Cambridge*, of which I can only say, that some Friend (to himself I mean) thought fit to borrow and never to restore those Lectures.

July 16. 1662. He was chosen to the Geometry Lecture at *Gresham College*, vacant by the death of Mr *Laurence Rook*, [of whom I could not forbear to speak, but that a large and true Character is given by Dr Barrow himself in his Inauguration Speech.] Dr *Wilkins*, who while *Trinity College* had the happiness of his Mastership, thoroughly observed and much esteemed him, and was always zealous to promote worthy men and generous designs, did interpose vigorously for his assistence, well knowing that few others could fill the place of such a Predecessour; he not only discharged the duty incumbent on him, but supplied the absence of his learned Colleague Dr *Pope*, Astronomy Professour; and among other of his Lectures were divers of the Projections of the Sphere, which he lent out also, and many other Papers we hear no more of. [About this Time he was offer'd a living of good Value; but the Condition annexed, of teaching the Patron's Son, made him refuse it, as too like a Simoniacal Contract. He was also invited to take charge of the *Cotton* Library; but upon a trial a while, he liked better to settle at *Cambridge*.] He so well answered all expectation and performed what Dr *Wilkins* had undertaken for him, that when (1663) Mr *Lucas* founded a Mathematick Lecture at *Cambridge*, the same good and constant Friend recommended him to the Executours, Mr *Raworth* and Mr *Buck*, who very readily conferr'd on him that employment;

and the better to secure the end of so noble and usefull a foundation, he took care that himself and Successours should be bound to leave yearly to the University 10 written Lectures; and those of his which have been, and others yet to be printed, will best given an account of how well he acquitted himself of that service. [Tho' his two Professorships were not inconsistent, yet he was content with that at *Cambridge*; and May 20, 1664, resign'd that at *Gresham* College. There was great Interest against Mr *Robert Hook*, who desir'd to succeed him, and by the assistance of Dr *Wilkins* obtained the Place; the appearance of Such a Patron were ⟨proof⟩ enough of Mr *Hook's* Merit, if the World were not satisfied of it by his own Works.] But after that learned piece *Geometricae Lectiones* had been some while in the world, he had heard of onely two Persons that had read it through; these two were Monsieur *Slusius* of *Liege*, and Mr *Gregory* of *Scotland*, two that might be reckoned instead of thousands, yet the little relish that such things met with did help to loosen him from these Speculations, and the more ingage his inclination to the study of Morality and Divinity, which had always been so predominant that when he commented on *Archimedes*, he could not forbear to prefer and admire much more *Suarez* for his book *de Legibus*; and before his *Apollonius* I find written this divine Ejaculation.

'Ο Θεὸς γεωμετρεῖ

Tu autem, Domine, quantum es Geometra? . . .

The last kindness and honour he did to his Mathematical Chair was to resign it (166⟨9⟩) to so worthy a friend and successour as Mr *Isaac Newton*, fixing his resolution to apply himself intirely to Divinity; and he took a course very convenient for his publick person as a Preacher and his private as a Christian; for those Subjects which he thought most important to be considered for his own use he cast into the method of Sermons for the benefit of others, and herein was so exact as to write some of them four or five times over.

[His Sermons were all large and finished, and fairly written, which he was very ready to preach, i.e. read or lend them as often as desired: Had he been a settled Preacher, he intended them shorter, and he would have trusted to his Memory.

The Method of Dr Barrow in his Sermons is such as the ablest Divines of the Church of *England* observe; but we may farther remark, that he having apply'd himself much to Mathematicks, had acquir'd a Habit to write with Exactness, to proceed directly toward his Scope, and to make use of solid Proofs rather than Figures of Rhetorick. *Le Clerc Bibl. Univ.* 3. 312.

The Sermons of this Author are rather Treatises or exact Dissertations, than Harangues to please the Multitude; if we had resolved to keep within the Bounds of a meer Historian, we might say we have never known a sermon-maker comparable to this Author. *Ib.* 326.]

And now he was onely a Fellow of *Trinity College*, till my L. Bishop of St *Asaph* gave him a small *Sine-cure* in *Wales*, and the R. Reverend *Seth* L. Bishop of *Salisbury* (who very much valued his conversation) a Prebend in his Church; the advantages of both which he bestowed in a way of charity, and parted with them as soon as he was made Master of his College (1672.) he and his Relations being by that time out of a necessitous condition; the Patent for his Mastership, being so drawn for him as it had been for some others, with permission to marry, he caused to be altered, thinking it not agreeable with the Statutes, from which he desired no dispensation.

He had hitherto possessed but a scanty Estate, which yet was made easie to him by a contented mind, and not made a trouble by envy at more plentifull fortunes; he could in patience possess his Soul when he had little else; and now with the same decency and moderation could maintain his character under the temptations of prosperity.

When the King advanced him to this dignity, he was

pleased to say, *he had given it to the best Scholar* in England; his Majesty had several times done him the honour to discourse him, and this preferment was not at all obtained by faction or flattery; it was the King's own act, though his desert made those of the greatest power forward to contribute to it, particularly *Gilbert* Lord Archbishop of Canterbury, and the Duke of *Buckingham* then Chancelour of *Cambridge*, and formerly a member of *Trinity College*.

It were a disrespect to his College, to doubt that, where he had spent so much time and obliged so many Persons, he should not be most welcome; they knew as his power increased, the effects of his goodness would do so too; and the Seniour Fellows so well and understood and esteemed him, that with good will and joy they received a Master much younger than any of themselves. Besides the particular assistence he gave to many in their studie, he concerned himself in every thing that was for the interest of his College; upon the single affair of building their Library, he writ out quires of Paper, chiefly to those who had been of the College; first to ingage them, and then to give them thanks, which he never omitted; these Letters he esteemed not enough to keep Copies of, but by the generous returns they brought in, they appeared to be of no small value; and these Gentlemen that please to send back their Letters will deserve to be accounted farther Benefactours to the Library. He had always been a constant and early man at the Chapel, and now continued to doe the same; and was therein encouraged not only by his own devotion, but by the efficacy his example had upon many others of his College.

In this place seated to his ease and satisfaction, a station wherein of all others in the world he could have been most usefull, and which he meant not to make use of as a step to ascend higher, he abated nothing of his studies, he yielded the day to his publick business, and took from his Morning sleep many hours to increase his stock of Sermons, and write his Treatise of the *Pope's Supremacy*. He understood Popery both at home and abroad, he had narrowly observed it, militant in *England*, triumphant in *Italy*, disguised in *France*, and had earlier apprehensions than most others of the approaching danger, and would have appeared with the forwardest in a needfull time; for his ingagement in that Cause and his place in your Friendship, I would (with the leave of the most worthy Dean of St *Paul's*, his highly respected Friend) call him another Dr *Stilling fleet*.

But so it pleased God, that being invited to preach the *Passion Sermon, April* 13. 1677. at *Guildhall Chapel* (and it was the second sermon for which he received a pecuniary Recompence) he never preached but once more, falling sick of a Fever; such a distemper he had once or twice before, otherwise of a constant health; this fatally prevailed against the skill and diligence of many Physicians his good Friends.

I think not my self competent to give an account of his life, much less of his sickness and death. If great grief had not forced silence, you Sir, his dearest and most worthy Friend, had perpetuated the remarkables of that sad scene, in a Funeral Sermon.

Our Passions, which have hitherto been kept within the banks, should now be permitted to overflow and they even expect to be moved by a breath of Eloquence, but that is not my talent. In short, his death was sutable to his life; not this imperfect slight life as I relate it, but that admirable heroick divine life which he lived.

He died the 4th, of May, 1677 and had it not been inconvenient to carry him to *Cambridge*, then Wit and Eloquence had paid their tribute for the Honour he has done them.

Now he is laid in *Westminster-Abby*, with a Monument erected by the contribution of his Friends, a piece of gratitude not usual in this Age, and a respect peculiar to him among all the glories of that Church. I wish they would (as I have adventured) bring in their Symbols toward the History of his Life: there are many who long before me had the advantage

of his Conversation, and could offer more judicious observations, and in a style fit to speak of Dr *Barrow*. [My Lord
Chancellor's Message of Condolence to his Father, was, that
he had too much cause to grieve, for no Father lost a better
son: But that was also a Reason to mitigate his Sorrow.]

In the Epitaph, Dr *Mapletoft*, his much esteemed Friend,
doth truly describe him; his Picture was never made from the
life, and the Effigies on his Tomb doth little resemble him.
He was in person of the lesser size and lean, of extraordinary
strength, of a fair and calm complexion, a thin skin, very
sensible of the cold; his Eyes gray, clear and somewhat short-
sighted, his Hair of a light aubrun, very fine and curling.
He is well represented by the Figure of *Marcus Brutus* on his
Denarii, and I will transfer hither what is said of that great Man.

> *Vertue was thy Life's centre, and from thence*
> *Did silently and constantly dispense*
> *The gentle vigorous influence*
> *To all the wide and fair circumference.*
>
> (Cowly)

The Estate he left was Books; those he bought, so well
chosen as to be sold for more than they cost; and those he
made, whereof a Catalogue is annexed, and it were not improper to give a farther account of his Works than to name
them: Beside their number, variety, method, style, fulness and
usefulness, I might thence draw many proofs to confirm what
I have before endeavoured to say to his advantage, and many
more important reflexions will be obvious to you than to such
a Reader as I am. I will only take leave to say, that for his
little piece of *the Unity of the Church*, he has better deserved
of the Church and Religion than many who make a greater
Figure in Ecclesiastick History and Politicks. [For upon his
Principles Ecclesiasticism would be for Edification, and not for
Destruction; it is the learned Mr. Thorndyke he disputes
against, but that did not abate the intimate Friendship that

was between them.] But such Remarks will be more fitly placed in what we expect from his learned Friends of the University. And to them I must also refer for the Observables at the taking his several Degrees, and discharging the Office of Vice-Chancelour.

There are beside other particulars which are gratefull to talk over among friends, not so proper perhaps to appear in a publick Writing. For instance, One morning going out ⟨of⟩ a Friend's House before ⟨which⟩ a huge and fierce Mastiff was chained up (as he used to be all day) the Dog flew at him, and he had that present courage to take the Dog by the Throat, and after much strugling bore him to the ground, and held him there till the People could rise and part them, without any other hurt than the streining of his Hands, which he felt some days after.

Some would excuse me for noting that he seem'd intemperate in the love of Fruit; But it was to him Physick as well as Food; and he thought that if Fruit kill hundreds in the Autumn, it preserves Thousands; and he was very free too in the use of Tobacco, believing it did help to regulate his thinking.

I did at first mention the uniformity and excellent tenour of his life, and proceeding on have noted several particulars of a very different nature. I therefore explain myself thus, that he was always one by his exact conformity to the rule in a vertuous and prudent conversation, he steered by the same compass to the same Port when the storms forced him to shift his Sails. His fortune did in some occasions partake of the unsetledness of the times wherein he lived; and to fit himself for the several works he was to do, he enter'd upon studies of several kinds, whereby he could not totally devote himself to one, which would have been more for the publick benefit, according to his own opinion, which was, that general Scholars did more please themselves, but they who prosecuted particular subjects did more service to others.

Being thus ingaged with variety of men and studies, his mind became stored with a wonderfull plenty of words wherewith to express himself; and it happened that some time he let slip a word not commonly used, which upon reflexion he doubtless would have altered, for it was not out affectation.

But his Life were a Subject requiring another kind of Discourses; and as he that acts another man, doth also act himself; so he that would give an account of the excellent qualities in Dr Barrow, would have a fair field wherein to display his own. Another *Camerarius*, or *Gassendus* would make another Life of *Melanchthon* or *Piereskius*. What I am doing will not prevent them; I shall be well satisfied with my unskilfulness if I provoke them to take the argument into better hands.

All I have said, or can say, is far short of the Idea which Dr *Barrow's* Friends have formed of him, and that Character under which he ought to appear to them who knew him not. Beside all the defects on my part, he had in himself this disadvantage of wanting foils to augment his lustre, and low places to give evidence to his heights; such vertues as his, Contentment in all conditions, Candour in doubtfull cases, Moderation among differing Parties, Knowledge without ostentation, are Subjects fitter for praise than narrative.

If I could hear of an accusation, that I might vindicate our Friend's fame, it would take off from the flatness of my expression; or a well-managed Faction, under the name of zeal, for or against the Church, would shew well in story; but I have no shadows to set off my Piece. I have laid together a few sticks for the Funeral-fire, dry Bones which can make but a Sceleton, till some other hand lay on the Flesh and Sinews, and cause them to live and move.

London. 10, *April*, 1683.

JOHN AUBREY

LIFE OF LANCELOT ANDREWES

LANCELOT ANDREWES, Lord Bishop of Winton, was born in London; went to school at Merchant Taylors schoole. Mr Mulcaster was his Schoolemaster, whose picture he hung in his studie (as Mr Thomas Fuller, *Holy State*).

Old Mr Sutton, a very learned man of those days, of Blandford St Maries, Dorset, was his school-fellowe, and sayd Lancelot Andrewes was a great long boy of 18 yeares old at least before he went to the university.

He was a Fellowe of Pembroke-hall, in Cambridge (called Collegium *Episcoporum* . . .)

The Puritan faction did begin to increase in those dayes and especially at Emanuel College. That party had a great mind to drawe in this learned young man, whom if they could make theirs, they knew would be a great honour to them. They carried themselves outwardly with great sanctity and strictness. . . . They preached up very strict keeping and observing the Lord's day; made, upon the matter damnation to breake it, and was less sin to kill a man. . . . Yet these Hypocrites did bowle in a private green at their colledge every sunday after Sermon; and one of the Colledge (a loving friend to Mr L. Andrewes) to satisfie him one time lent him the key of a private back dore to the Bowling green, on a Sunday evening, which he opening, discovered there zealous Preachers, with their gownes off, earnest at play. But they were strangely surprised to see the entry of one that was not of their Brotherhood.

There was then at Cambridge a good fatt Alderman that

was wont to sleep at Church, which the Alderman endeavoured
to prevent but could not. Well! this was preached against as
a signe of *Reprobation*. The good man was exceedingly
troubled at it, and went to Andrewes his chamber to be satisfied in point of Conscience. Mr Andrewes told him that was
an ill habit of body not of mind, and that it was against his
will; advised him on Sundays to make a more sparing meale
and mend it at supper. The alderman did so, but sleepe comes
upon ⟨him⟩ again for all that, and was preached at; comes
again to be resolved with tears in his eies; Andrewes tells him
he would have him make a good heartie meale as he was wont
to doe, and presently take out his full sleep; he followed his
advice, came to St Maries, where the Preacher was prepared
with a sermon to damne all who slept at sermon, a certain
signe of Reprobation. The good Alderman having taken his
full nap before, lookes on the preacher all sermon time, and
spoyled the designe. But I should have sayd Andrewes was
extremely spoken against and preached against for offering to
assoile or excuse a sleeper in Sermon time. But he had learning
and witt enough to defend himselfe.

His great learning quickly made him known to the University, and also to King James who much valued him for it,
and advanced him, and at last made him Bishop of Winchester,
which Bishoprick he ordered with great Prudence as to
government of the Parsons, preferring of ingeniose persons
that were staked to poore livings and did *delitescere*. He made
it his Enquiry to find out such men; amongst severall others
(whose names have escaped my memorie) Nicholas Fuller (he
wrote *Critica Sacra*), Minister of Allington neer Amesbury in
Wilts was one. The Bishop sent for him, and the poor man
was afrayd and knew not what hurt he had done. ⟨He⟩ makes
him sitt downe to Dinner; and after the Desert, was brought
in in a dish his Institution and Induction, or the donation, of a
Prebend: which was his way. He chose out always able men
to his Chaplaines, whom he advanced. Among others,

⟨Christopher⟩ Wren, of St John's in Oxon, was his Chaplaine, a good generall scholar and good Orator, afterwards Deane of Winsore, from whom (by his son in lawe Dr William Holder) I have taken this exact Account of that excellent Prelate.

His Life is before his Sermons also his Epitaph, which see. He dyed at Winchester house, in Southwark, and lies buried at a Chapell at St Mary overies, where his executors . . . Salmon, M.D. and Mr John Saintlowe, Merchant of London, have erected (but I beleeve according to his Lordship's will, els they would not have layd out 1000 li) a sumptuouse monument for him.

He had not that smooth way of Oratory as now. It was a shrewd and severe animadversion of a Scotish Lord, who, when King James asked him how he liked Bishop Andrewes' sermon, sayd that he was learned, but he did play with his Text, as a Jack-an-apes does, who takes up a thing and tosses and playes with it, and then he takes up another, and playes a little with it. Here's a pretty thing, and there's a pretty thing.

JOHN AUBREY

LIFE OF ROBERT BOYLE

THE honourable Robert Boyle Esq., the ⟨fifth⟩ son of Richard Boyle, the first Earle of Corke, was borne at Lismor in the country of Corke, the ⟨25⟩ day of January anno ⟨1626-7.⟩

He was nursed by an Irish nurse, after the Irish manner, wher they putt the child into a pendulous Satchell (insted of a Cradle), with a slitt for the child's head to peepe out.

Mr R. Boyle, when a boy at Eaton was verie sick and pale. Went to the University of Leyden. Travelled France, Italy, Switzerland. I have oftentimes heard him say that after he had seen the Antiquities and architecture of Rome, he esteemed none any where els.

He speakes Latin very well, and very readily, as most men I have mett with. I have heard him say that when he was young, he read over Cowper's dictionary: wherein I think he did very well, and I beleeve he is much beholding to him for his mastership of that language.

His father in his Will, when he comes to the Settlement and provision for his son Robert, thus,

Item, to my son Robert, whom I beseech God to blesse with a particular Blessing, I bequeath, &c.

Mr R. H., who has seen the Rentall, sayes it was 3000 *li.* per annum: the greatst part in Ireland. His father left him the Mannor of Stalbridge in com. Dorset, where is a great free-stone house; it was forfeited by the earle of Castle-haven.

He is very tall (about six foot high) and streight, very temperate, and vertuouse and frugall: a Batcheler; keeps a Coach, sojournes with his Sister, the lady Ranulagh. His greatest delight is Chymistrey. He haz at his sisters a noble Laboratory, and severall servants (Prentices to him) to looke to it. He is charitable to ingeniose men that are in want, and foreigne Chymists, for he will not spare for cost to gett any rare Secret. At his owne costs and chardges he gott translated and printed the New Testament in Arabique to send into Mahometan countreys. He has not only a high renowne in England, but abroad and when foreigners come hither, 'tis one of their curiosities to make him a Visit.

JOHN AUBREY

THE LIFE OF MR THOMAS HOBBES
OF MALMESBURIE

THE Writers of the Lives of the ancient Philosophers used in the first place to speake of their Lineage, and they tell us that in processe of time, severall illustrious, rich, great Families accounted it their Glory to be derived from such or such a *Sapiens*. Why now should that method be omitted in the *Historiola* of our Malmesburie Philosopher? who though but of Plebeian extraction his Renowne haz and will give brightness to his name and Familie which hereafter may arise glorious and flourish in riches, and may justly take it an honour to be of kin to this worthy Person so famous for his Learning both at home and abroad.

Thomas Hobbes, then whose Life I write, was second son of Thomas Hobbes, Vicar of Westport juxta Malmesbury, who married . . . Middleton of Brokenborough (a yeomanly family). He was also Vicar of Charlton (a mile hence) they are annexed, and are both worth 60 or 80 *li* per annum. Thomas the father was one of the ignorant Sir Johns of Queen Elizabeth's time, and could only read the Prayers of the Church, and the Homilies: and valued not learning, as not knowing the Sweetness of it. As to his father's ignorance and clownery, 'twas as good metall in the Oare, which wants excoriating and refineing; a witt requires much cultivation, much paines, and art, and good conversation to perfect a man. He ⟨i.e. Thomas the father⟩ had an elder Brother whose name was Francis, a wealthy man and had been Alderman of the Borough: by profession a Glover [shall I expresse or conceale this (Glover), the Philosopher would acknowledge it,] which is a great trade here, and in times past much greater. Having no child: he contributed much, or rather altogether maintained his Nephew Thomas at Magdalen-hall in Oxon; and when he dyed gave him *agellum* (a mowing ground, pasture) called the Gasten-ground lyeing near to the Horse-faire, worth 16, or 18 poundes per annum; the rest of his Landes he gave to his nephew Edmund.

Thomas, the Vicar, had two sonnes, and one daughter. Edmund his eldest was bred-up to his Uncle's profession of a Glover, and Thomas (Philosopher), second son, whose life I now write. Edmund was neer two years elder than his brother Thomas and something resembled him in face: not so tall, but much short of him in his Intellect; though he was a good plain understanding country-man. He had been bred at Schoole with his brother; could have made theame and verse, and understood a little Greeke to his dying day; he dyed about 13 yeares since, *aetat circiter* 80. This Edmund had only one son named Francis, and two daughters, maried to countrymen (Renters) in the neighbourhood. Francis pretty well resembled his Uncle Thomas, especially about the eie; and probably, had he had good education might have been ingeniose; but he drowned his witt in Ale; he was left by his Father, and Uncle Thomas 80 *li* or better per ann. but he was an ill husband; he dyed about 2 yeares after his father and left 5 children: his eldest son, Thomas, a clothier (now about 23) did live at Tedbury, the 2nd did live at Chippenham, has some lines of the Philosopher; when he was a Boy, his genius inclined him to pourtraying, and engraving in copper; he is now about 21.

Westport is the Parish without the West-gate, which is now demolished, which gate stood on the neck of land that joines Malmesbury to Westport. Here was before the late Warres a very pretty Church consisting of a nave and 2 aisles (which tooke up the whole area) dedicated to St Mary and a faire spire-steeple with five Tuneable Bells, which, when the Towne was taken (about 1644) by Sir W. Waller, were melted, converted into ordnance and the church pulled down to the ground, that the Enemy might not shelter themselves against the Garrison. The steeple was higher than that now standing in the Borough, which much adorned the Prospect. The Windowes were well painted and in them were Inscriptions that declared much Antiquitie. Now is here rebuilt a Church like a stable.

Thomas Hobbes, Malmesburiensis, *Philosophus* was borne at his father's house in Westport, being that extreme house that pointes into, or faces, the Horse-Fayre; the farthest house on the left hand as you go to Tedbury, leaving the Church on your right. To prevent mistakes, and that hereafter may rise no doubt what house was famous for this Famous man's Birth; I do here testifie that in April, 1659, his brother Edmond went with me into this house, and into the Chamber where he was borne. Now things begin to be antiquated, and I have heard some guesse it might be the house where his brother Edmond lived and dyed. But this is so, as I here deliver it. This house was given by Thomas the Vicar to his daughter, whose daughter or grand-daughter possessed it when I was there. It is a firme house, stone built and tiled, of one room (besides a buttery, or the like, within) below, and two chambers above. 'Twas in the innermost where he first drew breath.

The day of his Birth was April the fifth, Anno Domini 1588, on a Friday morning, which that year was Good Friday. His mother fell in Labour with him upon the fright of the Invasion of the Spaniards—he told me himselfe between the houres of four and six. . . .

At four yeares old he went to Schoole in Westport-church, till eight; by that time he could read well and number four figures. Afterwards he went to schoole to Malmesbury to Mr Evans, the Minister of the Towne and afterwards to Mr Robert Latimer, a young man of about 19 or so, newly come from the University, who then kept a private Schoole in Westport where the broad place is next dore north from the Smyths' shop, opposite to the 3 Cuppes (as I take it). He was a Batchelour and delighted in his Scholar T. H. company, and used to instruct him and 2 or 3 ingeniose youths more in the evening till nine a clock. Here T H. so well profited in his Learning, that at fourteen yeares of age he went away a good schoole-scholar to Magdalen hall in Oxford. It is not to be forgotten that before he went to the University he had turned *Euripidis Medea* out of Greeke into Latin Iambiques which he presented to his Master. Mr H. told me that he would faine have had them to have seen how he did grow. Twenty odde yeares agoe I searcht all old Mr Latimer's papers but could not find them: the good huswives had sacrificed them. I have heard his brother Edmond and Mr Wayte, his schoolfellowe, say that when he was a Boye he was playsome enough, but withall he had even then a contemplative Melancholinesse; he would gett him into a corner, and learne his Lesson by heart presently. His haire was black, and the boyes his schole-fellows were wont to call him Crowe. This Mr Latimer was a good Graecian, and the first that came into our Parts since the Reformation. He was afterwards Minister of Malmesbury and from thence, preferred to a better living of 100 *li* per annum or more at Leigh-delamere within this Hundred.

At Oxford Mr T. H. used in the summertime especially to rise very early in the morning, and would tye the Leaden Counters (which they used in those days at Christmas at Post and Payre) with pack threds which he did besmere with bird-lime, and bayte them with parings of cheese, and the Jack dawes[1] would spye them a vast distance up in the aire, as far as Osney Abbey, and strike at the bayte, and so be harled in the string, which the wayte of the counter would make cling round their wings. He tooke great delyte there to goe to the

---

[1] "This story he happened to tell me discoursing of the Optiques to instance such a sharpnes of Sight in so little an Eie." (Aubrey's marginal note.)

Book-binders' shops, and lye gaping on Mappes. He did not much care for Logick, yet he learned it, and thought himselfe a good Disputant. . . .

He came to Magdalen Hall in the beginning of an. 1603, at what time Dr James Hussee LLD. was Principall. This James Hussee was afterwards knighted by King James—was made Chancellour of Sarum—this Dr Hussee was a great encourager of towardly youths—but he resigning his princi-pallity about 1605 Mr John Wilkinson succeeded him—so that Mr Hobbes was under the government of two principalls— Thomas Hobbes was admitted to the reading of any book of logic (*ad Lectionem cujuslibet Libri Logices*) that is he was admitted to the degree of Bachelour of Arts 5, feb. 1607 in the Lent that then began did determine, that he did his exercise for the completion of that degree.

After he had taken his Batchelour of Arts degree the then Principall of Magdalen-hall Sir James Hussey recommended him to his young Lord when he left Oxon., who did believe that he should profitt more in his learning, if he had a Scholar of his owne age to wayte on him, than if he had the information of a grave Doctor: He was his Lordship's page, and rode a-hunting and hawking with him, and kept his privy-purse. By this way of life, he had almost forgott his Latin: He there-fore bought him bookes, of an Amsterdam print, that he might carry in his pocket (particularly Caesar's Commentarys) which he did read in the Lobby or Ante-chamber, whilst his lord was making his Visits.

The Lord Chancellour Bacon, loved to converse with him. (This, I believe was after his first Lord's death). He assisted his Lordship in translating severall of his Essayes into Latin, one I well remember was that of the Greatness of Cities: the rest I have forgott. His Lordship was a very contemplative person, and was wont to contemplate in his delicious walks at Gorambery, and dictate to Mr Thomas Bushell or some other of his Gentlemen, that attended him with inke and paper ready to sett downe presently his Thoughts. His Lordship would often say that he liked better Mr Hobbes's taking of his Notions than any of the other because he understood what he wrote; which the others not understanding my Lord would many times have a hard taske to make sense of what they writt.

It is to be remembered that about these times Mr T. H. was much addicted to Musique, and practised on the Base-Violl.

1634. This Summer (I remember 'twas in Venison season July or August) Mr T. H. came into his Native Country to visitt his Friends, and amongst others he came then to see his old school-master, Mr Robert Latimer at Leigh-de-la-mer where I was then at Schoole in the Church. I was then a little youth newly entered into my Grammar by him: here was the first place and time that ever I had the honour to see this worthy, learned man who was then pleased to take notice of me, and the next day came and visited my relations. He was then a proper man, briske, and in very good habit; his haire was then quite black. He stayed at Malmesbury and the neighbourhoode a weeke or better, 'twas the last time that ever he was in Wiltshire. His conversation about these times was much about Ben: Jonson, Mr Ayton etc:

He was 40 yeares old before he looked on Geometry which happened accidentally, being in a Gentleman's Library in . . . , a Euclid's Elements lay open, and 'twas the 47 *El: Lib.* 1, he read the Proposition: by G— sayd he, this is impossible (he would now and then sweare an oath by way of emphasis). So he reads the Demonstration of it, which referred him back to such a Proposition: which proposition he read and that referred him back to another, which he also read and *sic deinceps* that at last he was convinced of that truth. This made him in love with Geometry. I have heard Sir Jonas Moore (and others) say that 'twas a great pitty he had not begun the study of the Mathematics sooner for such a curious witt would have made great advancement in it. Had so he donne, he would not have layn so open to his learned Mathematicall

Antagonists; but one may say of him as one says of Joseph Scaliger that where he erres, he erres so ingeniously that one had rather erre with him than hit the marke with Clavius. I have heard Mr Hobbes say that he was wont to draw lines on his thigh, and on the sheetes abed, and also multiply and divide. He would often complain, that Algebra (though of great use) was too much admired, and followed after, and it made men not contemplate and consider so much the nature and power of Lines which was a great hinderance to the groweth of Geometrie: for that though Algebra did rarely well and quickly and easily in right lines yet 'twould not *bite* in *solid* (I think) Geometry.

After he began to reflect on the Interest of the King of England as watching his affairs between him and the Parliament for 10 yeares together his thoughts were much or altogether unhinged from the Mathematiques: but chiefly intent on his *de Cive,* and after that on his *Leviathan* which was a great putter back to his Mathematicall improvement for in ten yeares (or better) discontinuance of that study (especially) one's Mathematiques will become very rusty.

1640. When the Parliament sate that began in April, 1640, and was dissolved in May following, and in which many points of the Regall Power, which were necessary for the Peace of the Kingdome and safety of his Majestyes Person were disputed and denyed, Mr Hobbes wrote a little Treatise in English, wherein he did sett forth and demonstrate that the sayd Power, and Rights were inseparably annexed to the Soveraignty; which Soveraignty they did not then deny to be in the King; but it seems understood not, or would not understand that inseparability. Of the Treatise, though not printed, many Gentlemen had Copies, which occasioned much talk of the Author; and had not his Majestie dissolved the Parliament it had brought him in danger of his life. He told me that Bishop Manwaring of St David's preached his Doctrine, for which, among others he was sent prisoner to the Tower.

Then thought Mr Hobbes 'tis time now for me to shift for myselfe; and so withdrew into France and resided mostly at Paris. As I remember there were others likewise did preach his Doctrine. This little MS. treatise grew to be his Booke *De Cive* and at last grew to be the so formidable LEVIATHAN. The manner of writing of which Booke (he told me) was thus. He walked much and contemplated, and he had in the head of his staffe a pen and inkehorne, carried always a Note-booke in his pocket, and as soon as a notion darted, he presently entered it into his Booke or otherwise might perhaps have lost it. He had drawne the designe of the Booke into Chapters etc.; he knew whereabout it would come in. Thus the Booke was made.

"He wrote and published the Leviathan far from the intention either of disadvantaging his Majestie, or to flatter Oliver (who was not made Protector till 3 or 4 yeares after) on purpose to facilitate his returne; for there is scarce a page in it that does not upbraid him. 'Twas written in the behalfe of the faithfull subjects of his Majestie, that had taken his part in the War or otherwise donne their utmost to defend his Majesties Right and Person—against the Rebells; whereby, having no other means of Protection, or (for the most part) of subsistence, were forced to compound with your Masters, and to promise obedience for the saving of their Lives and Fortunes which in his book he hath affirmed they might lawfully doe, and consequently not bear Arms against the Victors. They had done their utmost endeavour to performe their obligation to the King, had done all they could be obliged unto, and were consequently at liberty to seeke the safety of their Lives and Livelihood wheresoever and without Treachery.

His Majestie was displeased with him (at Paris) for a while, but not very long, by means of some's complayning of and misconstruing his writing. But his Majestie had a good opinion of him and sayd openly, that he thought Mr Hobbes never meant him hurt.

During his stay at Paris he went through a Course of Chymistry with Dr Davison and he there also studied Vesalius's Anatomie. This I am sure was before 1648 for Sir W. Petty (then Dr Petty Physician) studyed and dissected with him.". . .

Anno 165– ('twas 1650 or 1651) he returned into England and lived most part in London in Fetter Lane where he writt or finished his booke *de Corpore* in Latin, and then in English, and writt his Letters against the Savillian Professors at Oxon.

1655 or 1656. About this time he settled the piece of land (aforesayd) given to him by his uncle, upon his nephew Francis for life, the Remaynder to his nephew's eldest son Thomas Hobbes: he also discharged a Mortgage (to my knowledge to Richard Thorne an Attorney) of two hundred pounds, besides the Interest thereof; with which his Nephew Francis (a careless husband) had incumbred his Estate.

He was much in London till the restauration of his Majesty, having here convenience not only of Bookes, but of learned Conversation, as J. Selden, Dr W. Harvey, John Vaughan whereof anon in the catalogue of his acquaintance. I have heard him say that in his Lord's House in the Country (Derbyshire) there was a good library and bookes enough for him, and that his Lordship stored the Library with what bookes he thought fitt to be bought,; but he sayd the want of good learned conversation was a very great inconvenience, and that, though he conceived he could order his Thinking as well perhaps as another man yet he found a great defect. Amongst other of his acquaintance I must not forget our common friend Mr Samuel Cowper (the Prince of Limners of this last Age) who drew his Picture as like as art could afford, and one of the best pieces that ever he did, which his Majestie at his returne bought of him, and conserves, as one of his great rarities in his Closet at White-hall.

1659. In 1659 he was at Little Salisbury house (now the Middle Exchange) where he wrote among other things a

Poeme in Latin Hexameter and Pentameter of the Encroach-
ment of the Clergie (both Roman and Reformed) on the Civil
power. I remember I saw 500 or more verses (for he numbred
every 10th he wrote). I remember he did read Cluverius's
Historia Universalis, and made up his poem from thence. His
place of meditation was then in the Portico in the garden. He
sayd that he sometimes would sett his thoughts upon research-
ing and contemplating always with this proviso that he very
much and deeply contemplated one thing at a time (*scilicet* a
weeke or sometimes a fortnight).

There was a report (and surely true) that in Parliament not
long after the King was setted some of the Bishops made a
motion to have the good old Gentleman burn't for a Heretique;
which he hearing, feared that his papers might be search't by
their Order and he told me that he burn't part of them. I have
received word from his Amanuensis and Executour that he
remembers there was such Verses, for he wrote them out, but
he knows not what became of them, unlesse he presented them
to Judge Vaughan, or burned them, as I did seem to intimate.

(But I understand since by W. Crooke that he can retrieve
a good many of them.)

1660. The Winter-time of 1659 he spent in Derby-shire, in
March following was the dawning of the coming in of our
gracious Soveraigne and in April the Aurora. I then sent a
letter to him in the Country to advertise him of the Advent of
his Master the King, and desired him by all meanes to be in
London before his Arrivall; and knowing his Majestie was a
great lover of good Painting I must needs presume, he could
not but suddenly see Mr Cowper's curious pieces, of whose
fame had had so much heard, and seen some of his Work; and
likewise that he could sitt to him for his Picture, at which place
and time he would have the best opportunity of renewing his
Majestie's graces to him. He thanked for my friendly intima-
tion, and came to London in May following. It happened
about 2 or 3 dayes after his Majestie's happy returne that he

M

was passing in his coach through the Strand, Mr Hobbes was standing at little Salisbury-house gate (where his Lord then lived) the King espied him, putt off his hatt very kindly to him and asked him how he did; about a weeke after he had orall conference with Majesty and Mr S. Cowper, when as he sat for his picture, he was diverted by Mr Hobbes' pleasant discourse. Here his Majestie's favours were redintegrated to him and order was given that he should have free accesse to his Majestie who was always much delighted in his witt and smart repartees: the witts at Court were wont to bayte him; but he feared none of them and would make his part good. The King would call him the Beare: Here comes the Beare to be bayted. He was marvellous happy and ready in his replies; and that without rancour (except provoked); but now I speake of his readinesse in replies as to witt and drollery. He would say that he did not care to give neither was he adroit at a present answer to a serious quaere; he had as lieve they should have expected an extemporaneous solution to an Arithmeticall probleme, for he turned and winded and compounded in philosophy, politiques etc., as if he had been at mathematicall worke. He alwayes avoided as much as he could, to conclude hastily.

From 1660, till the time he went into Derbyshire, he spent most part of his time in London at his Lord's (viz: at little Salisbury-house, then Queen Street, lastly Newport-house: following his contemplation and study: he contemplated and invented (set down a hint with a pencill or so) the morning, but penned in the afternoon.

1664. In 1664, I sayd to him, methinks 'tis pitty that you that have such a cleare reason and working head did never take into consideration, the learning of the Lawes. I endeavoured to persuade him to it; but he answered that he was not like to have Life enough left to goe through with such a long, and difficult taske. I then presented him the Chancellor Bacon's Elements of the Lawe (a thin quarto) in order thereunto and to draw him on, which he was pleased to accept, and perused, and the next time I came to him he shewed me therein 2 cleare Paralogismes in the 2nd page, which I am heartily sorry are now out of my remembrance. I desponded that he should make any attempt towards this Designe. But afterwards it seemes in the Country he writt his Treatise *de Legibus* (unprinted) of which Sir John Vaughan Lord Chiefe Justice of Common pleas has a Transcript, and I doe affirme that he much admired it . . .

In a letter to me dated Aug. 18, 1679 among severall other things, he writes:—

> I have been told that my book of the Civill Warr is come abroad, and am sorry for it, especially because I could not get his Majestie to license it, not because it is ill printed or hath a foolish Title set to it. For I believe that an ingeniose man may understand the wickednesses of that time notwithstanding the errors of the Presse.
>
> The Treatise *de legibus* at the end of it is imperfect. I desire Mr Horne to pardon me that I cannot consent to his notion; nor shall Mr Crooke himselfe get my consent to print it. I pray you present my humble thanks to Mr Sam: Butler.
>
> The Privilege of the Stationers is in my opinion a very great hindrance to the advancement of humane learning.
>
> > I am, Sir,
> >
> > > Your very humble servant,
> > >
> > > > TH. HOBBES.

1665. This yeare he told me that he was willing to doe some good to the Towne where he was borne: that his Majestie loved him well and if I could find out something in our countrey that was in his guift, he did believe he could beg it of his Majestie, and seeing he was bred a Scholar, he thought it most proper to endowe a Free-schoole there; which is wanting *now*: for before the Reformation all Monasteries had great schooles appendant to them (e.g. Magdalen Schoole and New College Schoole). After enquiry I found out a piece of land in Braden-forest that was in his Majestie's guift (of about 25 *li* per annum value), which he desired to have obtained of his Majestie for a Salary to a School-master: but the Queene's Priests, smelling out the Designe; and being his Enemies hindred this publique and charitable Intention.

1669-70–1674. Anno Domini 1674 Mr Anthony à Wood sett forth an elaborate worke of eleven yeares study, intituled the *History and Antiquities* of the University of *Oxford*; wherein, in every respective Colledge and Hall, mentions the Writers educated there and what Bookes they wrote. The Dean of Christ-church having Plenipotentiary power of the Presse there, perused every sheet, before 'twas sent to the presse, and maugre the Author and to his sore displeasure did expunge and inserted what he pleased. Among other authors, he made divers alterations in Mr Wood's copie, in the account of Mr Th. Hobbes of Malmesbury's Life, pag. 445, 44J Lib. II. "Vir sane etc.," . . . This and much more was dashed out of the Author's copie by the sayd Deane.

These additions and expunctions being made by the sayd Deane of Christ-Church without the advice and quite contrary to the mind of the Author, he told him it was felt Mr Hobbs should know what he had done, because that his name being set to the Booke, and all people knowing it to be his, he should be liable to an answer, and so consequently be in perpetuall controversie. To this the Dean replied, Yea in God's name, and great reason it was that he should know what he had done, and what he had donne he would answer for.—etc.,

1674. Hereupon in the beginning of 1674 the Author acquaints J.A. Mr Hobbes' correspondent, with all that had passed—J.A. acquaints Mr Hobbes. Mr Hobbes taking it ill was resolved to vindicate himselfe in an Epistle to the Author —accordingly an Epistle dated April 20. 1674 was sent to the Author in MS., with an intention to publish it, when the History of Oxford was to be published—upon the receipt of Mr Hobbes' Epistle by Anthony à Wood he forthwith repaired very honestly and without any guile to the Deane of Christ-church to communicate it to him. The Deane read it over carelessly, and not without scorne, and when he had donne bid Mr Wood tell Mr Hobbes, that he was an old man, had one foote in the grave, that he should mind his latter end and not trouble the world any more with his papers etc., or to that effect.

In the meane time Mr Hobbes meetes with the King in the Pall-mall in St James's Parke—tells Him how he had been served by the Deane of Christ-church, in a booke then in the Press entituled the *History and Antiquities of the Universitie of Oxon.*—and withall desires his Majestie to be pleased to give him leave to vindicate himselfe—The King seeming to be troubled at the dealing of the Deane gave Mr Hobbes Leave conditionally, *that he touch nobody but him who had abused him, neither that he should reflect upon the Universitie.*

Mr Hobbes understanding that this History would be pub-lished at the common Act at Oxon. about 11 July the said yeare 1674, prints his Epistle at London, and sends down divers Copies to Oxon, which being disperst at Coffee-houses and Stationers' shops, a Copie forthwith came to the Deanes hands, who upon reading of it fretted and fumed, sent for the Author of the History, and chid him, telling him withall that he had corresponded with his Enemie (Hobbes)—the Author replied, that surely he had forgott what he had donne—for he had communicated to him before what Mr Hobbes had sayd and written—whereupon the Deane recollecting himselfe told him that Hobbes should suddenly heare more of him, so that the last sheet of paper being then in the presse, and one leafe thereof being left vacant, the deane supplied with this answer; both the Epistle and the answer I here exhibit . . . To this Angry answer the old gentleman never made any reply, but slighted the Doctor's passion and forgave it. But 'tis supposed that was the cause why Mr Hobbes was not afterwards so indulgent (or spared the lesse to speake his Opinion) concerning the Universities and how much their Doctrine, and Method had contributed to the Troubles (e.g. in his Historie of the Civill Warre).

1675. Mense . . . he left London *cum animo nunquam rever-tendi*, and spent the remaynder of his dayes in Derbyshire with the E. of Devon, at Chatsworth and Hardwyck, in contemplation and study . . . Extracted out of the Executor's lettre (January 16, 1679) to me:

"He fell sick about the middle of October last. His disease was Strangury and the Physitians judged it incurable by reason of his great age and naturall decay. About the 20th of November, my lord being to remove from Chatsworth to Hardwick, Mr Hobbes would not be left behind; and therefore with a featherbed laid onto the coach, upon which he lay warme clad, he was conveyed safely, and was in appearance as well after that little journey as before it. But seven or eight days after, his whole right side was taken with the dead palsey, and at the same time he was made speechlesse. He lived after this seven days, taking very little nourishment, slept well, and by intervalls—endeavoured to speake, but could not. In the whole time of his sicknesse he was free from fever. He seemed therefore to dye rather for want of the Fuell of Life (which was spent in him) and meer weaknesse and decay, than by the power of his disease, which was thought to be only an effect of his old age and weaknesse. He was born the 5th April in the year 1588 and died the 4th of December, 1678. He was putt into a Woollen Shroud and Coffin, which was covered with a white sheet and upon that a black herse cloth, and so carried upon men's shoulders a little mile to the Parish Church. The company consisting of the family and neighbours that came to his funerall and attended him to his Grave were very handsomely entertained with Wine, burned and raw, cake, biscuit etc., He was buried in the Parish Church of Hault Hucknall, close adjoining to the Raile of the Monument of the Grandmother of the present Earle of Devonshire, with the service of the Church of England by the Minister of the Parish."

In his Youth he was unhealthy; of an ill complexion, yellow-ish. His Lord (who was a waster) sent him up and downe to borrow money and he putt Gentlemen to be bound for him, being ashamed to speake him selfe; he took colds being wett in his feet, (then were no hackney coaches to stand in the streetes), and trod both his shoes aside in the same way. Notwithstanding he was well-beloved; they loved his company for his pleasing facetiousness and good-nature, from 40 or better he grew healthier, and then had a fresh-ruddy com-plexion; he was a Sanguineo-melancholicus, which the Physi-ologists say is the most ingeniose complexion. He would say, that there might be good witts of all complexions; but good natured impossible. In his old age he was very bald which claymed a veneration; yet within dore, he used to study, and sitt bareheaded; and sayd he never tooke cold in his head but that the greatest trouble was to keepe off the Flies from pitch-ing on the baldness. His head was . . . inches in compass and of a mallet form approved by the Physiologers.

His Skin was soft and of that kind which the Lord Chan-cellor Bacon in his *History of life and death* called a goose skin i.e. of a wide texture.

Crassa cutis, crassum cerebrum, crassum ingenium. Face not very great, ample forehead, whiskers yellowish-redish which natur-ally turned-up which is a signe of a Brisque witt e.g. James Howell, Henry Jacob of Merton College; belowe he shaved close except a little tip under his lip. Not but that nature would have afforded a venerable beard; but being naturally of a cheerfull and pleasant humour, he affected not at all Austerity and gravity, and to looke severe. . . . He desired not the reputation of his Wisdome from the cutt of his Beard but from his Reason.

He had a good Eie and that of a hasell colour, which was full of life and spirit even to his last: when he was in discourse,

there shone (as it were) a bright live-coale within it. He had
two kinds of looks: when he laught, was witty, and in a merry
humour, one could scarce see his Eies; by and by when he was
serious and earnest he open'd his eies round (i.e. Eyelids); he
had middling eies, not very big, nor very little.

He was six foote high and something better and went
indifferently erect; or rather considering his great age, very
erect. His Sight and Witt continued to his laste. He had a
very curious sharp sight, as he had a sharp Witt; which also
so sure and steady, (and contrary to what men would call
Brodewittednes) that I have heard him oftentimes say that in
Multiplying and Dividing he never mistooke a figure; and so
in other things. He thought much and with excellent method,
and stediness, which made him seldom take a false step. He
had read much, if one considers his long life, but his Contemplation was much more than his Reading. He was wont to
say that if he had read as much as other men, he should have
continued still as ignorant as other men. He had very few
Bookes. I never saw (nor Sir William Petty) above a half a
dozen about him in his Chamber. Homer and Virgil were
commonly on his table. Sometimes Xenophon or some
probable Historie, and Greek Testament or so.

Though he left Malmesbury (his native country) at 14 yet
(sometimes) one might find a little touch of our pronunciation;
old Dr Thomas Malette (one of the Judges of the Kings
(bench), knew Sir Walter Raleigh, and sayd that notwithstanding his great Travell, conversation, learning etc., he
spoke broade Devonshire to his dyeing day.

He seldome used any Physique. . . . He was even in his
youth (Generally) temperate as to wine and women (*et tamen
haec omnia mediocriter. Homo sum nihil humani a me alienum puto*).
'Tis not consistent with an Harmonicall soule to be a woman-
hater neither had he an abhorrence of good wine. I have
heard him say he did beleeve he had been in excesse 100 times
which, considering his great age did not amount to above

once a yeare; when he did drinke, he would drink to excesse to
have the benefit of vomiting which he did easily by which
benefit neither his witt was disturbt (longer than he was
spuing) nor his stomach oppressed; but he never was nor
would endure to be habitually a good fellow i.e. to drinke
every day wine with company; which, though not to drunken-
nesse spoiles the Braine.

Insert the love verses he made not long before his death:

1

Tho' I am now past ninety, and too old
   To expect preferment in the Court of Cupid
And many Winters made mee ev'n so cold
   I am become almost all over stupid.

2

Yet I can Love, and have a Mistresse too,
   As fair as can be, and as Wise as fair,
And yet not proud, nor any thing will doe
   To make me of her favour to despair.

3

To tell you who she is were very bold:
   But, if i th'Character your Selfe you find,
Thinke not the man a Foole, tho' he be old,
   Who loves in Body fair, a fairer mind.

For his last 30 or more yeares, his dyet etc., was very
moderate and regular: after sixty he drank no wine. His
stomach grew weake and he did eate most fish, especially
Whitings: for he sayd he digested Fish better than Flesh. He
rose about seaven, had his breakfast of Breade and butter, and
tooke his Walke, meditating till ten. Then he did put down
minutes of his thoughts: which he penned in the afternoon.
His dinner was provided for him exactly by eleaven for he
could not stay till his Lord's houre *scilicet* about two. His
stomach would not beare. After dinner he took a pipe of
Tobacco, and then threw himselfe immediately on his bed with

his band off, and slept (tooke a nap) of about halfe an houre. In the afternoon he penned his morning thoughts.

He had an inch thick board about 16 inches square where paper was pasted; on this board he drew his lines (schemes). When a line came into his head, he would as he was walking take a rude Memorandum of it, to preserve in his memory, till he came to his chamber. He was never idle, his Thoughts were always working.

Besides his dayly Walking, he did twice or thrice a yeare play at Tennis (at about 75 he did it) then went to bed there and was well rubbed. In the Country for want of a Tennis court he would walk uphill, and downe-hill in the Parke, till he was in a good sweat, and then give the servant some money to rubbe him.

He gave to his Ammanuensis James Wheldon (the Earle of Devonshire's Baker), who writes a delicate hand, his pention at Leicester yearly to wayte on him and take care of him, which he did performe to him living and dying with great respect and diligence for which consideration he made him his Executor.

In cold weather, he commonly wore a black velvet coate lined with Furr: if not some other coate so lined, but all the yeare he wore a kind of bootes of Spanish leather laced or tyed along the sides with black ribons.

He had alwayes bookes of prick-song lying on his Table e.g. of H. Lawes etc., Songs: which at night when he was a bed and the dores made fast, and was sure nobody heard him he sang aloud (not that he had a very good voice) but for his health's sake; he did believe it did his lunges good, conduced much to prolong his life.

He had the shaking palsey in his hands; which began in France before the yeare 1650, and has growne upon him by degrees ever since, so that he has not been able to write legibly since 1665 or 1666, as I find by some of his letters he honoured me withall.

nothing

His Goodnes of Nature, and Willingnes to instruct anyone who was willing to be informed, and modestly desired it, which I am a witnesse of as to my owne part and also to others.

His brotherly love to his kinred hath already been spoken of; he was very charitable (*pro suo modulo*) to those that were true objects of his bounty. One time I remember goeing in the Strand, a poor and informe old man craved his Almes. He, beholding him with eies of pitty and compassion, putt his hand in his pocket and gave him 6d. Sayd a divine (*scilicet* Dr Jasper Mayne) that stood by, would you have done this if it not been Christ's command? Yea, sayd he. Why, quoth the other? Because, sayd he, I was in paine to consider the miserable condition of the old man, and now my almes, giving him some reliefe, doth also ease me.

His Work was attended with Envy, which threw severall aspersions and false reports on him: for instance one (common) was that he was afrayd to lye alone in his Chamber. I have often heard him say, that he was not afrayd of Sprights, but afrayd of being knockt on the head for 5 or 10 pounds which rogues might thinke he had about him in his Chamber: and severall other tales as untrue.

I have heard some positively affirme, that he had a yearly Pension from the King of France; possibly for having asserted such a Monarchie as the King of France exercises; but for what other grounds I know not; unless it be that the present King of France is reputed an Encourager of choice and able men in all Faculties; who can contribute to his Greatnes. I never heard him speake of any such things, and since his death I have enquired of his most intimate friends in Derbyshire, who write to me they never heard of any such thing. Had it been so, he nor they ought to have been ashamed of it: and it had been becoming the munificence of so great a Prince to have don it.

For his being branded with Atheisme, his writings and vertuous life testifie against it. . . . And that he was a Christian 'tis cleare, for he received the Sacrament of Dr Pierson, and in

his Confession to Dr John Cosens, at . . . on his (as he thought)
death-bed declared that he liked the religion of the Church
of England best of all other. (He would have the worship of
God performed with Musique.)

Mr J. Dreyden Poet Laureate to his great admirer, and often-
times makes use of his Doctrine in his Playes (from Mr Dreyden
himselfe).

When he was in Florence—he contracted a friendship with
the famous Galileo Galileo . . . whom he extremely venerated
and magnified; and not only so he was a prodigious Witt, but
for his sweetness of nature and manners. They pretty well
resembled one another in their countenances, as by their
Pictures may appeare, were both cheerfull and melancholique
—sanguine; and such a consimilitie of Fate to be hated and
persecuted by the Ecclesiastiques.

Petrus Gassendus S. Th. Doctor et Regius Professor Parisus
. . . whom he never mentions but with great love and respect.
Doctissimus humanissimus, and they loved each other entirely,
as also the like love and friendship was betwixt him and
Maximus Mersennus and Monsieur Renatus Descartes.

'Tis of custom, in the Lives of wisemen to putt downe their
sayings: now if Trueth (uncommon) delivered clearly and
wittily may go for a Saying; his common discourse was full of
them; which for the most part were sharpe and significant.

Mr Hobbes was wont to say that had Monsieur Descartes,
(for whom he had a high respect) kept himselfe to his Geometrie, he had been the best Geometer in the World: but he
could not pardon him for writing in Defence of Transubstan-
tiation, which he knew was absolutely against his opinion and
donne meerly to putt a compliment (flatter) the Jesuites.

T. Hobbes (said) if it were not for the Gallows, some men
are of so cruell a nature, as to take a delight in killing men—
more than I should to kill a Bird.

When Spinosa *Tractatus Theologico-Politicus* first came out,
Mr E. Waller sent it to my Lord of Devonshire and desired

him to send him word what Mr Hobbes sayd of it. Mr Hobbes told his Lordship *Ne judicate, ne judicemini*; he told me he had out throwne him a barres length, for he durst not write so boldly.

I have heard him say, that Aristotle was the worst Teacher that ever was, the worst Politician and Ethick, that a Countrey-fellow that could live in the world, as good, but his rhetorique, and his discourse of Animals was rare. I have heard him inveigh much against the Crueltie of Moyses for putting so many thousands to the Sword for Bowing to ⟨the Golden Calf⟩.

T. Hobbes's saying—rather use an old woman that had many yeares been at sick peoples' bedsides than the learnedst young unpractised Physitian.

⟨From Elizabeth Viscountesse Purbec⟩ when Mr Hobbes was sick in France the Divines came to him and tormented him (both Catholic, Church of England and Geneva) ⟨he⟩ said to them, let me alone, or else I will detect all your Cheates from Aaron to your-selves. I think I have heard him speake something to this purpose.

Mr Waller sayd to me when I desired him to write some Verses in praise of him that he was afrayd of the Churchmen; he quoted Horace: *incedo per ignes suppositis cineri doloso*—that, what was chiefly to be taken notice of in Elogie was that he being but one and a private Person pulled downe all the Churches, dispelled the Mists of Ignorance, and layd open their Priestcraft.

JOHN AUBREY

MR ANDREW MARVELL

MR ANDREW MARVELL: his father was minister of ⟨Hull⟩. He had good Grammar-Education: and was after sent to Cambridge.

In the time of Oliver the Protector he was Latin Secretarie. He was a great master of the Latin tongue: an excellent poet in Latin or English: for latin verses there was no man would come into competition with him. The verses called *The Advice to the Painter* were of his making.

His native towne of Hull loved him so well that they elected him for their representative in Parliament, and gave him an honourable pension to maintaine him.

He was of a middling stature, pretty strong sett, roundish faced, cherry cheek't, hazell eie, browne haire. He was in his conversation very modest, and of very few words: and though he loved wine he would never drink hard in company: and was wont to say, *that he would not play the good-fellow in any mans company in whose hands he would not trust his life.*

He kept bottles of wine at his lodgeing, and many times he would drinke liberally by himselfe to refresh his spirits, and exalt his Muse. I remember I have been told that the learned . . . (an High German) was wont to keep bottells of good Rhenish-wine in his studie, and when he had spent his spirits he would drink a good Rummer of it.

James Harrington, Esq. (autor *Oceana*) was his intimate friend. John Pell, D.D. was one of his acquaintance. He had not a generall acquaintance.

I remember I heard him say that the Earle of Rochester

was the only man in England that had the true veine of satyre.

He wrote *The Rehersall transprosed* against Samuel Parker, D.D. *Mr Smirke* (stich't, 4to about 8 sheets); *The naked Trueth*.

Obiit Londini, Aug. 18. 1678; and is buryed in St Giles church in-the-fields, about the middle of the south aisle. Some suspect that he was poysoned by the Jesuites, [but I cannot be positive.]

He lies interred under the pewes in the south side of St Giles church in the fields, under the window wherein is painted in glasse a Red lyon, (it was given by the inneholder of the Red Lyon Inne in Holborne). . . . This account I had from the sexton who made his grave.

JOHN AUBREY

LIFE OF JOHN MILTON

MR JOHN MILTON was of an Oxfordshire familie: his Grand-
father, (a Roman Catholic) of Holton in Oxfordshire neer
Shotover. His mother was a Bradshaw. His father was
brought-up in the University of Oxon: at Christ-church and
his grandfather disinherited him because he kept not the
Catholique Religion (he found a Bible in English in his
chamber) so that thereupon he came to London, and became
a Scrivener (brought up by a friend of his, was not an Appren-
tice) and gott a plentifull estate by it and left it off many yeares
before he dyed; he was an ingeniose man, delighted in Musique
composed many Songs now in print especially that of *Oriana*;
his son John was borne in Bread Street in London at the
Spread Eagle which was his house, he had also in that street
another house the Rose and other houses in other places.

I have been told, that the Father composed a Song of four
score parts, for the Lantgrave of Hess, for which ⟨his⟩ High-
nesse sent a medall of Gold or a noble present. He dyed about
1647, in that yeare the Army marched through the City,
buried in Cripple-gate-church from his house in the Barbican.
John Milton was born the 9th of december 1608 *die veneris*
half an hour after 6 in the morning: Anno domini 1619, he
was ten yeares old, as by his picture: and was then a Poet;
his schoolmaster was a puritan in Essex, who cutt his haire
short. He went to schoole to old Mr Gill at Paules schoole;
went at his own chardge only to Christs College in Cambridge,
at fifteen, where he stayed at least eight yeares: then he travelled
into Franc and Italie. At Geneva he contracted a great friend-

ship with [Carolo Diodati son of] the learned Dr Diodati of
Geneva. Had Sir H. Wotton's commendatory letters (Vide
his Poems.) He was acquainted beyond sea with Sir Henry
Wotton, Ambassador at Venice who delighted in his company.
He was severall yeares beyond sea, and returned to England
just upon the breaking out of the Civil Warres. He was
Latin Secretary to the parliament.

(From his Brother Christopher Milton). When he was at
Schoole, when he was very young, he studied very hard, and
sate-up very late, commonly till 12 or one aclock at night, and
his father ordered the mayd to sitt-up for him, and in those
yeares composed many Copies of Verses, which might well
become a riper age. And he was a very hard student in the
University, and performed all his exercises there with very
good Applause. His 1st Tutor there was Mr Chapell, from
whom receiving some unkindnesse (whip't him), he was
afterwards (though it seems against the Rules of the College)
transferred to the Tuition of one Mr Tovell, who dyed Parson
of Lutterworth. He went to travell about the year 1638 and
was abroad about a years space cheifly in Italy; immediately
after his return he took a lodging at Mr Russell's a Taylour in
St Brides churchyard and took into his tuition his sisters two
sons Edward and John Philips the first 10 the other 9 years
of age and in a years time made them capable of interpreting
a Latin authour at sight and within 3 years they went through
the best of Latin and Greec Poetts: Lucretius and Manilius
(and with him the use of the Globes and some Rudiments of
Arithmetic and Geometry) of the Latins; Hesiod, Aratus,
Dionysus Afer, Oppian, Apollonii *Argonautica* and Quintus
Calaber, Cato, Varro, and Columella de *Re rustica* were the
very first Authors they learn't.

As he was severe on one hand, so he was most familiar and
free in his conversation to those to whome most soure in his
way of education—N.B. he made his Nephews Songsters, and
sing from the time they were with him.

N

He married his first wife ⟨Mary⟩ Powell of Fosthill in Oxfordshire Anno Domini ⟨1643⟩, by whom he had 4 children; hath two daughters living: Deborah was his Ammanuensis, he taught her Latin, and to read Greeke (and Hebrew) to him when he lost his eiesight, which was Anno Domini ⟨1651⟩.

Two opinions doe not well on the same Boulster. She was a Royalist, and went without her husband's consent to her mother in the King's quarters neer Oxford. He parted with her Anno Domini [1643] and wrote the triple chord, about Divorce. She dyed Anno Domini ⟨1652⟩. I have so much charity for her that she might not wrong his bed but what man (especially contemplative) would like to have a young wife environed and stormd by the sons of Mars, and those of the enemi partie?

His first wife (Mrs Powell a Royalist) was brought up and lived where there was a great deale of company and merriment, dancing etc., and when she came to live with her husband at Mr Russells in St Brides churchyard, she found it very solitary: no company came to her, often-times heard his Nephews beaten and cry. This life was irkesome to her; and so she went to her Parents at Fosthill: he sent for her (after some time) and I think his servant was evilly entreated, but as for matter of wronging his bed, I never heard the least suspicion: nor had he of that, any Jealousie.

He had a middle wife whose name was Katharine Woodcock. No child living by her.

He married his wife Mrs Elizabeth Minshull Anno Domini [1663] the yeare before the Sicknesse. A gentle person, a peacefull and agreable Humour.

His sight began to faile him at first upon his writing against Salmasius, and, before 'twas fully compleated, one eie absolutely failed; upon the writing of other books after that his other eie decayed. His eiesight was decaying about 20 years before his death. Q. when stark Blind his father read without spectacles at 84, his mother had very weake eies and used spectacles presently after she was thirty yeares old.

After he was blind he wrote these following Bookes viz. Paradise lost Paradise regained Grammar Dictionarie (imperfect. Q.). I heard that after he was blind, that he was writing a Latin Dictionary in the hands of Moyses Pitt. Vidua Affirmat she gave all his papers to his Nephew (among which this Dictionary imperfect), that he brought up a sister's son [Edward] Phillips, who lives near the Maypole in the Strand. She has a great many letters by her from learned men his acquaintance, both of England and beyond sea.

He lived in several places e.g. Holborn neer King's gate. He died in Bunhill opposite to the Artillery garden-wall.

He died of the gowt struck in, the 9th or 10th of November, 1674, as appeares by his Apothecaryes Booke [about the 64th yeare of his age].

He lies buried in St Giles Cripplegate, upper end of chancell at the right hand, his stone is now removed; about 2 yeares since [now 1681] the steppes to the communion table were raised. I ghesse John Speed and He lie together.

He was scarce so tall as I am, of middle stature. He had light abroun hayre, his complexion very (exceeding) faire, His widowe has his picture drawne very well and like when a Cambridge schollar, [he was so faire that they called him the Lady of Christ's Coll:] which ought to be engraven: for the Pictures before his bookes are not at all like him; he was a Spare man. His harmonical, and ingeniose soule did lodge in a beautifull & well proportioned body—*in toto nusquam corpore menda fuit*—Ovid. He had a very good memory: but I believe that his excellent method of thinking and disposing did much to helpe his memorie. Of a very cheerful humour. He was very healthy, seldome tooke any Physique, only sometimes he tooke Manna and only towards his later end he was visited with the gowte spring and fall: he would be chearfull even in his Gowte-fitts; and sing. He was an early riser . . . at 4 a clock mane. yea after he lost his sight. He had a man read to him: the first thing he read was the Hebrew bible, & that was at 4 h. mane—½ h. then he contemplated. At 7 his man came to him again & then read to him and wrote till dinner: the writing was as much as the reading. His daughter Deborah could read to him Latin: Italian and French and Greeke. Maried in Dublin to one Mr Clarke (a mercer) sells silke etc. very like her father. The other sister is Mary, more like her mother. After dinner he used to walke 3 or 4 houres at a time he alwayes had a Garden where he lived: went to bed about 9. Temperate man rarely drank between meales. Extreme pleasant in his conversation, and at dinner, supper etc.: but Satyricall. He pronounced the letter R (*littera canina*) very hard a certaine signe of a Satyricall Witt (from John Dreyden). He had a delicate tuneable Voice and good skill: his father instructed him: he had an Organ in his house: he played on that most. His exercise was chiefly walking.

He was visited much by learned ⟨men⟩: more than he did desire. He was mightily importuned to goe into France and Italie (foraigners came much to see him) and much admired him, and offered him great preferments to come over to them, and the only inducement of severall foreigners that came over into England, was chiefly to see O. Protector and Mr J. Milton, and would see the house and chamber wher he was borne: he was much more admired abrode then at home.

Mr Theodore Haak R.S.S. hath translated halfe his Paradise lost into High Dutch in such blank verse as is very well liked of by Germanus Fabricius Professor at Heidelberg who sent to Mr Haak a letter upon this Translation . . .

His familiar learned Acquaintance were Mr Andrew Marvell, Mr Skinner, Dr Pagett M.D. Mr ⟨Daniel⟩ Skinner, who was his disciple. John Dreyden Esq. Poet Laureate, who very much admires him, and went to him to have leave to putt his Paradise—lost into a Drama in Rhyme: Mr Milton received him civilly, and told him that he would give him leave to tagge his Verses.

His widowe assures me that Mr Hobbs was not one of his acquaintance: that her husband did not like him at all: but he would grant him to be a man of great parts, a learned man. Their Interests and tenets were diametrically opposite, did run counter to each other. Vide Mr Hobbes *Behemoth.*

(from Mr E. Philips). His Invention was much more free and easie in the Aequinoxes than at the Solstices; as he more particularly found in writing his Paradise lost. All the time of writing *Paradise lost*, his veine began at the Autumnall Aequinoctiall and ceased at the Vernall or thereabouts (I believe about May) and this was 4 or 5 yeares of his doeing it. He began about 2 yeares before the King came-in, and finished about 3 yeares after the King's Restauracion.

In the 4th Booke of Paradise lost, there are about 6 verses of Satan's exclamation to the Sun, which Mr E. Phillips remembers, about 15 or 16 yeares before ever his Poem was thought of which verses were intended for the Beginning of a Tragoedie which he had designed, but was diverted from it by other businesse.

(from Mr Abraham Hill) memorandum his sharp writing against Alexander More of Holland upon a mistake notwithstanding he had given him by the *Ambassador* all satisfaction to the contrary, viz. that the book called *Clamor* was writt by Peter du Moulin. Well that was all one; he having writt it, it should goe into the world; one of them as bad as the other.

Whatever he wrote against Monarchie was out of no animosity to the Kings person, or out of any faction, or Interest, but out of a pure zeall to the Liberty of Mankind, which he thought would be greater under a free state than under a Monarchall government. His being so conversant in Livy and the Roman authors and the greatness he saw donne by the Roman commonwealth and the virtue of their great Captaines induc't him to.

Mr John Milton made two admirable panegyricks, as to sublimitie of witt, one on Oliver Cromwel, and the other on Thomas, lord Fairfax, both which his nephew Mr Philip<s> hath. But he hath hung back these two yeares, as to imparting copies to me. . . . Were they made in commendation of the devill, 'twere all one to one: 'tis the ὕψος that I looke after. I have been told 'tis beyond Waller's or anything in that kind.

APPENDIX

BURNET AND DRYDEN ON THE ART OF BIOGRAPHY

I. Extract from the Preface to "The Life and Death of Sir
Matthew Hale, Kt.," by Gilbert Burnet (London, 1682)

No part of History is more instructive and delighting than the
Lives of great and worthy Men. The shortness of them invites many
Readers, and there are such little and yet remarkable passages in
them, too inconsiderable to be put in a general History of the Age
in which they lived; that all people are very desirous to know them.
This makes *Plutarks* Lives to be more generally read than any of
all the Books which the ancient *Greeks* or *Romans* writ.

But the lives of Hero's and Princes, are commonly filled with
accounts of the great things done by them, which do rather belong
to a general than a particular History; and do rather amuse the
Reader's fancy with a splendid shew of greatness than offer him
what is really so useful to himself; And indeed the Lives of Princes
are either writ with so much flattery, by those who intended to
Merit by it at their own hands, or others concerned with them: Or
with so much spite, by those who being ill used by them, have
revenged themselves on their Memory, that there is not too much
to be built on them: And though the ill nature of many makes what
is satyricaly writ to be generally more read and believed, than when
the flattery is visible and course, yet certainly Resentment may make
the Writer corrupt the truth of History, as much as Interest: And
since all Men have their blind sides, committ errors, he that will
industriously lay there together, leaving out, or but slightly touching
what should be set against them, to ballance them, may make a
very good man appear in very bad Colours: So upon the whole
matter, there is not that reason to expect either much truth or great
instruction, from what is written Concerning Hero's or Princes

for few have been able to imitate the patterns Suetonius set the
World in writing of the Lives the Roman Emperours with the same
freedom that they led them: But the Lives of private Men, though
they seldom entertain the Reader with such a variety of passages as
the other do; Yet certainly they offer him things that are more
imitable, and do present Wisdom and Virtue to him, not only in a
fair *Idea*; which is often look'd on as a piece of the Invention or
Fancy of the Writer, but in such plain and familiar instances, as do
both direct him better and perswade him more; And there are not
such temptations to biass those who write them, so that we may
generally depend more on the truth of such relations as are given in
them.

II. Extract from "The Life of Plutarch," by John Dryden,
Prefixed to "Plutarch's Lives, translated from the Greek
by Several Hands" (London, 1683)

History is principally divided into three species. *Commentaries* or
Annals; *History* properly so called; and *Biographia*, or the Lives of
particular Men . . .
Biographia, or the History of particular Mens Lives, comes next
to be considered; which in dignity is inferiour to the other two; as
being more confin'd in action, and treating of Wars, and Counsels,
and all other publick affairs of Nations, only as they relate to him,
whose Life is written, or as his fortunes have a particular dependance
on them, or connection to them: All things here are circumscrib'd,
and driven to a point, so as to terminate in one: Consequently if
the action, or Counsel were managed by Collegues some part of it
must be either lame or wanting; except it be supply'd by the
Excursion of the Writer: Herein likewise must be less of variety
for the same reason; because the fortunes and actions of one Man
are related, not those of many. Thus the actions and atchievements
of *Sylla*, *Lucullus*, and *Pompey* are all of them but successive parts
of the *Mithridatick War*: Of which we cou'd have no perfect image,
if the same hand had not given us the whole, tho at several views,
in their particular Lives.
Yet tho we allow, for the reasons above alledg'd that this kind of

writing is in dignity inferiour to *History* and *Annalls*, in pleasure and instruction it equals, or even excells both of them. 'Tis not only commended by ancient practice, to celebrate the memory of great and worthy Men, as the best thanks which Posterity can pay them; but also the examples of vertue are of more vigor, when they are thus contracted into individuals. As the Sun beams, united in a burning-glass to a point, have greater force than if they were darted from a plain superficies; so the vertues and actions of one Man, drawn together into a single story, strike upon our minds a stronger and more lively impression, than the scatter'd Relations of many Men, and many actions; and by the same means that they give us pleasure they afford us profit too. For when the understanding is intent and fix'd on a single thing, it carries closer to the mark, every part of the object sinks into it, and the Soul receives it unmixt and whole. For this reason *Aristotle* Commends the unity of action in a Poem; because the mind is not capable of digesting many things at once, nor of conceiving fully any more than one Idea at a time. Whatsoever distracts the pleasure, lessens it: And as the Reader is more concerned with one Mans fortune, than those of many; so likewise the Writer is more capable of making a perfect Work, if he confine himself to this narrow compass. The lineaments, features, and colourings of a single picture may be hit exactly; but in a History-piece of many figures, the general design, the ordinance or disposition of it, the Relation of one figure to another, the diversity of the posture, habits, shadowings, and all the other graces conspiring to an uniformity, are of so difficult performance, that neither is the resemblance of particular persons often perfect, nor the beauty of the piece compleat: For any considerable errour in the parts, renders the whole disagreeable and lame. Thus then the perfection of the Work, and the benefit arising from it are both more absolute in *Biography* than in History. . . .

Biographia, or the Histories of particular Lives, tho circumscrib'd in the subject, is yet more extensive in the stile than the other two:[1] For it not only comprehends them both, but has something superadded, which neither of them have. The stile of it is various, according to the occasion. There are proper places in it, for the plainness and nakedness of narration, which is ascrib'd to Annals;

[1] *i.e.*, "*Commentaries* or *Annals*" and "*History* properly so called."

there is also room reserv'd for the loftiness and gravity of general History, when the actions related shall require that manner of expression. But there is withal, a descent into minute circumstances, and trivial passages of life, which are natural to this way of writing, and which the dignity of the other two will not admit. There you are conducted only into the rooms of state; here you are led into the private lodgings of the Heroe: you see him in his undress, and are made Familiar with his most private actions and conversations. You may behold a *Scipio* and a *Lelius* gathering Cockle-shells on the shore, *Augustus* play at bounding stones with *Boyes*; and *Agesilaus* riding on a Hobby-horse among his Children. The Pageantry of Life is taken away; you see the poor reasonable Animal, as naked as ever nature made him; are made acquainted with his passions and his follies, and find the *Demy-God a Man.*

NOTES

Life of Mr George Herbert

p. 47. *George Herbert* (1593–1633). Poet and priest. For full biographical details see the Introduction to *The Works of George Herbert*, edited by F. E. Hutchinson (Oxford University Press). This is the best modern edition; there is also an excellent critical study by J. B. Leishman in his *Metaphysical Poets* (Oxford University Press, 1934).

p. 48. *Edward, the eldest.* Better known as Lord Herbert of Cherbury, philosopher and poet. His poetry had considerable merit. The standard modern edition is that of G. C. Moore Smith (Oxford University Press, 1923). His poems are also included in R. G. Howarth's *Minor Poets of the Seventeenth Century*, "Everyman's Library." His most important philosophical works are *De Veritate* (1624) and *De Religione Gentilium* (1663). He is generally considered to be the first of the English deists, who rejected Christianity in favour of a "religion of nature." For an account of his opinions see Basil Willey, *The Seventeenth Century Background*, pp. 121–132. His *Autobiography*, a lively and entertaining work, was first printed by Horace Walpole in 1764.

p. 49. *Master of the Revels; a place that requires a diligent wisdom.* Sir Henry Herbert (1595–1673) was Master of the Revels under Charles I and II. He claimed the right of licensing all forms of public entertainments, and even certain books. It is to these functions of the Master of the Revels that Walton probably refers in this passage, and he may be thinking of Herbert's action in licensing Middleton's play *The Game of Chess* in 1624, which was suppressed because of the protests of the Spanish Ambassador.

p. 51. *Mr John Donne* (? 1571–1631). The famous poet, whose life was also written by Walton. The best modern edition of his poems is that of Sir H. J. C. Grierson (Oxford University Press). The poem addressed to Lady Magdalen Herbert which Walton quotes is his Ninth Elegy, *The Autumnall* (*Poems*, edited by Grierson, i, 92–94). Walton's quotation is slightly inaccurate.

The reading of the two couplets which he quotes (lines 1 and 2, and 23 and 24) in Grierson's edition is as follows:

No *Spring*, nor *Summer* Beauty hath such grace,
As I have seen in one *Autumnall* face.
In all her words, unto all hearers fit,
You may at *Revels*, you at Counsaile sit.

p. 51. *St Chrysostom.* John Chrysostom (Χρυσόστομος = golden-mouthed), the most famous of the Greek Fathers of the Church. Born about A.D. 345, he was trained under the pagan philosopher Libanius, converted to Christianity about 370, and ordained presbyter in 386. He became famous as a preacher in Antioch and was appointed Archbishop of Constantinople. He incurred the enmity of the Court and of the Empress Eudoxia, whose vices he attacked fearlessly in his sermons. Through the influence of the Empress he was condemned for heresy and banished. The people of Constantinople, however, rose in revolt and demanded his recall. The Emperor restored him to his see, but Eudoxia forced him to go into exile again, and he died in an obscure retreat in Asia Minor in 407. See Gibbon, *Decline and Fall of the Roman Empire*, chapter xxxii, and Rev. R. W. Stephens, *St John Chrysostom, his Life and Times* (1871).

p. 51. *St Hierome.* The more common modern form of the name is St Jerome (Hieronymus), (*c.* A.D. 320–340). Father of the Church, renowned for his piety and scholarship, and particularly his translation of the Bible into Latin called the Vulgate, which became the official version of the Church. Paula was a wealthy Roman widow, who with her daughter Eustochium, one of Jerome's pupils, made a pilgrimage to Palestine and in company with Jerome visited various places mentioned in the Bible. St Jerome wrote an account of this tour. Paula founded a nunnery at Bethlehem where she died in 404. See F. W. Farrar, *Lives of the Fathers* (1889).

p. 52. *To the Lady Magdalen Herbert.* See *The Poems of John Donne*, edited by Grierson, i, 317, 318.

p. 53. *such, as they two now sing in Heaven.* Professor Butt points out that this was a favourite turn of phrase of Walton's. *Cf.* p. 95, ll. 13, 14: "Where they at this time interchangeably and constantly sing, etc." Similar expressions occur twice in the *Life of Sanderson*, and on the fly-leaf of Walton's copy of Eusebius's *Ecclesiastical History*, now in Salisbury Cathedral Library, he is twice to be found practising a similar phrase.

p. 55. *Orator for the University.* The office of Orator still exists in the

universities of Oxford and Cambridge. The Orator's chief duties
in the seventeenth century were to write Latin ceremonial letters
and addresses on behalf of the university and to present eminent
persons for honorary degrees.

p. 56. *Lady Elizabeth Queen of Bohemia* (1596–1662). Eldest daughter
of James I, married Frederick V, elector of the Palatinate, who
became King of Bohemia in 1619, but was driven from his kingdom by the Catholic League in the following year. This is the
Queen of Bohemia to whom Sir Henry Wotton addressed his
well-known poem.

p. 56. *Basilicon Doron*. The title of a Latin work by James I meaning "The Royal Gift," published in 1599 and containing a defence
of episcopacy and an attack on Presbyterianism. Actually James
presented to the University on this occasion not only the *Basilicon
Doron* but his *Opera Latina*, or complete Latin works in one
volume.

p. 56. *Quid Vaticanam*, etc. This Latin couplet is a compliment to
James I on his learning, of which he was very proud. It can be
rendered into English as follows:

Why, stranger, boast your libraries at Oxford or at Rome,
When we have a whole library packed in a single tome.

p. 56. *Andrew Melvin* or Melville (1545–1622). Scottish scholar and
theologian, a man of prodigious learning, who became Principal
of Glasgow University in 1574 and Rector of St Andrew's in 1590.
He was a strong Presbyterian and stoutly opposed the attempts of
King James to force episcopacy on the Scottish Kirk. He had the
"strange confidence" to call the King "God's silly vassal" at the
Hampton Court conference in 1606, and was imprisoned in the
Tower for several years. After his release, he went to the Continent and became professor at the University of Sedan, where he
died in 1622. The "bitter verses" to which Walton refers are
Melville's *Anti-Tami-Cami-Categoria*, a Latin poem in which he
attacks the Universities of Oxford and Cambridge for their hos-
tility to Presbyterianism and makes rather heavy-handed fun of
the Anglican ritual. Herbert wrote in reply to Melville's poem a
series of Latin epigrams called *Musae Responsoriae* which were not
published till 1662, when they appeared in a collection called
Solomonis Ecclesia, edited by Dr Duport. This passage is a good
illustration of the careful way in which Walton revised his work
in the interests of accuracy. In the first edition of his *Life of
Herbert*, published in 1670, he stated that the occasion of Herbert's
answer to Melville was the return of Melville from abroad, "some

short time before or immediately after Mr *Herbert* was made *Orator*" (January 21, 1619–20). Actually Melville remained abroad from 1611 till his death in 1622. In the second edition (1675), which contains the text printed in this volume, Walton revised the passage, having apparently obtained more reliable information. He omits the statement quoted above and substitutes the account of the introduction of Melville's verses into Westminster School and of the replies to them made by the young Herbert "then, and often after." Some of the epigrams in Herbert's collection are not beyond the powers of a clever schoolboy, and it is probable that Herbert wrote these while he was at Westminster between 1605 and 1609, and that he took up the collection and added to it when Melville's satire was printed in 1620. It is pleasant to find that, in a later Latin poem addressed to Melville, Herbert pays a tribute to his learning and poetic gifts. See *The Works of George Herbert*, edited by F. E. Hutchinson, pp. 384, 587.

p. 57. *Lady Arabella.* Arabella Stuart (1575–1615), next heir to the throne of England after James I, her first cousin. She was imprisoned by Elizabeth, but released by James on his accession to the throne in 1603. However, she incurred the King's displeasure by a secret marriage to Edward Seymour, a descendant of Henry VII. She and her husband tried to escape, but she was captured in the Channel and imprisoned in the Tower, where she died in 1615.

p. 57. *Causa tibi mecum*, etc. The effect of these two Latin verses cannot be given in an English rendering as it depends on a pun on the name Arabella (*Ara bella*=fair altar): "You and I have a common reason for our imprisonment: Arabella (a fair altar) is yours; *Ara sacra* (a holy altar—*i.e.*, my defence of my religious principles) is mine."

p. 58. *Dr Duport.* James Duport (1606–79), Master of Magdalene College, Cambridge, and Regius Professor of Greek. See p. 153 *and n.*

p. 58. *Sir Francis Bacon, Lord Verulam.* See Introduction, p. 24.

p. 58. *Dr Andrews, Bishop of Winchester.* Lancelot Andrewes (1555–1626), one of the translators of the Authorized Version of the Bible and a famous preacher. See *Life* by Aubrey; p. 177.

p. 59. *Sine Cure.* An office carrying a salary but involving no duties. A number of such offices were "in the gift of the Crown" in the seventeenth century. It has been supposed that the sinecure given by James I to George Herbert was the Rectory of Whitford in

Flintshire, which was held by Sir Philip Sidney for a few months. According to Hutchinson, however, there is no mention of Herbert in the list of rectors of Whitford (*Works*, edited by Hutchinson, p. 32). It is to be noted that Walton's statement is hesitating ("I think"), and that he may well have been mistaken.

p. 60. *Mr Herbert Thorndike* (1598–1672). Prebendary of Westminster, 1661. Thorndike was a distinguished theologian and the author of numerous works which were reprinted in six volumes of the "Library of Anglo-Catholic Theology" (1844–56). He helped in the editing of Bishop Walton's great Polyglot Bible, and Cardinal Newman considered him to be the only writer of any authority in the English Church who held the true Catholic theory of the Eucharist.

p. 60. *Affliction.* Walton's quotation consists of the last three stanzas of the first of four poems with this title in *The Temple*. The poem begins, "When first thou didst entice me to thy heart," and will be found on p. 46 of Hutchinson's edition.

p. 62. *Deacon.* The exact date and place of George Herbert's ordination as Deacon are unknown, but the Lincoln Chapter Acts describe him as Deacon when he was instituted by proxy, on July 5, 1626, into the canonry and prebend of Leighton Ecclesia (see *Works*, edited by Hutchinson, p. 31). Professor Butt points out that the taking of deacon's orders did not commit Herbert to taking priest's orders later. Herbert's struggles were not, therefore, ended, as Walton recognizes.

p. 62. *John, then Lord Bishop.* John Williams (1582–1660), afterwards Archbishop of York, the last cleric to hold the office of Lord Keeper.

p. 63. *costly Mosaick.* Professor Butt in his article on "Izaak Walton's Methods in Biography" (see Bibliography) has shown that Walton was misled here by Barnabas Oley, whose short biography of Herbert was prefixed to the poet's *Remains* published in 1650. There is no mosaic work at Leighton Ecclesia, as Zouch, the eighteenth-century editor of Walton's *Lives*, points out in a puzzled note. Oley, summarizing Herbert's work at Leighton, writes "*so that the Church of England owed to him . . . the reparation of a* Church-materiall"; he then passes on to speak of Herbert's volume of poems entitled *The Temple*, adding "and the erection of that costly piece (*of Mosaick or Solomonick work*) The Temple." Walton, who probably never saw Leighton Church, took Oley's metaphorical expression literally, and imagined he was speaking of actual mosaic work at Leighton instead of the "mosaick" of

Herbert's poetry. Herbert himself probably never went to Leighton. His installation was merely to the prebend at Lincoln Cathedral and he had no responsibility for the cure of souls. The rebuilding began in 1626 and was not completed till after his death. He rebuilt the nave and west walls of the transepts, re-roofed the church, and furnished it throughout. Excellent photographs will be found in the Huntingdonshire volume (1926) of the Royal Commission on Historical Monuments.

p. 64. *Mr Nicholas Farrer* or Ferrar (1592–1637). One of the most remarkable Englishmen of his time. He graduated at Cambridge, became a Fellow of Clare Hall, then studied medicine and travelled on the Continent. On his return he engaged in business, entered Parliament, and took a prominent part in the affairs of the Virginia Company. In 1625 he retired to Little Gidding in Huntingdonshire, where he founded a High Anglican religious community of some thirty persons which was broken up by the Puritans after his death. The life of this community is well described in J. H. Shorthouse's novel *John Inglesant*, first published in 1880. Ferrar edited Herbert's *The Temple* and wrote a short preface to the first edition of 1633.

p. 64. *Mr Arthur Woodnot or Wodenoth* (?1590–?1650). Cousin of Nicholas Ferrar and a London goldsmith and colonial pioneer. He was a member of the Virginia Company and Deputy-governor of the Somers Island Company.

p. 65. *our Commencement*. Commencement Day at Cambridge was a day near the end of the summer term when degrees were granted. The Public Orator had important functions to perform at the degree ceremonies. The day when degrees are granted at Cambridge is still known as Commencement Tuesday.

p. 65. *snarles*. Tangles.

p. 68. *Jane*. Jane Danvers was a kinswoman of John Aubrey, who describes her as "a handsome *bona roba* and ingeniose."

p. 68. *Platonick—i.e.*, Platonic lover. 'Platonic' love, or purely spiritual affection between persons of different sexes, was much discussed in court circles in the early seventeenth century. James Howell, in a letter dated June 3, 1634, writes, "The Court affords little news at present, but that there is a love called platonic love, which much sways there of late. It is a love abstracted from all corporal gross impressions and sensual appetite, but consists in contemplations and ideas. . . ." It was satirized by Davenant in his comedy *The Platonic Lovers* (1636).

p. 70. *more pleasant, than healthful*. The village of Bemerton is about one and a half miles from Salisbury on the road to Wilton. The river Neder flows at the bottom of the rectory garden, and there is a delightful view of Salisbury Cathedral across the meadows. The damp, low-lying situation could not have been very good for a man with a delicate constitution like George Herbert.

p. 72. *The Odour. Works*, edited by Hutchinson, p. 174. The lines to which Walton refers are the first two stanzas:

> How sweetly doth *My Master* sound! *My Master*!
>   As Amber-greese leaves a rich scent
>   Unto the taster;
>   So do these words a sweet content,
> An orientall fragrancie, *My Master*.
>
> With these all day I do perfume minde
>   My minde ev'n thrust into them both:
>   That I might finde
>   What cordials make this curious broth,
> This broth of smells that feeds and fats my minde.

p. 72. *The Pearl*. One of Herbert's finest poems. See *Works*, edited by Hutchinson, pp. 88, 89. Walton summarizes the first three stanzas and quotes the last lines of the fourth, changing the first word of the first line quoted from "Yet" to "That."

p. 75. *Dr Humphrey Henchman* (1592–1675). Appointed canon and precentor of Salisbury in 1623, assisted Charles II to escape after the battle of Worcester, was Bishop of Salisbury from 1660 to 1663, when he became Bishop of London.

p. 75. *The Countrey Parson. A Priest to the Temple or The Country Parson* was first printed by Oley in Herbert's *Remains*, 1652. See note above. The best modern edition is in *The Works of George Herbert* edited by F. E. Hutchinson. Much of Walton's long account of Herbert's parochial practice can be paralleled from *The Country Parson*, from which he probably drew it.

p. 76. *Mr Barnabas Oly*. Fellow and afterwards President of Clare College, Cambridge. He edited a volume of George Herbert's *Remains*, published in 1652, and prefixed to it a "Prefatory View of the Life of Mr Geo. Herbert" which Walton knew and used.

p. 87. *Mr Edmund Duncon*. Edmund Duncon (d. 1673), afterwards Rector of Friern Barnet in Middlesex.

p. 91. *John Valdesso*. Juan de Valdes (*c*. 1500–41), Spanish religious writer and reformer. He attacked the corruptions of the Roman Church, and, to escape the Spanish Inquisition, settled at Naples

o

in 1530. His name became Italianized as Valdesso. The work which Ferrar translated was his *Ciento Diez Conçideraçiones*, a book which had been suppressed in Spain by the Inquisition. An Italian translation of it was published in Rome in 1550, and it was this version which Ferrar translated into English.

p. 93. *The Temple*. This was the first edition of Herbert's poems, printed by the Cambridge University Press in 1633.

p. 93. *Religion stands a Tip-toe, etc.* This couplet is from Herbert's poem *The Church Militant*, ll. 235, 236 (*Works*, edited by Hutchinson, p. 196). The correct reading of the first line is as follows: "Religion stands on tip-toe in our land."

p. 95. *The Sundays of Mans Life*. This is the fifth stanza of George Herbert's poem *Sunday*. See Works, edited by Hutchinson, pp. 75, 76.

p. 96. *All must to their cold graves*, etc. Walton is adapting the last four lines of James Shirley's fine poem "The glories of our blood and state," first printed in his *Ajax and Ulysses* (1659). Shirley's lines are as follows:

> Your heads must come,
> To the cold Tomb;
> Onely the actions of the just
> Smell sweet, and blossom in their dust.

p. 97. *Andrew Melvin*. Walton does not seem to have known that Andrew Melville died in 1622, ten years before Herbert.

Some Passages of the Life and Death of John Earl of Rochester

p. 98. *John Earl of Rochester* (1647–80). Poet, courtier, and wit. A pirated and unreliable edition of Rochester's works appeared in 1680. The first authentic collection, edited by Thomas Rymer, was published in 1691. For a full account of the career of Rochester, see V. de S. Pinto, *Rochester, Portrait of a Restoration Poet* (1935). For his works see the complete edition by J. Hayward (1920), and the selection edited by R. Duncan (1949).

p. 98. *Henry Earl of Rochester*. Henry Wilmot (1612–58), one of the most prominent Royalist generals in the Civil War, created Baron Wilmot in 1643. After the execution of Charles I he became one of the chief advisers of the young Charles II. He fought at the battle of Worcester in 1651, and, after the Royalist defeat, helped the young King to escape. He was created Earl of Rochester by Charles II in 1652 and died at Sluys in 1657–58. See Clarendon's *History of the Great Rebellion*.

p. 98. *his Mother*. Anne St John, daughter of Sir John St John and a relative of Oliver St John, the great Parliamentary leader, who was killed early in the Civil War.

p. 99. *Dr Blanford*. Walter Blandford (1619–75), Fellow of Wadham, afterwards Bishop of Oxford and Bishop of Worcester.

p. 99. *Mr Phineas Berry or Bury*. Fellow of Wadham, Proctor in 1665.

p. 99. *Dr Balfour*. Sir Andrew Balfour, M.D., an eminent Scottish physician and naturalist. An account of his travels in France and Italy appeared in *Letters Written to a Friend by the Learned and Judicious Sir Andrew Balfour*, published in 1700. A Latin record of his tour with Rochester was printed by Sir R. Sibbald in his *Memoria Balfouriana* (1699). See Pinto, *Rochester, Portrait of a Restoration Poet*, pp. 7, 8.

p. 100. *Boileau among the French, and Cowley among the English Wits*. The Satires of Nicolas Boileau (1636–1711), the French poet, were appearing in Paris at about the time when Rochester returned from his travels. A collected edition of the poems of Abraham Cowley had appeared in 1656. His works were published in 1668 and went through many editions.

p. 100. *Earl of Sandwich*. Edward Montagu (1625–72), one of Cromwell's admirals, played a prominent part in bringing about the restoration of Charles II, who created him Earl of Sandwich in 1660. He distinguished himself at the battle of Lowestoft in the Second Dutch War in 1664 and commanded the fleet which put to sea in the summer (not the winter) of 1665 to intercept the Dutch East India Fleet off the coast of Norway. Rochester joined the fleet in July with a letter from Charles II recommending him to the Admiral as a volunteer. When the Dutch fleet took refuge in the port of Bergen Sir Thomas Teddiman was sent with twenty frigates to seize the treasure ships. Rochester volunteered for service with Teddiman's squadron and was present at the attack on Bergen. He took part in the action on board the *Revenge*, where he is said to have shown "as brave and resolute a Courage as was possible." He wrote an interesting account of the battle in a letter to his mother which is preserved in the British Museum. See Pinto, *op. cit.*, pp. 51–54.

p. 100. *Lord Clifford*. Thomas Clifford (1630–73), created Baron Clifford of Chudleigh in 1672. Served under Sandwich in the Second Dutch War, 1665–66.

p. 101. *Sir Edward Spragge*. Rochester volunteered again for service at sea in May 1666. He joined the ship commanded by Sir Edward Spragge on May 31 and took part in the sanguinary four days' battle in the Channel between the English, under Monk and Rupert, and the Dutch, under Van Tromp and Ruyter. He was in the thick of the fighting and was one of the few volunteers in Spragge's ship that were not killed.

p. 102. *Libels* and *Satyrs*. A number of these survive and were printed in various collections after Rochester's death. They cover a wide range from the sombre and philosophic *Satyr against Mankind* to such squibs as the famous epigram on Charles II:

> We have a pritty witty king,
>> Whose word no man relys on,
> He never said a foolish thing,
>> And never did a wise one.

p. 103. *Mr Mountague*. Edward Montagu, son of Lord Montagu of Boughton, killed at the attack on Bergen in 1665.

p. 104. *Lady Warre*. Widow of Sir John Malet of Enmore and wife of Elizabeth Malet whom Rochester married on January 29, 1666–67.

p. 106. *Tower-street. Italian Mountebank.* In 1676 Rochester was banished from Court, and, disguising himself as a quack doctor practised at lodgings on Tower Hill under the name of Dr Alexander Bendo with the help of his servant Thomas Alcock. According to Alcock, the Earl wore "an old overgrown green gown" and sold nostrums compounded out of "buck, slate, soot, and ashes, soap and nastier things" which he dispensed to his credulous patients. He wrote a witty and amusing Bill to advertise the skill of "Dr Bendo," which was printed in the edition of his works published in 1691.

p. 140. *Mr Parsons, his Mothers Chaplain.* This is Robert Parsons, M.A., who preached a Funeral Sermon on Rochester which was published at Oxford in 1680.

p. 144. *He had overcome all his Resentments to all the World.* According to Aubrey, "He sent for all his servants, even the piggard-boy, to come and heare his palinode." See Aubrey, *Brief Lives*, edited by Clark, ii, 304.

Some Account of the Life of Dr Isaac Barrow

p. 149. *Isaac Barrow* (1630–77). Mathematician and divine; he published many works on mathematics and optics and is regarded as one of Newton's chief predecessors. His theological works include a *Treatise of the Pope's Supremacy* (1680) and his clear and vigorous sermons, which were regarded as models of the new simple method of preaching. Barrow's *Works* were edited by

A. Napier (9 vols., 1859), and there is a modern study by **P. H. Osmond** (1944).

p. 149. *To the Reverend Dr Tillotson, Dean of Canterbury.* Hill's biography of Barrow is in the form of a letter addressed to John Tillotson (1630–94), a contemporary of Barrow at Cambridge, who became one of the most famous preachers of his time and a leader of the Broad Church or latitudinarian party in the Church of England. Tillotson became Dean of Canterbury in 1670, Dean of St Paul's in 1680, and Archbishop of Canterbury in 1691.

p. 149. *Isaac Barrow, late L. Bishop of St Asaph* (1614–80), uncle of the famous Isaac Barrow. Fellow of Peterhouse, Cambridge, Bishop of St Asaph, 1669–80.

p. 150. *Viscount Fairfax of Emley.* This is Thomas Fairfax, fourth Viscount Fairfax of Emley, who succeeded his father in the peerage in 1648 and died, according to Cokayne's *Peerage*, "young and unmarried" in 1651. According to Aubrey, he married "a gentleman's daughter while still a schoolboy, and 'tis thought he dyed for want."

p. 150. *Dr Hammond.* Henry Hammond (1605–60), Canon of Christ Church, Public Orator of Oxford University, and Chaplain to Charles I. Author of numerous theological works.

p. 150. *excellent Epitaph.* This Latin epitaph on Dr Hammond is printed on p. 301 of vol. iv of the 1683 edition of Barrow's *Works*. It describes Hammond as "Theologorum sui seculi coryphaeus. Literatorum princeps. Anglicae gentis decus. Ecclesiae columen. Veritatis assertor peritissimus."

p. 150. *the Covenant.* The Solemn League and Covenant, a document binding Englishmen to abjure episcopacy and adopt Presbyterianism, was accepted by the Parliamentary party as a result of the agreement with the Scottish Presbyterians in 1643. When the universities came under parliamentary control all their members were asked to sign the Covenant.

p. 150. *Dr Hill.* Thomas Hill, Master of Trinity College (d. 1653), Vice-Chancellor of Cambridge, 1646, a strong Calvinist.

p. 150. *the Ingagement.* This was the "engagement" to be faithful to "the Commonwealth of England, as the same is now established without a King or House of Lords" imposed on all officials, as well as graduates and officers of the universities in October 1649 (see Gardiner's *History of the Commonwealth and Protectorate*, vol. i, p. 176).

p. 151. *Physiology.* In the old sense of "the study and description of natural objects: natural science or philosophy."—*New English Dictionary.*

p. 151. *the Lord Verulam.—i.e.*, Francis Bacon.

p. 151. *Monsieur des Cartes, Galileo.* See Introduction, p. 26.

p. 152. *Tractare res multi norunt, aestimare pauci.* "Many knew how to handle affairs, few how to judge them."

p. 152. *Cardan.* Girolamo Cardano, Italian physician, mathematician, autobiographer (1501–76). See Introduction, pp. 27, 28.

p. 152. *Scaliger.* Joseph Justus Scaliger (1540–1609), one of the greatest scholars of the Renaissance. The book to which Hill refers here is his *De Emendatione Temporum*, a work on ancient chronology, in which he made considerable use of the surviving fragments of the chronicle of the ancient ecclesiastical historian Eusebius of Cæsarea (*c.* A.D. 260–*c.* 340).

p. 152. *Ptolomy's Almagest.* The Almagest was a famous treatise on astronomy by Ptolemy of Alexandria (second century A.D.).

p. 152. *Euclide's Elements.* Euclid of Alexandria (*c.* 300 B.C.), the first famous geometrician of antiquity. His *Elementa* were translated into all the European languages and used as a school textbook for generations. Barrow published in 1655 *Euclidis Elementorum Libri XV Breviter Demonstrati*. This is "Euclide in a less form" referred to below.

p. 152. *Mr John Ray* (1627–1705). The greatest English naturalist of the seventeenth century and a pioneer of modern botanical science. Fellow of Trinity College, Cambridge, 1649–62.

p. 152. *Apollonius.* The book referred to is the *Conics*, a work by Apollonius of Perga, Greek geometer of the Alexandrian period (*c.* 260–205 B.C.).

p. 152. *intra haec temporis, etc.* "This work was performed between these two dates."

p. 152. *Labore et constantia.* "By labour and perseverance."

p. 152. *Bonae*, etc. "Good if they are combined with humility and serve the cause of charity."

p. 152. *Poetry.* Barrow was an early admirer of Milton's poetry and is the author of the Latin commendatory verses prefixed to the second edition of *Paradise Lost* in 1674. Barrow's own poems are all in Latin.

p. 152. *Hyperboles.* Probably a reference to the 'conceits' of the metaphysical poets of the school of Donne.

p. 152. *Plays.* Barrow is certainly criticizing the morality of the fashionable plays of Charles II's reign, such as the comedies of Etherege, Dryden, Wycherley, and Shadwell.

p. 153. *Dr Duport.* See above, p. 58 *and n.* Duport resigned from the Chair of Greek in 1654. He was succeeded by Ralph Widdrington, who, according to Aubrey, was "putt in" by Cromwell.

p. 153. *Dr Whichcote*. Benjamin Whichcote (1609–83), Provost of King's College, Cambridge, 1644–60, Vice-Chancellor of Cambridge University, 1650, famous preacher and latitudinarian divine, generally considered to be the inaugurator of the Cambridge Platonist movement. See account of him in *The Cambridge Platonists* by F. M. Powicke, extracts from his sermons in *The Cambridge Platonists*, edited by E. T. Campagnac, and his interesting *Religious and Moral Aphorisms*, edited by W. R. Inge.

p. 153. *the English Court*. The exiled Court of Charles II.

p. 153. *viaticum*, "journey money."

p. 153. *Great Duke's Library*. The Medicean Library, or Bibliotheca Mediceo-Laurenziana, founded by Cosimo de' Medici the Elder.

p. 153. *Mr Fitton*. Probably a member of the family of Fitton of Gawsworth in Cheshire.

p. 153. *Livorn*. Leghorn.

p. 154. *In this Voyage*. Barrow described his voyage in a long poem called *Iter Maritimum* in Latin elegiac verse. It is printed in vol. iv of the 1683 edition of his *Works*, pp. 211–226.

p. 154. *Vitali charior aura*, etc. A quotation from Barrow's *Iter Maritimum*, where he describes the fight in a lively passage.

> Almaque libertas vitali charior aura,
>   Libertas! bullit cor, animusque tumet.

> Fair freedom, than the breath of life more dear,
> Freedom that swells the heart and casts out fear.

p. 154. *Non te*, etc. The quotation is from Cicero, *Letters to Atticus*, xiv, 20. (Complete Correspondence, edited by Tyrrell and Purser, v. 267.) The meaning is, "Does not the severe face (*vulticulus*) of Brutus keep you from talk of that kind?" Atticus had mentioned Epicurus and his advice not to take part in politics.

p. 154. *St Chrysostome*. See above, p. 204.

p. 155. *Te magis*, etc. This satiric epigram can be translated as follows:
"No one wished more for your return, O Charles, in all the nation
And no one felt the difference less after your Restoration."

p. 155. *Gresham College*. An institution founded by Sir Thomas Gresham, the famous Elizabethan merchant. The bequest of Gresham provided for seven professors to lecture on astronomy, geometry, physic, law, divinity, rhetoric, and music.

p. 155. *Mr Laurence Rook* (1622–62). Astronomer and geometrician. Professor of Astronomy at Oxford and of Geometry at Gresham College. One of the founders of the Royal Society.

p. 155. *Dr Wilkins.* John Wilkins (1614–72), Warden of Wadham College, Oxford, and afterwards Bishop of Chester. He was the moving spirit of the group who formed the Royal Society and was its first Secretary.

p. 155. *Dr Pope* (d. 1714). Astronomer and physician, Fellow of Wadham College, Oxford.

p. 155. *Cotton Library.* The great collection formed by Sir Robert Cotton, acquired by the Nation in 1702 and now in the British Museum.

p. 156. *Mr Robert Hook.* Robert Hook (1635–1703), one of the most distinguished English physicists of the seventeenth century. Secretary of the Royal Society in 1677.

p. 156. *Monsieur Slusius.* René François de Sluse, Canon of Liége. Walloon scholar and mathematician (1622–85), a corresponding member of the Royal Society.

p. 156. *Mr Gregory.* David Gregory (1661–1708), Scottish astronomer. Professor of Mathematics at Edinburgh 1683–91, and afterwards Savilian Professor of Astronomy at Oxford.

p. 156. *Archimedes.* The famous ancient Greek mathematician (287–212 B.C.).

p. 156. *Suarez.* Francisco Suarez (1548–1617). Spanish theologian and political philosopher.

p. 156. *Apollonius.* See p. 152 *n.*

p. 156. '*Ὁ Θεὸς γεωμετρεῖ.*' "God is a geometrician." One of the sayings of the ancient Pythagoreans. It is followed in the original text by a Latin meditation, or prayer, by Barrow, beginning, "Tu autem, Domine, quantus es Geometra." ("How great a geometrician art thou, O Lord.")

p. 156. *Mr Isaac Newton* (1642–1727). The great mathematician and physicist. He succeeded Barrow as Lucasian Professor of Mathematics at Cambridge in 1669.

p. 157. *Le Clerc Bibl. Univ.* The reference is to the *Bibliothèque Universelle et Historique* by the French Protestant divine Jean Le Clerc (1657–1736), published at Amsterdam in 25 vols. in 1686–93.

p. 157. *The King.* Charles II.

p. 158. *Gilbert Lord Archbishop of Canterbury.* Gilbert Sheldon (1598–1677), Archbishop of Canterbury 1663–67.

p. 158. *Duke of Buckingham.* George Villiers, second Duke of Buckingham (1628–87), the Zimri of Dryden's *Absalom and Achitophel.*

p. 158. *Treatise of the Pope's Supremacy.* Barrow's most considerable controversial work, first published in 1680.

p. 159. *Approaching danger.* Hill's *Life of Barrow* appeared at the time when Charles II had routed the exclusionists and the succession to the throne of his brother, the Roman Catholic James, seemed certain.

p. 159. *Dr Stillingfleet.* Edward Stillingfleet (1635-99). Dean of St Paul's 1678-89, and afterwards Bishop of Worcester. Famous as a preacher and controversialist. Hill is referring particularly to his polemics against the Roman Catholic Church.

p. 159. *Symbols.* In the obsolete sense of a summary or synopsis (see *Oxford English Dictionary*).

p. 160. *My Lord Chancellor.* Heneage Finch, Earl of Nottingham (1621-82), to whom the 1683 edition of Barrow's *Works* is dedicated.

p. 160. *Dr Mapletoft.* Physician and divine (1631-1721), F.R.S. 1676, friend of John Locke. He wrote the Latin epitaph for Barrow's tomb which is printed at the head of Barrow's *Works* after Hill's *Life*.

p. 160. *Marcus Brutus.* The famous Roman republican leader who died at Philippi in B.C. 42. The *denarii* are Roman coins on which the head of Brutus appears. Hill quotes from the first stanza of Abraham Cowley's *Ode to Brutus*, first published in his *Poems* of 1656.

p. 162. *Camerarius.* Joachim Camerarius (1500-74), German scholar, friend of Philip Melanchthon, the Reformer, whose life he wrote in Latin.

p. 162. *Gassendus.* Pierre Gassendi (1592-1655), French philosopher and scientist. For his *Life of Peireskius* see Introduction, pp. 28, 29.

Aubrey's Life of Lancelot Andrewes

p. 163. *Lancelot Andrewes* (1555-1626). Divine and theologian. His sermons were famous in his day. A collected edition of them appeared in 1629 and was frequently reprinted. His *Preces Privatae* are a classic of Anglican devotional literature. See *Lancelot Andrewes and the Reaction*, by D. Macleane (1910), and T. S. Eliot's essay (first published in 1928) in his *Selected Essays*.

p. 163. *Mr Mulcaster.* Richard Mulcaster (1530-1611). Headmaster of Merchant Taylor's School 1561-86, and a notable Elizabethan humanist scholar and teacher. See his book *The Elementarie*, edited by Campagnac (Oxford University Press, 1925). Edmund Spenser was one of his pupils.

p. 163. *Mr Thomas Fuller, Holy State.* Thomas Fuller (1608–61), author of *The Holy State and the Profane State*, published in 1642. See the selection from his works edited by E. K. Broadus (Clarendon Series, Oxford, 1928). Aubrey is probably referring to the chapter in *The Holy State* called "The Good School-master." There is a modern edition by M. G. Walton (Columbia University Press, 1938).

p. 164. *Nicholas Fuller* (?1557–1626). A learned Hebraist, author of three books of *Miscellanea Theologica* published in 1612.

p. 165. *Christopher Wren* (1591–1658). Dean of Windsor, father of the famous architect of the same name.

Aubrey's Life of the Honourable Robert Boyle

p. 166. *Robert Boyle.* The Hon. Robert Boyle (1627–91), seventh (not fifth) son of Richard Boyle, the great Earl of Cork, was one of the most distinguished English scientists of the seventeenth century and the great pioneer of modern chemistry. He was also a man of wide general learning and culture. In his notes on the Boyle family Aubrey describes him as "that honourable and well known name Robert Boyle, esquier, that profound philosopher, accomplished humanist, and excellent divine, I had almost said lay-bishop, as one hath stiled Sir Henry Savil; whose works alone may make a library." The best modern study of Boyle is *The Life and Works of the Honourable Robert Boyle*, by Louis Trenchard More (Oxford University Press, 1944). Boyle's most famous work, *The Sceptical Chymist*, has been reprinted in "Everyman's Library."

p. 166. *Cowper's Dictionary.* This is *Thesaurus Linguae Latinae*, by Thomas Cooper, an Elizabethan scholar and divine, first published in 1565.

p. 166. *R.H.* Robert Hooke; see above, p. 216.

p. 166. *Lady Ranulagh.* Katherine Boyle, wife of Richard Jones, Viscount Ranelagh. She was a beautiful and talented woman, and a friend of Milton.

p. 167. *New Testament in Arabique.* The Gospels and Acts actually in Malay, printed in Arabic characters (Oxford, 1677).

Aubrey's Life of Thomas Hobbes

p. 168. *Mr Thomas Hobbes* (1588–1679). Philosopher. His most famous work, *Leviathan*, was published in 1651. The standard edition of Hobbes's *Works* is that of Sir W. Molesworth (16 vols.;

London, 1839–45). There are useful modern editions of *Leviathan* by Pogson Smith (1909) and M. Oakeshott (1946). For biography and criticism see Leslie Stephen, *Thomas Hobbes* ("English Men of Letters"), and J. Laird, *Thomas Hobbes* (1934). The chapter on Hobbes in Basil Willey's *Seventeenth Century Background* is particularly valuable. Hobbes wrote a short autobiography in Latin verse, which was published in 1680. Aubrey lent his MS. life to Dr Richard Blackburne, who used it in the compilation of his Latin life of Hobbes which appeared in 1681. A book called *Mr Hobbes Considered* appeared anonymously in 1662 and was reprinted in 1680. It contained a defence of Hobbes's life and opinions, and was, according to Aubrey, actually by Hobbes himself. Aubrey quotes this book in his *Life of Hobbes*; see below, p. 221.

p. 168. *Writers of the Lives,* etc. Aubrey is probably thinking of Diogenes Laertius.

p. 168. *Sir Johns.* Parish priests. The ignorance of many Elizabethan parish priests is satirized by Spenser in *Mother Hubberd's Tale*, ll. 379–401.

p. 168. *Homilies.* Printed sermons. Two official *Books of Homilies* were issued in the sixteenth century, the first in 1547 and the second in 1562.

p. 168. *ignorance and clownery.* Among the letters which Aubrey appends to his life of Hobbes is one from his brother William Aubrey containing the following account of the elder Hobbes. "The old vicar Hobs was a good fellow, and had been at cards all Saturday night, and at church in his sleep he cries out Trafells is Troumps [viz., clubs]. Then quoth the clark, Then, master, he that hath ace doe rub [*i.e.*, he that has the ace wins]. He was a collerice man, and a parson (which I thinke succeeded him at Westport) provoked him (a purpose) at the Church doore, so Hobs stroke him and was forcd to fly for it and . . . in obscurity beyond London, died there, was about 80 yeares since."

p. 168. *Alderman.* Aubrey adds a footnote: "Alderman is the title of the chiefe magistrate here."

p. 168. *Glover.* Aubrey's question in brackets is addressed to Anthony Wood. It is highly significant that he is doubtful about the propriety of alluding to the trade of Hobbes's uncle. Sprat in his *Life of Cowley* conceals the fact that Cowley's father was a grocer and writes that his parents were "citizens of vertuous life and of a sufficient estate."

p. 169. *agellum.* "A little field."

p. 169. *Gasten-ground.* Aubrey adds a note on the etymology of "Gasten," suggesting first that it was originally "Garsten" and derived from the British word Gaer meaning the "*vallum* or bulwarkes" of a castle, and then that "Gasten-ground" means ground for the guests "probably to putt the horses of the guests (that came to lie at the abbey) to grasse."

p. 169. *theame and verse.* Latin prose and verse composition.

p. 170. *Sir W. Waller.* One of the generals of the Parliamentary army in the Civil War.

p. 170. *father's house.* Aubrey gives a sketch plan of Westport and a drawing of the house where Hobbes was born. They are reproduced in Clarke's edition.

p. 170. *houres of four and six.* After this Aubrey gives astrological details concerning Hobbes's horoscope.

p. 171. *Graecian.* Greek scholar.

p. 171. *Post and Payne.* A card game said to have been "once a favourite game in the West of England.—*Oxford English Dictionary*."

p. 171. *harled.* Entangled, twisted.

p. 172. *Disputant.* Here Aubrey adds, "of which he took notice in his life written by himself in verse," and quotes the couplets from Hobbes's autobiography in Latin verse.

p. 172. *his young lord.* William Cavendish, Lord Hardwick, eldest son of William Cavendish, first Earl of Devonshire; who succeeded to his father's earldom in 1626. He died in 1628 at the age of 37. In his Latin autobiography Hobbes describes the years which he spent with this young nobleman as the happiest in his life and declares that "Non Domiuns tantum, verum et Amicus erat."

After his first patron's death in 1628 Hobbes acted for a time as travelling tutor to Sir Gervase Clifton of Clifton Hall, Nottinghamshire, but was recalled from Paris in 1631 to become tutor to William Cavendish, his former pupil's eldest son, third Earl of Devonshire (1617–84), in whose service he remained for the rest of his life. For a short time when he was in Paris (1646–1647) he acted as mathematical tutor to the Prince of Wales, afterwards Charles II.

p. 173. *then a little youth.* Aubrey was born in 1626 and must have been about eight years old when Hobbes saw him at Mr Latimer's school. He writes in the margin, "I was not a vulgar boy, and carried not a Satchell on my back but *hoc inter nos*. I had then a a fine little horse and commonly rode, but this is impertinent."

p. 173. *Ben Jonson.* According to one of Aubrey's notes elsewhere,

"Mr Benjamin Johnson Poet-Laureat was his (Hobbes's) loving, familiar friend and acquaintance."

p. 173. *Mr Ayton*. Sir Robert Ayton (1570–1638), Scottish knight, and writer of English and Latin verse.

p. 173. *Euclid's Elements*. 47 *El. lib.* 1. This is the famous 47th Proposition of the First Book of Euclid (known as the Theorem of Pythagoras): "In right-angled triangles the square on the side subtending the right angle is equal to the squares on the sides containing the right angle."

p. 173. *learned Mathematicall Antagonists*. Probably John Wallis and Seth Ward. See below, note on "Savillian Professors."

p. 174. *Joseph Scaliger*. Joseph Justus Scaliger (1540–1609), famous Renaissance scholar. See above, p. 152 *n*.

p. 174. *Clavius*. Christopher Clavius (1537–1612), Bavarian Jesuit astronomer and mathematician.

p. 174. *Leviathan*. Hobbes's most famous work, published in 1651.

p. 175. "*He wrote and published*, etc. The passage in quotation marks is from *Mr Hobbes Considered*; see above, p. 219. Only the first three paragraphs of a long quotation copied out by Aubrey are given here.

p. 176. *Vesalius*. Andreas Vesalius (1514–64), the greatest anatomist of the Renaissance, and one of the founders of modern medicine.

p. 176. *Sir W. Petty*. Sir William Petty (1623–87), physician and political economist, an original Fellow of the Royal Society.

p. 176. *Savillian Professors*. Seth Ward, Savilian Professor of Astronomy (see above, p. 157), and his more celebrated colleague John Wallis, Savilian Professor of Geometry (both of the University of Oxford), with whom Hobbes had a violent controversy.

p. 176. *J. Selden*. John Selden (1584–1654), famous jurist and scholar. The work by which he is chiefly remembered now is his *Table Talk*. See the edition by S. H. Reynolds (Oxford, 1892), with biographical preface.

p. 176. *Dr W. Harvey*. William Harvey (1578–1657), discoverer of the circulation of the blood.

p. 176. *John Vaughan*. Sir John Vaughan (1603–74), judge, created Lord Chief Justice of the Common Pleas in 1668.

p. 176. *Mr Samuel Cowper* (1609–72). One of the most fashionable and successful English portrait-painters of the period. His works are all miniatures, and he painted most of the celebrities of the day, including Cromwell and Charles II.

p. 176. *Limners*. Miniature painters.

p. 177. *Cluverius's Historia Universalis.* The work which Hobbes used was probably the *Historiarum Totius Mundi Epitome* of Joannes Cluverius, the fourth (revised) edition of which appeared in 1645.

p. 178. *his Lord. I.e.,* the town house of William Cavendish, Earl of Devonshire, Hobbes's patron.

p. 179. *book of the Civil Warr. Behemoth: the History of the Causes of the Civill Wars of England* (in the form of a dialogue), published without Hobbes's consent in 1679.

p. 180. *Mr Anthony à Wood* (1632–95). The famous Oxford anti-quary; see Introduction, p. 44. The work which occasioned Hobbes's dispute with Dr Fell was Wood's *Historia et Antiquitates Universitatis Oxoniensis,* published in 1674.

p. 180. *Dean of Christ-church.* John Fell (1625–86), Vice-Chan-cellor of the University, 1666–69; Bishop of Oxford, 1675. He was the subject of Thomas Brown's epigram:

> I do not love you, Doctor Fell
> The reason why, I cannot tell;
> But this I know, and know full well,
> I do not love thee, Doctor Fell.

p. 180. *Vir sane,* etc. There follows a commendatory passage in Latin on Hobbes from Wood's *Historia et Antiquitates Univer-sitatis Oxoniensis.*

p. 180. *J.A.—i.e.,* John Aubrey.

p. 181. *common Act.* In seventeenth-century Oxford the 'Common' or 'Public Act' took place early in July. It was the occasion on which the candidates for degrees 'kept acts' or publicly defended their theses, and it corresponded roughly to the modern 'Schools' or Final Degree examinations. As the University was crowded with visitors at that time it was obviously suitable for the pub-lication of new books.

p. 182. *Historie of the Civill Warre—i.e., Behemoth*; see above, p. 227.

p. 182. *cum animo nunquam revertendi.* "With the intention of never returning."

p. 182. *Extracted out of the Executor's lettre.* Among the letters which Aubrey appends to his *Life of Hobbes* is one from James Wheldon, Hobbes's servant and executor, giving an account of his death. He certainly meant to give an extract from it at this point, as his note indicates. I have therefore inserted here the passage in which Wheldon describes Hobbes's death and funeral.

p. 183. *Crassa cutis,* etc. A stout skin, a stout skull, and stout intellect.

p. 184. *et tamen haec omnia mediocriter. Homo sum*, etc. "And never-theless all these things in moderation: 'I am a man and think nothing human outside my province'." The quotation is a famous line from Terence, *Heauton timorumenos*, I, i, 25.

p. 186. *Tennis.* Not the modern lawn tennis, but the more ancient and strenuous game played in a covered court with a penthouse.

p. 186. *prick-song.* Originally 'pricked song.' Music sung from notes written or 'pricked' as distinguished from that sung from memory or by ear; vocal music.—*Oxford English Dictionary.*

p. 186. *H. Lawes.* Henry Lawes (1596–1662), one of the most eminent English musicians of the seventeenth century, friend of Milton and composer of music for *Comus.* Hobbes probably used one of his books of Ayres for "one, two or three voyces."

p. 187. *pro suo modulo*, after his own fashion.

p. 187. *Dr Jasper Mayne* (1604–72). Poet and divine. He was Archdeacon of Chichester and author of *The City Match* and other plays and poems.

p. 187. *King of France.—i.e.*, Louis XIV.

p. 188. *Mr J. Dreyden . . . Playes.* Aubrey is, doubtless, thinking of such passages in Dryden's plays as Act V, scene 2 of *The Indian Emperor*, where Cortez is made to denounce the priests in language that is clearly influenced by Hobbes's doctrines:

> And you,
> Who sawcily, teach Monarchs to obey,
> And the wide World in narrow Cloysters sway;
> Set up by Kings as humble aids of power,
> You that which bred you, Viper-like, devour,
> You Enemies of Crowns.

p. 188. *Maximus Mersennus.* Marin Mersenne (1588–1648), French mathematician and fellow-pupil of Descartes.

p. 188. *Descartes.* René Descartes, the famous French philo-sopher; see Introduction, p. 25.

pp. 188, 189. *Tractatus Theologico-Politicus.* The reference is to the *Tractatus Theologico-Politicus* of Baruch Spinoza, the great Dutch-Jewish philosopher (1632–77), which was published anonymously in 1670 and aroused a storm of controversy throughout Europe because of its outspoken rationalistic criticism of the Bible. There is a good English translation of the *Tractatus* by R. M. Elwes (1895). The best modern English work on Spinoza is by Leon Roth (E. Benn, 1929). See also the trans-lation of his *Ethics* by A. J. Boyle in "Everyman's Library."

p. 189. *out throwne him a barres length.* Clark in his edition of the

Brief Lives, reads, "cut thorough him a barre's length." I am convinced that this is a misreading of Aubrey's hastily scribbled note, in which "out" (easily misread as "cut") comes at the end of one line and a scrawled "throwne" at the beginning of the next. The phrase certainly refers to the old game of throwing "a thick rod of iron or wood as a trial of strength, the players contending which of them could throw it farthest."—*Oxford English Dictionary*, 'bar,' sense 2, s.a. The *Oxford English Dictionary* quotes North's *Lives*, ii, 37: "the objectors . . . outdo, many bars, all that themselves found fault with." Hobbes's meaning was obviously that Spinoza had gone a great deal further than he dared to go in the criticism of traditional religious beliefs.

p. 189. *incedo per ignes suppositis cineri doloso.* A slightly adapted quotation of Horace, *Odes*, II, i, 8. Conington translates the passage as follows:

> As one on fire should tread
> Scarce hid by treacherous ashes' crust.

Aubrey's Life of Andrew Marvell

p. 190. *Mr Andrew Marvell* (1621–78). Poet and politician. The first collection of his poetry appeared in 1681. The best modern edition of his *Poems and Letters* is that of H. M. Margoliouth (2 vols.; Oxford, 1927). See also the very full study in French by Pierre Legouis, *André Marvell, Poète, Puritain, Patriote, 1621–78* (Paris, 1928).

p. 190. *to Cambridge.* Aubrey wrote "to . . . in Cambridge." He apparently did not know the name of Marvell's college: actually it was Trinity.

p. 190. *Latin Secretarie.* Marvell was appointed Latin Secretary to Thurloe, Cromwell's Secretary of State, in September 1657. Milton, who had hitherto been Latin Secretary, but who was now blind, retained his office at a reduced salary. See Margoliouth's edition, ii, 350.

p. 190. *excellent poet in Latin.* See the admirable Latin versions of *On a Drop of Dew* (Ros) and *The Garden* (Hortus) in Margoliouth's edition.

p. 190. *Advice to the Painter.* In 1666 Waller published a complimentary poem on the Duke of York called *Instructions to a Painter*. Numerous satiric rejoinders to this work were written. Seven of these were printed in *Poems on Affairs of State* (1697). Of these only *Last Instructions to a Painter* is certainly by Marvell. See Margoliouth, *op. cit.*, I, 269.

p. 190. *James Harrington, esq.* (*autor Oceanae*) (1611–77). One of the most famous English political theorists of the seventeenth century. His *Commonwealth of Oceana* appeared in 1656. He founded the Rota Club for political discussion in 1659. They met at the Turk's Head Tavern in New Palace Yard. Aubrey used to attend their meetings, and, in his *Life of Harrington*, writes that their discourses were "the most ingenious and smart that ever I heard. . . . the arguments in the Parliament House were but flat to it."

p. 190. *John Pell, D.D.* (1611–85). An eminent mathematician, employed by Cromwell as a diplomatist in Switzerland. He was also a friend of Milton.

p. 191. *Samuel Parker, D.D.* (1640–88). This divine was originally a Presbyterian, but after the Restoration became "as warm a member of the Church of England as any." He became Archdeacon of Canterbury in 1670, and Bishop of Oxford in 1686. He had a vigorous controversy with Marvell, who attacked him in several of his pamphlets.

p. 191. [*but I cannot be positive*]. These words are scored out by Aubrey in his MS.

Aubrey's Life of John Milton

p. 192. *John Milton* (1608–74). *A Milton Handbook*, by J. Holly Hanford (Bell, 1935), is the most useful short guide to Milton's life and works. It contains a full bibliography.

p. 192. *he found a Bible.* Aubrey writes before this statement "Q" for "*quaere*," meaning probably that he is not quite sure and wants to make further inquiries.

p. 192. *Scrivener.* A seventeenth-century scrivener combined the functions of a notary or solicitor with those of a banker and moneylender.

p. 192. *Oriana.* This is *The Triumphes of Oriana to 5 or 6 voices composed by divers severall aucthors*, published in 1601. It consists of a series of madrigals in honour of Queen Elizabeth edited by Thomas Morley. John Milton, the elder, contributed No. xviii to the collection. Other contributors included such distinguished Elizabethan musicians as John Mundy, Thomas Weelkes, and John Wilbye. The words will be found in *English Madrigal Verse*, edited by E. H. Fellowes, pp. 143–151.

p. 192. *ten yeares old, as by his picture.* This is the famous picture of Milton as a boy which was in the possession of his widow when

P

she died in 1727. It is now in the Pierpont Morgan Library in New York. An inscription on the canvas reads, "Aetatis suae: 10 An. 1618. John Milton."

p. 193. *Carolo Diodati son of.* These words are scored through in Aubrey's MS. Actually Aubrey is mistaken about the Diodatis. Milton did not make their acquaintance at Geneva, but in London. The elder Diodati was an Italian Protestant exile who settled first in Geneva and then in England. He was a doctor of medicine and was practising in London when Milton was at St Paul's School, where he met the son Charles (Carolo), who became one of his most intimate friends. Milton addressed two Latin letters to the younger Diodati, which were printed in his *Epistolae Familiares*, and an Italian sonnet. When he died in 1638 Milton lamented his loss in his famous Latin elegy *Epitaphium Damonis.*

p. 193. *Sir Henry Wotton* (1568–1639). Diplomatist and poet. See Introduction, pp. 34, 35. Wotton's letter of advice to Milton concerning his travels was printed in the 1645 edition of Milton's *Poems* at the head of *Comus*, which is specially commended in the letter. Aubrey is mistaken in his statement that Milton knew Wotton "beyond sea." Actually Wotton had retired from the Venetian embassy in 1624 and, when Milton knew him, he was living in retirement as Provost of Eton.

p. 193. *Christopher Milton* (1615–93). Younger brother of the poet; a Royalist and Roman Catholic. He was knighted and made Baron of the Exchequer by James II.

p. 193. *Mr Chapell.* William Chapell (1582–1649), Fellow of Christ's College and afterwards Bishop of Cork.

p. 193. *Mr Tovell.* The person to whom Aubrey refers is apparently Nathaniel Tovey, Fellow of Christ's College, afterwards Rector of Lutterworth from 1637 till about 1647, when he was expelled from his living.

p. 193. *Edward and John Philips.* These were the nephews of Milton's only sister Ann, who married Edward Phillips, an official in the Court of Chancery. Both brothers published works in verse and prose, and Edward was the author of the interesting book on the English poets called *Theatrum Poetarum* (1675), which is supposed to embody some of the critical opinions of his famous uncle.

p. 194. *Triple chord.* This seems to be a reference to *Tetrachordon* (1645) (the fourfold chord), one of Milton's four pamphlets on divorce. It is an examination of four passages of Scripture "which treat of marriage or nullities of marriage."

p. 194. *writing against Salmasius.* Claude Saumaise (1588–1653), who Latinized his name to Claudius Salmasius, was a French scholar who wrote a Latin defence of Charles I which appeared in 1651. Milton replied to it in his famous *Defensio pro Populo Anglicano.*

p. 195. *Moyses Pitt.* A London bookseller in St Paul's Churchyard, who printed Milton's Latin *Letters of State* in 1676.

p. 195. *John Speed.* Historian and cartographer (1552–1629).

p. 195. *His widowe has his picture.* This is the picture known as the Onslow portrait. It was inherited by Milton's daughter Deborah, and was bought by Speaker Onslow and engraved by Vertue (see H. Darbishire *loc. cit.,* pp. 333, 334).

p. 195. *in toto,* etc. "There was no blemish in the whole body." Aubrey's quotation is from Ovid, *Amores,* I, v, 18.

p. 195. *Manna.* My colleague, Mr G. E. Trease, B.Pharm., informs me that this is Ash Manna, a saccharine exudation from the manna ash found chiefly in Sicily, and used as a mild laxative. See *Text Book of Pharmacognosy* by G. E. Trease (5th edition, 1949), p. 461.

p. 196. *Mr Theodore Haak* (1605–90). A German who came to England at the age of twenty, studied at Oxford and Cambridge, and became one of the early Fellows of the Royal Society. R.S.S. probably stands for *Regiae Societatis Socius.*

p. 196. *Mr Skinner.* This is Cyriac Skinner (b. 1627), grandson of Sir E. Coke, to whom Milton addressed two famous sonnets.

p. 196. *Mr [Daniel] Skinner.* Aubrey left a blank before the surname which I have filled in. He is referring to Daniel Skinner, Fellow of Trinity College, Cambridge, the son of a London merchant, to whom Milton entrusted the MS. of his *De Doctrina Christiana* (see H. Darbishire, *Four Lives of Milton,* p. 335).

p. 196. *putt his Paradise—lost into a Drama in Rhyme.* Dryden's drama in rhyme, based on *Paradise Lost,* is the opera called *The State of Innocence,* published in 1677, but never performed.

p. 197. *Mr Hobbes Behemoth.* The reference is to *Behemoth: The History of the Causes of the Civil Wars of England.* An imperfect edition of this work was published in 1679 and a complete, authorized edition in 1680. Hobbes's work is in the form of a dialogue. It contains a defence of the monarchy and a strong condemnation of the Puritans and those "who are furnished with arguments for liberty out of the works of Aristotle, Plato, Cicero, and Seneca." Milton is mentioned as an "English Independent" in connexion with his controversy with Salmasius. Of Salmasius's defence of Charles I and Milton's defence of the English people Hobbes writes, "they are very good Latin both, and hardly to be judged which was better; and both very ill reasoning, hardly to be judged which is worse."

p. 197. *In the 4th Booke of Paradise lost.* Edward Phillips in his *Life of Milton* (1694) quotes the lines in question: they are the opening lines of Satan's address to the sun (*Paradise Lost*, iv, 33–41).

p. 197. *Alexander More* (1616–70). A French Protestant divine of Scottish descent. On the appearance of the anonymous Royalist pamphlet called *Regii Sanguinis Clamor ad Cælum* (1652) it was generally ascribed to More, and Milton, believing the common report, replied to it in his *Pro Populo Anglicano Secunda Defensio,* which contains a scurrilous personal attack on More. Actually *Regii Sanguinis Clamor* was the work of Peter Du Moulin, another French Protestant clergyman (1601–84).

p. 197. *Whatever he wrote against Monarchie.* The reference is probably to *The Tenure of Kings and Magistrates* (1648), in which Milton argued in favour of the deposition and punishment of Charles I, and *Eikonoklastes* (1650), his slashing reply to *Eikon Basilike*, the work which purported to be the prayers and meditations of the King before his execution.

p. 197. *conversant in Livy and the Roman authors.* Aubrey seems to be echoing the opinion of Hobbes, who in his *Behemoth* blamed the universities for furnishing scholars "with arguments for liberty out of the works of Aristotle, Plato, Cicero, Seneca, and out of the histories of Rome and Greece, for their disputation against the necessary power of their sovereigns."

p. 198. *Two admirable panegyricks.* These are Milton's famous sonnets on Fairfax and Cromwell. Edward Phillips printed them for the first time with his *Life of Milton* prefixed to the edition of Milton's *Letters of State* which appeared in 1694.

p. 198. *Waller's.* Aubrey is referring to Waller's *A Panegyric to my Lord Protector*, published on the death of Cromwell in 1658.

CHRONOLOGICAL TABLE

1555. Lancelot Andrewes born at Barking.

1588. Thomas Hobbes born at Westport, Malmesbury. **Spanish Armada.**

1589. Lancelot Andrewes elected Fellow of Pembroke Hall, Cambridge.

1593. Izaak Walton born at Stafford. George Herbert born at Montgomery Castle.

1602-3. Thomas Hobbes enters Magdalen Hall, Oxford.

1603. **Death of Elizabeth, accession of James I.**

1605. Herbert enters Westminster School. Bacon's *Advancement of Learning* published.

1607-8. Hobbes graduates B.A. and becomes tutor to Lord Hardwick.

1608. John Milton born in London.

1609. George Herbert enters Trinity College, Cambridge.

1612-13. Herbert graduates B.A.

1616. Herbert proceeds M.A., and is elected Fellow of Trinity, Cambridge.

1619. Herbert appointed Public Orator at Cambridge.

1621. Andrew Marvell born at Winestead, Yorks.

1624. Milton enters Christ's College, Cambridge.

1626. Izaak Walton marries Rachel Floyd. Lancelot Andrewes dies. John Aubrey born at Easton Piers, Wilts.

1627. Robert Boyle born.

1627-40. Izaak Walton living in Chancery Lane.

1629. Milton takes B.A. degree.

1630. Isaac Barrow born in London. George Herbert presented to living of Bemerton.

1631. Death of John Donne.

1632. Milton proceeds M.A. and leaves Cambridge.

1633. George Herbert dies at Bemerton. Marvell enters Trinity College, Cambridge.

1634. Hobbes visits Mr Latimer's School at Leigh Delamere, and sees Aubrey for the first time.

1635. Abraham Hill born in London. Boyle enters Eton.

1637. Descartes' *Discours de la Méthode* published.

1638. Milton starts on his Continental journey. Marvell graduates B.A. and leaves Cambridge.

1639. Milton returns to England.

1640. Donne's *LXXX Sermons* published with first version of Walton's *Life of Donne*.

1641. Gassendi's *Vita Peireskii* published.

1642. Hobbes publishes *De Cive*. Aubrey enters Trinity College, Oxford. **Outbreak of the Civil War.**

1643. Barrow enters Peterhouse, Cambridge. Gilbert Burnet born. Aubrey leaves Oxford without a degree. Cardan's *De Vita Propria* published in Paris.

1645. Milton's early Poems published. Barrow transferred to Trinity College, Cambridge.

1646. John Aubrey enters the Middle Temple.

1647. Rochester born at Ditchley, Oxfordshire.

1648. Barrow graduates B.A.

1649. **Execution of Charles I.** Barrow elected Fellow of Trinity, Cambridge. Milton appointed Latin Secretary to Council of State.

1651. *Leviathan* published.

1652. Richard Aubrey dies; John Aubrey inherits his estates. George Herbert's *Remains* with Prefatory Life by Barnabas Oley published.

1653. Burnet enters Marischal College, Aberdeen. **Cromwell establishes Protectorate.**

1655–59. Barrow travelling in France, Italy, and Turkey.

1657. W. Rand's translation of the *Life of Peireskius* published.

1658. **Death of Cromwell. Richard Cromwell Protector.**

1659. Aubrey friendly with John Harrington: attends meetings of the Roto Club in the Strand. Hobbes's *De Homine* published.

1659–60. Abraham Hill inherits his father's fortune and devotes himself to study. Rochester admitted to Wadham College, Oxford.

1660. **Restoration of Charles II.** Barrow elected Professor of Greek at Cambridge.

1661. Boyle publishes *The Sceptical Chymist*. Rochester takes M.A. degree.

1662. Barrow elected Gresham Professor of Geometry. **The Royal Society receives its Charter from Charles II.**

1661–64. Rochester travelling on the Continent with Sir A. Balfour.

1663. Aubrey elected F.R.S.

1664. Burnet elected F.R.S. Rochester appears at Court.

1665. Rochester serving in the Fleet against the Dutch. Walton's *Life of Hooker* published.

1666. Revised version of Walton's *Life of Hooker* published with new edition of Hooker's *Works*.

1667. Aubrey meets Anthony à Wood, and promises Hobbes to write his life. *Paradise Lost* published.

1669. Aubrey starts to collect *Brief Lives* to help Wood with *Athenæ Oxonienses*.

1670. Walton publishes *Life of George Herbert*.

1672–73. Barrow elected Master of Trinity, Cambridge.

1674. Second edition of *Paradise Lost* with prefatory poems by Marvell and Barrow. Death of Milton.

1675. Second (revised) edition of Walton's "Lives" of Donne, Wotton, Hooker, and Herbert published. Hobbes retires to Derbyshire. Barrow Vice-Chancellor of Cambridge.

1677. Death of Barrow.

1678. Death of Andrew Marvell.

1679. Death of Hobbes at Hardwick.

1679–80. Burnet's conversations with Rochester on religion.

1680. Walton helps Aubrey with life of Ben Jonson. Rochester dies at High Lodge, Woodstock. Burnet publishes *Some Passages of the Life and Death of John Earl of Rochester*.

1682. Burnet publishes *The Life and Death of Sir Matthew Hale*.

1683. Izaak Walton dies at Winchester. Publication of the *Works* of Barrow with *Some Account of the Life of Isaac Barrow* by Abraham Hill and of *Plutarch's Lives translated from the Greek by Several Hands* with *Life of Plutarch* by Dryden.

1685. Burnet publishes *Life of Bishop Bedell*. **Death of Charles II, Accession of James II.**

1688–89. **Flight of James II. The Revolution. William and Mary King and Queen.**

1691. Death of Robert Boyle.
1691–92. Wood's *Athenæ Oxonienses published.*
1697. Death of Aubrey at Oxford.
1715. Death of Burnet.
1716. Publication of third edition of *Works* of Barrow with enlarged version of Hill's *Life of Barrow.*
1721. Death of Abraham Hill.

SELECT BIBLIOGRAPHY

ALDINGTON, RICHARD: *A Book of Characters Compiled and Translated by Richard Aldington* (London, 1924). Contains the chief collections of "Theophrastan" Characters.

AUBREY, JOHN: *Brief Lives Chiefly of Contemporaries . . . set down by John Aubrey*, edited by Andrew Clark (Oxford; 2 vols., 1898).

Brief Lives and Other Selected Writings by John Aubrey, edited with an Introduction and Notes by Anthony Powell (London, 1949).

See also *John Aubrey and his Friends*, by Anthony Powell (London, 1944).

BACON, SIR FRANCIS: *The Twoo Bookes of Francis Bacon of the Proficience and Advancement of Learning divine and humane* (London, 1605).

The Advancement of Learning, edited by W. Aldis Wright (Oxford, 1869).

The Historie of the Raigne of King Henry the Seventh (London, 1622).

The History of the Reign of Henry VII, edited by J. R. Lumby (Cambridge, 1902).

BARROW, ISAAC: *The Works of the Learned Isaac Barrow, D.D. Late Master of Trinity College in Cambridge, Published by the Reverend Dr Tillotson* (London; 4 vols., 1683). Vol. i contains "Some Account of the Life of Dr Isaac Barrow," by Abraham Hill.

The Works of the Learned Isaac Barrow, D.D. . . . . (Being All his English Works) (London; 3 vols., 1716). Vol. i contains an enlarged version of "Some Account of the Life of Dr Isaac Barrow."

BOSWELL, JAMES: *The Life of Samuel Johnson, LL.D.* (London; 2 vols., 1791).

Boswell's Life of Johnson, edited by G. Birkbeck Hill (Oxford; 6 vols., 1887).

BURNET, GILBERT: *The Memoires of the Lives and Actions of James and William Dukes of Hamilton and Castle-Herald* (London, 1677). (Modern edition, Oxford, 1852).

Some Passages of the Life and Death of the Right Honourable John Earl of Rochester (London, 1680). Many later editions.

The Life and Death of Sir Matthew Hale Kt. Sometime Lord Chief Justice of His Majesties Court of King's Bench (London, 1682).

Life of William Bedell D.D. Lord Bishop of Kilmore in Ireland (London, 1685).

History of his Own Time.

BUTT, JOHN: *Essays and Studies by Members of the English Association,* Vol. XIX, collected by D. Nichol Smith (Oxford, 1934). Pp. 67–85: "Izaak Walton's Methods in Biography" by John Butt.

BUTTERFIELD, HERBERT: *The Origins of Modern Science, 1300–1800* (London, 1949).

CARDAN, JEROME (GIROLAMO CARDANO): *Hieronymi Cardani Mediolanensis de Propria Vita Liber Ex Bibliotheca. Gab. Naudæi Parioris apud Jacobum Villery, in Palatio sub Portici Delphinati MCDCXLIII.*

The Book of My Life (De Vita Propria Liber), by Jerome Cardan, translated from the Latin by Jean Stoner (London, 1931).

CAVENDISH, GEORGE: *The Negotiations of Thomas Woolsey, the great Cardinal of England, Containing his Life and Death* (London, 1641.

The Life and Death of Thomas Wolsey, edited by F. S. Ellis (London, 1893–99).

COWLEY, ABRAHAM: *The Works of Mr Abraham Cowley* (London, 1668). *An Account of the Life and Writings of Mr Abraham Cowley*, by Thomas Sprat, is prefixed to this and subsequent editions.

DESCARTES, RENÉ: *A Discourse on Method etc.*, translated by John Veitch, Introduction by A. D. Lindsay. ("Everyman's Library.")

DRYDEN, JOHN: *Plutarch's Lives, translated from the Greek by several hands. To which is prefixt the life of Plutarch* (London; 5 vols., 1683–6). Dryden's life of Plutarch is prefixed to vol. i.

DUNN, WALDO H.: *English Biography* (London, 1916).

FONTENELLE, BERNARD LE BOVIER DE: *Eloges des Academiciens de l'Academie Royale des Sciences* (la Haye; 2 vols., 1731).

Eloges de Fontenelle Avec Une Introduction et des Notes par M. Francisque Bouillier (Garnier, Paris). A good modern selection.

GASSENDI, PIERRE: *Viri illustris N. C. Fabricii de Peiresc . . . vita* (Paris, 1641).

The Mirrour of true Nobility & Gentility being the Life of The Renowned Nicolaus Claudius Fabricius Lord of Peiresk etc. *Englished by W. Rand Doctor of Physick* (London, 1657).

GREVILLE, FULKE: *The life of the renowned Sr Philip Sidney* (London, 1652).

Sir Fulke Greville's Life of Sir Philip Sidney . . . with an Introduction by Nowell Smith (Oxford, 1906).

HEYLYN, PETER: *Cyprianus Anglicus: or the History of the Life and Death, of the Most Reverend and Renowned Prelate William by Divine Providence Lord Archbishop of Canterbury* etc. (London, 1668). (Life of Archbishop Laud.)

HILL, ABRAHAM: See Barrow, Isaac.

JOHNSON, SAMUEL: *The Works of Samuel Johnson, LL.D.* (Oxford; 9 vols., 1825).

The Rambler 1750–52 (Essay on Biography, No. 60, October 13, 1750).

An Account of the Life of Mr Richard Savage (London, 1744).

Prefaces Biographical and Critical to the Works of the English Poets (London, 1779–81).

JOSSELIN, JOHN: *The life of the 70th Archbishop of Canterbury presently Sittinge Englished* (London, 1574). Life of Archbishop Parker translated from Latin original probably by John Stubbs.

MAUROIS, ANDRÉ: *Aspects of Biography,* translated by S. C. Roberts (Cambridge, 1929).

MORE, SIR THOMAS: *The Workes of Sir Thomas More* (London, 1557).

The English Works of Sir Thomas More, edited by W. E. Campbell (London; 2 vols., 1931).

See also R. W. Chambers: *Thomas More* (London, 1935).

NICOLSON, HAROLD: *The Development of English Biography* (London, 1928).

NYXON, ANTHONY: *London's Dove: or a Memoriall of the life and death of Maister Robert Dove Citizen and Marchant Taylor of London* (London, 1612).

PINTO, VIVIAN DE SOLA: Article on biography in *Chambers's Encyclopædia* (new edition), vol. ii, 1950, pp. 320–322.

PLUTARCH: *The Lives of the Noble Grecians and Romanes* (translated by Sir Thomas North), 1579. Modern edition by G. Wyndham in "The Tudor Translations" (6 vols., 1895).
Parallel Lives, with an English Translation by B. Perrin (Loeb Classical Library, 11 vols., 1914–28).
See also under Dryden, J.
See also Trench, R. C.: *Plutarch: his Life, his Lives and his Morals* (London, 1873).

ROPER, WILLIAM: *The Mirrour of Vertue in worldly greatness, or the life of Syr Thomas More Knight, Sometime to Chancellour of England* (Paris, 1626).

SMITH, D. NICHOL: *Characters from the Histories and Memoirs of the Seventeenth Century With an Essay on the Character and Historical Notes* (Oxford, 1918).

SPRAT, THOMAS: *The History of the Royal Society of London* (London, 1667).
See also under Cowley, Abraham.

STAUFFER, DONALD: *English Biography before 1700* (Harvard, 1930).

STRACHEY, GILES LYTTON: *Eminent Victorians* (London, 1918). See Preface for remarks on biography.

SUETONIUS: *The Historie of the twelve Cæsars, Emperours of Rome. Written in Latine . . . and newly translated into English by P. Holland* (1606). Modern edition in "The Tudor Translations," edited by C. Whibley, 1897.
De Vita Cæsarum Libri VII–VIII with Introduction, Translation, and Commentary by G. W. Mooney (London, 1930).

TACITUS: *The Ende of Nero and Beginning of Galba. Fower bookes of the Histories of Cornelius Tacitus. The Life of Agricola*, translated by Sir Henry Savile (Oxford, 1591). *Corneli Taciti De Vita Agricolæ*, edited by H. Furneaux. Second Edition, revised by J. G. C. Anderson (Oxford, 1922).

WALTON, IZAAK: *The Lives of Dr John Donne, Sir Henry Wotton, Mr Richard Hooker, Mr George Herbert . . . To which are added some letters by Mr George Herbert* (London, 1670).
The Lives of Dr John Donne, Sir Henry Wotton, Mr Richard Hooker, Mr George Herbert Written by Izaak Walton, the Fourth Edition (London, 1675). This is actually the second collected edition.

The Lives . . . with Notes and Life of the Author by T. Zouch.
Third Edition (York, 1817).
See also Butt, John.

WILLEY, BASIL: *The Seventeenth Century Background* (London, 1934).

WOOD, ANTHONY À: *Athenæ Oxonienses,* edited by P. Bliss (London; 4 vols., 1813–20). It was to help Wood with this work that Aubrey compiled his *Brief Lives.*

DATE DUE

MAY 2 0 1991			